*An Introduction
to Wisdom Literature
and the Psalms*

Festschrift Marvin E. Tate

Marvin E. Tate

An Introduction to Wisdom Literature and the Psalms

Festschrift Marvin E. Tate

edited by
H. Wayne Ballard, Jr.
and
W. Dennis Tucker, Jr.

MERCER UNIVERSITY PRESS

ISBN 0-86554-652-5   MUP/P194

An Introduction to Wisdom Literature and the Psalms.
Festschrift Marvin E. Tate.
Copyright ©2000
Mercer University Press, Macon, Georgia 31210-3960
All rights reserved
Printed in the United States of America

The paper used in this publication meets the minimum requirements
of American National Standard for Information Sciences—
Permanence of Paper for Printed Library Materials, ANSI Z39.48-1984.

∞

Library of Congress Cataloging-in-Publication Data

An introduction to wisdom literature and the Psalms :
festschrift Marvin E. Tate /
edited by H. Wayne Ballard, Jr. and W. Dennis Tucker, Jr.
pp. cm.
Includes bibliographical references and index.
ISBN 0-86554-652-5 (alk. paper).
1. Wisdom literature—Criticism, interpretation, etc.
2. Bible. O.T. Psalms—Criticism, interpretation, etc.
I. Tate, Marvin E.
II. Ballard, Harold Wayne, 1963–
III. Tucker, W. Dennis.

BS1455 .I58 2000
223'.061—dc21

00-022187

Contents

Foreword

Marvin E. Tate: Professor Exemplar

Roy L. Honeycutt

For a half-century Professor Marvin Tate and I shared maturing relationships as fellow students, professorial and administrative colleagues, and a continuing personal friendship. Out of the matrix of those bonding associations my appreciation for his professorial career reflects fifty years of close association during which I experienced firsthand his life's stellar quality. So, this prefatory assessment to a *Festschrift* honoring Professor Tate comes not from a stranger but from one who has closely interacted with him in a variety of contexts. What then shall one say about Marvin E. Tate? How shall one summarize his academic and professional career?

Notable among Professor Tate's enduring qualities have been his dedication and commitment to his academic career. Whether during his student years, collegiate faculty tenure, or his long career of almost forty years at Southern Seminary he has been steadfast, dependable, and determined as he implemented high standards of academic excellence. During my direct associations with him during the past half-century one never needed to inquire about locating Dr. Tate. Almost without exception one witnessed his involvement in both preparation and implementation of classroom responsibilities. Or, one might locate him in the library or his seminary office, hard at work in research. Often he shared his extensive bibliographic awareness with faculty colleagues, making the faculty-staff lounge a place of academic interchange and learning. Whatever the locale, however, dedication and commitment to his calling as a professor marked his career with excellence.

As much or more than any other area of his professorship Dr. Tate magnified classroom responsibilities and other student relationships. Although his students can better assess that role than I, it has been my observation that it was in classroom teaching, graduate seminars and colloquia, and supervision of Ph.D. students that he made his most enduring contribution. To be sure, his publication of articles, translation of the Hebrew text for contemporary English Bible publication, and contributions to book manuscripts were significant aspects of his career. Yet, it remains that those accomplishments found their most significant and enduring value through Professor Tate's classroom and seminar leadership.

Editors who planned this *Festschrift* captured outstanding qualities of Professor Tate's career. Psalms and Wisdom Literature mark a central focus of his research and teaching career. Both the choice of subject matter and the selection of uniquely gifted scholars as authors of the several components of the *Festschrift* well summarize crucial elements of his decades of research and teaching. Central to that career but also evident in peripheral conversations was the bibliographic scope of his scholarship. Not only in Old Testament studies but in other areas also, he possessed an amazing range of bibliographic awareness. Following a chapel address or otherwise I recall his saying to me on occasion something such as, "By the way, have you read so-and-so's book on that subject?" During the 1980s an internationally recognized Old Testament scholar from Oxford University was an invited guest for a semester at Southern Seminary. Toward the end of that visit he remarked to me that he enjoyed and thought it quite remarkable to interact with someone of such wide-ranging bibliographic knowledge as Marvin Tate.

Beyond those qualities more directly related to his professorial career, there are several personal qualities which have continued to impress me during our half century of relationship. For example, during my presidency at Southern Seminary I developed a growing appreciation for his practical wisdom and clear judgment. To this commendable quality one should add also his personal stability and balanced perspective. This is not to say that Professor Tate agreed with every proposal or action by colleagues, whether administrative or professorial. It is to say, however, that his judgment was clear and more often than not his wisdom was sound.

At a more personal level Professor Tate's career remains one characterized by his churchmanship and personal devotion. Some might question the inclusion of such personal qualities in a reflection on a colleague's career. Yet, without being self-evident or superficial, such commitment inevitably shaped the whole of his life, as it does for anyone committed to such ideals. Far from allowing those qualities to become parochial and limiting, Professor Tate's career reached beyond boundaries, which might have stifled or otherwise limited his career. Since his first sabbatical leave from Southern Seminary I have continued to be impressed with his ecumenical associations and professional interaction with scholars of differing traditions. His professorial career was institutional but never parochial, faithful to valued traditions yet never limited by their restrictive powers.

Reflecting on the outstanding career of a professor-friend who has gone about his calling quietly and without great fanfare, I rediscovered his true greatness. Perhaps the title I have chosen summarizes my evaluation most appropriately: "Professor Marvin E. Tate: Professor Exemplar."

Editors' Preface

H. Wayne Ballard, Jr. and W. Dennis Tucker, Jr.

It is an honor and privilege to present this *Festschrift* to Marvin E. Tate. On behalf of the many bachelors-, masters-, and doctoral-level students Professor Tate has taught over the years and the countless parishioners who have gleaned from his pulpit ministry we offer a simple word of appreciation. It is only fitting that this *Festschrift* come in the form of a textbook because Marvin Tate's passion has always been in the class-room. It is our hope that this volume will aid in introducing students to the Wisdom Literature and the Psalms—much as Marvin Tate ably did for so many years.

As we have reflected on our journey with Marvin Tate through the Ph.D. program, two words best summarize the experience: excruciatingly pleasant. Tate is well known for his breadth of knowledge in many areas, but he is a walking bibliography in the field of Old Testament studies. As an advisor, Tate was meticulous and demanding. Thus, during graduate studies the word "excruciating" describes the attention to detail Tate gave to his student's work. However, after completing the program, we have developed a sincere sense of gratitude for the investment Tate made in our educational experiences. And like many other students, his influence has been felt academically, professionally, and spiritually. This *Festschrift* is a small token of appreciation from his students.

This *Festschrift* is also a symbol of the appreciation of Tate's many colleagues. We would like to thank the contributors who have provided the "flesh" for this project. Their willingness made the editors' job an enjoyable experience. Thank you for your help.

One other word of gratitude must be offered to Don Keyser, professor emeritus at Campbell University. Keyser provided another set of critical eyes during the editing process. His help was insightful and timely. Thanks, Don, for your support and friendship. Last, but not least, we would like to thank Marc A. Jolley and Edmon L. Rowell, Jr. at Mercer University Press for their encouragement and help.

Acknowledgments

A special word of thanks is due those who have supported this project from the very beginning. The following groups provided resources to help defray the cost of publication.

The School of Christian Studies
Ouachita Baptist University

The Department of Religion and Philosophy
Campbell University

Chapter 1

Introduction to the Psalms and Wisdom Literature

H. Wayne Ballard, Jr.

Introduction

Ordinary descriptive words do not do justice to the beauty and complexity of the portion of the Hebrew Bible named *Ketuvim* or Writings. The heart of the *Ketuvim* is the Book of Psalms. Psalms captivate the hearts of worshipers in every age. This collection of poems is a timeless expression of the angst of humanity in pursuit of relationship with a divine being generally referred to in the Psalms as *Adonai* (LORD) or *Elohim* (God). The psalms reflect the sentiments of both individuals and communities. A rich diversity exists in these expressions. The religions of Judaism and Christianity have equally valued their depths. The Psalms include polarities such as praise and lament, repentance and haughtiness, forgiveness and imprecation. This diverse collection constitutes a "profile of Old Testament theology" spanning the time of David in the tenth century BCE to the postexilic community in the fourth century BCE.

If the Psalms are indeed the heart of the *Ketuvim*, then the wisdom books (Proverbs, Ecclesiastes, and Job[1]) can be described as its soul. As the Psalms emphasize humanity's relationship to a divine being, the Wisdom Literature focuses on humanity's relationship to one another and to the universe at large. Belief in God as creator and sustainer of universal order supports the admonitions of wisdom. Aside from this foundational affirmation, however, there is little expressly religious content in much of the Wisdom Literature. Wisdom Literature as a distinct category of

---

[1]The remaining books of the *Ketuvim* include the festal scrolls (also called the *megilloth* ["scrolls"], which include Ruth, Song of Songs, the Ecclesiastes, Lamentations, and Esther), Daniel, and the works associated with the Chronicler (Ezra, Nehemiah, and 1 and 2 Chronicles).

biblical literature is foreign to the Hebrew Bible itself. It takes its name from the Hebrew word *hokmah*, "wisdom." More than half of the occurrences of this word occur in the books of Proverbs, Job, and Ecclesiastes.[2]

The Wisdom Literature of the Hebrew Bible is found in two basic forms, practical wisdom and speculative wisdom.[3] Practical wisdom is best observed in the Book of Proverbs. The cornerstone of the Book of Proverbs is the short aphoristic statement called a *mashal* in Hebrew. These maxims are usually very short and pregnant with meaning. They are often devoid of anything necessarily religious. The statements are generally true for all people of any generation. Speculative wisdom delves into the deeper and more vexing issues confronting humanity. Job and Ecclesiastes are both prime examples of speculative wisdom. Speculative wisdom is characterized by a thoughtful, reflective approach to the difficult questions concerning humanity's relationship to each other and to God. Speculative wisdom is closely related to philosophical issues raised in many ancient Near Eastern cultures.

The Psalms and Wisdom Literature are indeed the heart and soul of the *Ketuvim*. These works provide the matrix for this third section of the Hebrew Bible. They also demonstrate a corresponding relationship to the *Torah*, the Law, and the *Nevi'im*, the Prophets. The *Torah* is at the heart of many psalms in the Psalter.[4] The wisdom materials also acknowledge the importance of obeying the *Torah*. Habakkuk 3 is an example of a psalm included in the *Nevi'im*. The *Nevi'im* also includes many wisdom sayings. Hosea 14:9 is a wisdom saying serving as a conclusion to this prophetic book.

> Those who are wise understand these things;
>   those who are discerning know them.
> For the ways of the LORD are right,

---

[2]For further discussion see James Crenshaw, *Old Testament Wisdom: An Introduction* (Atlanta: John Knox Press, 1981) 27, 28, and 245.

[3]For a discussion of the characteristics of wisdom literature see Donald K. Berry, *An Introduction to Wisdom and Poetry of the Old Testament* (Nashville: Broadman & Holman Publishers, 1995) 4-6.

[4]Psalm 119 is a classic example of a psalm dedicated to the instruction of the Torah. It is an acrostic poem built on the succession of eight lines devoted to a succeeding letter of the Hebrew alphabet. Acrostic poems are also found in the Wisdom Literature, for example, Proverbs 31:10-31.

and the upright walk in them,
but transgressors stumble in them. (NRSV)

The Psalms and the Wisdom Literature of the Hebrew Bible provide the careful reader insights into theology, faith, the human condition, the history of Israel, and a host of other areas. Studying these works acquaints the reader with the pulse of Israelite faith, worship, and ultimately with the God of Israel.

Purpose

The purpose of the present book is threefold. First, this is a *Festschrift* in honor of Marvin E. Tate. Marvin Tate has spent his career as a teacher, student, and admirer of the Psalms and Wisdom Literature of the Hebrew Bible. Tate's involvement in the study of the *Ketuvim* has profoundly impacted this field of study through both his own writings and the contributions of his many students. This volume is offered as a testament to the ongoing legacy of Marvin E. Tate.

Second, this book is designed to be an entry-level textbook for university or divinity school students of the Wisdom Literature and the Psalms. It is a thorough yet readable introduction for students who are enrolled in classes that combine the study of the Psalms with Wisdom Literature. While there are many books written on each particular area, there are very few introductory textbooks that combine the study of these two areas in a brief introductory manner. This book is a compilation of essays from leading Baptist scholars in the fields of Psalms and Wisdom study.

Third, this book may also prove helpful to interested laypersons and ministers who seek a greater understanding of the Psalms and the Wisdom Literature. It is designed to help foster one's knowledge and appreciation for the biblical books contained in these segments of Hebrew/ Christian Scripture.

Scope

It is necessary from the outset to discuss some limitations placed as boundaries for this project. There are many other Old Testament and apocryphal texts one can classify as psalms or wisdom literature that lie beyond the pages of this book. The contributors for this project have focused their efforts on the canonical literature associated with the book of Psalms and the Wisdom Literature, namely, Proverbs, Ecclesiastes, and Job.

A proper understanding of Hebrew poetry plays an important role in understanding these texts. All of the Book of Psalms and most of the Wisdom Literature is in poetic form.[5] The study of Hebrew poetry has been the lifework of scholars such as Robert Alter and Adele Berlin.[6] These scholars have greatly influenced the study of the Psalms and Wisdom Literature.

Overview

Study of the Psalms and Wisdom Literature flourished in the last half of the twentieth century. These fields constitute separate areas of Old Testament research. Specialists spend whole careers investigating the intricacies of these individual books. Much if not all of Psalm scholarship in the twentieth century was affected by the work of Hermann Gunkel.[7] Gunkel turned away from the traditional historical-critical methodologies of his day as applied to biblical texts and introduced Form Criticism to the Psalms. The result is known today as the discussion of the various "types" of the Psalms.[8] Though Form Criticism is a fairly subjective exercise in naming the "types" of given texts, it has provided a framework by which Psalm scholars have been able to operate and maneuver for the last seventy-five years. Gunkel's work was continued by Sigmund Mowinckel.[9] Some of the more prominent names in recent Psalm studies include

---

[5]The narrative framework found in the book of Job is the lone exception to this poetic formula. See Job 1, 2, and 42:7-17.

[6]Robert Alter, *The Art of Biblical Poetry* (San Francisco: Basic Books, 1985). See also Adele Berlin, *The Dynamics of Biblical Parallelism* (Bloomington: Indiana University Press, 1985).

[7]Gunkel believed the Psalms could be best understood in the context of the cult rather than in the context of a given historical time period because there is little historical data on which to firmly base the dating of individual psalms. He looked for common characteristics in the Psalms and classified them into various *Gattungen* or types. Gunkel's major works on the Psalms include *The Psalms: A Form Critical Introduction*, trans. Thomas M. Horner (Philadelphia: Fortress Press, 1967); *An Introduction to the Psalms*, ed. Joachim Begrich, trans. James D. Nogalski (Macon GA: Mercer University Press, 1998); *Die Psalmen* (Göttingen: Vandenhoeck & Ruprecht, 1929).

[8]The various types referred to by Gunkel include Hymns, Laments of the People, Laments of the Individual, Songs of Thanksgiving of the Individual, and Spiritual Poems. See *An Introduction to the Psalms*, 1-21.

[9]Sigmund Mowinkel, *The Psalms in Israel's Worship*, vols. 1 and 2, trans. D. R. Ap-Thomas (Nashville: Abingdon Press, 1962). Mowinkel believed the psalms were the

Claus Westermann, H. J. Krauss, Patrick Miller, Walter Brueggemann, Clinton McCann, Bernard Anderson, and William Holladay.[10]

The study of Wisdom Literature also grew immensely popular during the latter half of the twentieth century. One of the most important contributions is the work of Gerhard von Rad, specifically his seminal work, *Wisdom in Israel*.[11] Von Rad helped lead other scholars to turn their attention to the wisdom texts. Other prominent scholars who have written in this area include Roland Murphy, R. E. Clements, and James Crenshaw.[12]

Though largely absent from the field in the early part of the twentieth century, there have been some prominent women who are making significant contributions to the study of the Psalms and Wisdom Literature. Nancy deClaissé-Walford is making an impact in Psalms studies by applying a canonical approach to the Psalms.[13] Claudia Camp has established herself as a leading scholar in the field of Wisdom Literature.[14]

---

exclusive product of the cult. Thus they could be used to re-create the worship of Israel. His approach became known as the Cult-Functional approach.

[10]This is only a representative list of many Psalms scholars in the twentieth century. See Claus Westermann, *The Praise of God in the Psalms*, trans. Keith R. Crim (Richmond: John Knox Press, 1961); Hans Joachim Kraus, *Psalms: A Commentary*, 3 vols., trans. Hilton C. Oswald (Minneapolis: Augsburg Publishing House, 1988); Patrick Miller, *Interpreting the Psalms* (Philadelphia: Fortress Press, 1986); Walter Brueggemann, *The Message of the Psalms: A Theological Commentary* (Minneapolis: Augsburg Publishing House, 1984); Clinton McCann, *A Theological Introduction to the Book of Psalms: The Psalms as Torah* (Nashville: Abingdon Press, 1993); Bernard Anderson, *Out of the Depths: The Psalms Speak for Us Today* (Philadelphia: Westminster Press, 1983); and William Holladay, *The Psalms Through Three Thousand Years: Prayerbook of a Cloud of Witnesses* (Minneapolis: Fortress Press, 1996).

[11]Gerhard von Rad, *Wisdom in Israel*, trans. James D. Marton (Nashville: Abingdon Press, 1972).

[12]See Roland Murphy, *The Tree of Life: An Exploration of Biblical Wisdom Literature* (Grand Rapids MI: Eerdmans, 1990). Also see *Wisdom Literature and the Psalms* (Nashville: Abingdon Press, 1983); R. E. Clements *Wisdom in Theology* (Grand Rapids: Eerdmans, 1992); James Crenshaw, *Old Testament Wisdom: An Introduction* (Atlanta: John Knox Press, 1981); and *Education in Ancient Israel: Across the Deadening Silence* (New York: Doubleday, 1998).

[13]Nancy deClaissé-Walford, *Reading from the Beginning: The Shaping of the Hebrew Psalter* (Macon GA: Mercer University Press, 1997).

[14]Claudia Camp, *Wisdom and the Feminine in the Book of Proverbs*, Bible and Literature Series 11 (Sheffield: Almond Press, 1985).

Introduction to Wisdom Literature and the Psalms stands in a long tradition of scholarship in the fields of Psalm and Wisdom study. This book is designed as an introduction to these fields. It is only a beginning point for study. Six areas within these respective fields provide the framework for this text: the history of interpretation; literary and poetic features; canonical shape; relationship to other ancient Near Eastern texts; the scope of theology; and an overview of contemporary or other related issues.

Three major divisions serve as the framework for this text: Introduction, Psalms, and Wisdom Literature. Chapters 1 and 2 serve as introductory material. Chapter 2 is a biographical sketch of Marvin E. Tate. Bob Dunston traces Tate's journey from Hope, Arkansas to educational endeavors at Ouachita Baptist University and the Southern Baptist Theological Seminary, and to his professional career as a pastor and longtime professor at the Southern Baptist Theological Seminary.

An introduction to the Psalms comprises the second major section of the text. In chapter 3, John Watts outlines in broad strokes the history of interpretation of the Psalms. He discusses the earliest use of the Psalms in Israel through their use in today's context. A particular emphasis is given to twentieth-century scholarship of the Psalms.

In chapter 4, "From Psalm to Psalms to Psalter," James Nogalski traces the development of various collections of Psalms into an organic whole. Nogalski introduces the reader to the issues of authorship, the nature of superscriptions (psalm titles), and the editorial activity evident throughout the various collections in the Psalms.

In chapter 5, "The Poetry and Literature of the Psalms," Danny Mynatt provides the beginning reader with the tools to comprehend the nuances of poetic features characteristic of the Psalms. Mynatt introduces the reader to the building blocks of Hebrew poetry, lines and parallelism. The reader is also introduced to the work of Hermann Gunkel and his form-critical approach to the Psalms. An overview of the various types of psalms provides a helpful introduction to the poetic literature of the Psalms.

In chapter 6, Joel Drinkard discusses the ancient Near Eastern Influences in the Psalms. Psalms were an important component of the fabric of many ancient Near Eastern societies. The work of Mitchell Dahood, specifically his work on Ugaritic poetry, has tremendously impacted today's Psalms scholarship.

"The Canonical Shape of the Psalms" is the title of chapter 7. Nancy deClaisse-Walford introduces the reader to the canonical shaping of the Psalms. She makes a strong case for a purposeful construction of the Psalter. It is described as telling the story of Israel through the lens of King David from the rise of the monarchy to an age of promise beyond the postexilic community.

William Bellinger discusses the scope of theology in the Psalms in the final chapter on the Psalms. Bellinger uses the title "Portraits of Faith" to describe the Psalms. With insight and precision, he discusses some of the more pronounced theological themes found in the Psalms: covenant theology, creation theology, and prophetic theology.

The third and final section is an introduction to the Wisdom Literature. In chapter 9, Pierce Matheney gives an overview of the history of interpretation of the personification of Wisdom as a lady. He traces this personification from biblical times through the time period of Medieval Christianity. Matheney argues against the idea of the hypostatization of wisdom in favor of the personification of wisdom as a foreshadowing of Jesus Christ.

In chapter 10, "Literary and Poetic Forms in the Wisdom Literature," Dennis Tucker summarizes the important literary characteristics and features of Wisdom Literature. Tucker treats the major wisdom literary forms: sayings, riddles, allegories, hymns, disputations, and autobiographical narratives. He also gives a helpful overview of the possible contextual settings for the rise of Wisdom Literature: the family, the royal courts, and wisdom schools.

In chapter 11, "Biblical Wisdom in Its Ancient Middle Eastern Context," Tom Smothers offers the reader a glimpse into the milieu of wisdom texts found in the cultures surrounding ancient Israel. The ancient wisdom texts are divided into two major categories: prudential wisdom and speculative wisdom. The corresponding wisdom texts of Egypt, Mesopotamia, and Ugarit are examined.

In chapter 12, Gerald Keown discusses the "Canonical Shape of the Wisdom Literature." In a thoughtful manner, Keown addresses the issues surrounding the final shaping and form of Proverbs, Job, and Ecclesiastes.

In chapter 13, Carol Grizzard provides a helpful glimpse into the scope of theology in the Wisdom Literature. Grizzard summarizes the theological issues in the Wisdom Literature in four probing questions:

How do we learn? How can we be satisfied in life? What is the relationship between our actions and our lives? What can we expect from God?

In the concluding chapter, James Crenshaw discusses "Unresolved Issues in Wisdom Literature." Crenshaw offers four major questions for the reader's consideration. First, is the designation "wisdom literature" valid for Proverbs, Job, and Ecclesiastes? Second, does a specific type of literature exist that can be classified as uniquely "wisdom"? Third, Crenshaw raises the serious question of disunity within the books themselves and throughout the corpus as a collection. Fourth, the issue of consistency over time throughout the wisdom corpus is the final focus of this chapter. In other words, are the literary elements that constitute biblical wisdom constant throughout Israel's history?

Conclusion

The Psalms and Wisdom Literature are indeed the heart and soul of not only the *Ketuvim*, but perhaps of the entire Hebrew Bible. A body without its heart is destined to die. A body without a soul is devoid of purpose or meaning for life. In his lesser known prayerbook on the Psalms, *Psalms: The Prayerbook of the Bible*, Dietrich Bonhoeffer calls the church to give its fullest attention to the words of the Psalms.

> Therefore whenever we no longer pray the Psalms in our churches, we must take up the Psalter that much more in our daily and evening prayers, reading and praying together at least several Psalms every day so that we succeed in reading through this book a number of times each year, getting into it deeper and deeper. We also ought not to select Psalms at our own discretion, thinking that we know better what we ought to pray than does God himself. To do that is to dishonor the prayerbook of the Bible. In the ancient church it was not unusual to memorize "the entire David." In one of the eastern churches this was a prerequisite for the pastoral office. The church father St. Jerome says that one heard the Psalms being sung in the fields and gardens in his time. The Psalter impregnated the life of early Christianity. Yet more important than all this is the fact that Jesus died on the cross with the words of the Psalter on his lips.

Whenever the Psalter is abandoned, an incomparable treasure vanishes from the Christian church. With its recovery will come unexpected power.[15]

May this collection of essays help keep the study of the Psalms and Wisdom Literature before the church and the biblical scholars of our day.

---

[15]Dietrich Bonhoeffer, *Psalms: The Prayerbook of the Bible* (Minneapolis: Augsburg Publishing House, 1970) 25-26.

Chapter 2

A Biographical Sketch of Marvin E. Tate

Robert C. Dunston

Marvin Embry Tate, Jr. was born in his family's farmhouse, three miles outside Hope, Arkansas, in 1925. Two older brothers welcomed him into the world. Later a sister joined the family. When he was five years old the family moved to outside Washington, Arkansas. His father became ill with tuberculosis in the 1930s, making life on the farm difficult. His older brothers worked the farm as best they could but when Tate was about seventeen years old, the family left the farm and moved into the town of Washington. The farm near Hope where he was born no longer exists. A country club and golf course now occupy the site.

Early in life Tate had his own health difficulties. Shortly after beginning fourth grade he fell ill and spent the next two years recuperating at home. His family did not own many books so he read some of the high school textbooks his brothers had used, as well as the newspaper, which despite his family's hard times, was a household staple. With these resources Tate developed his reading abilities.

Following his recuperation Tate began school again in the fourth grade, two years behind and physically much bigger than the other students in class. The next year he began the fifth grade but after a month his teacher moved him to the sixth grade. Later in high school he doubled up one year but still completed high school a year late at the age of nineteen.

While growing up, Tate attended the Presbyterian church in Washington. Rev. J. C. Williams, the pastor, had a good background in biblical languages and in the Old Testament. One day in a school assembly, he spoke to the students and faculty. His text was Isaiah 40:1-9, which he read in Hebrew and then translated into English. Tate never forgot the ability of the pastor to read Hebrew and his knowledge of the Old Testament.

While in high school, Tate also became involved in Baptist Training Union at the local Baptist church. Like many small towns in the South,

Washington had three churches: Presbyterian, Baptist, and Methodist. Young people might be members of one church but would attend activities at other churches if for no other reason than having something to do. He recalls that his willingness to read the Bible more than the Baptist students, coupled with his ability to speak, led to his election as Bible Readers Leader which was against the rules of the Baptist Training Union at the time.

As Tate approached high school graduation, he faced a major decision. The local Baptist pastor, Erwin McDonald, had been encouraging him to enter the ministry, something Tate was not enthusiastic about at all. His Presbyterian pastor, J. C. Williams, was also interested in him becoming a minister and wanted Tate to attend Arkansas College (now Salem College), a Presbyterian school, and perhaps move on to Columbia Theological Seminary in Decatur, Georgia, for seminary work. McDonald, who later served as editor of the Arkansas Baptist newspaper, *Arkansas Baptist Newsmagazine*, encouraged him to attend Ouachita Baptist College. Tate journeyed to Ouachita for the summer terms of 1944. During the summer terms he answered God's call to ministry and planned to become a Presbyterian pastor. After completing the summer terms and returning home he decided, after much personal struggle, that ministry in the Baptist tradition would be more amenable to his understanding of the Bible and theology than would ministry in the Presbyterian tradition. He returned to Ouachita in the fall with the goal of becoming a Baptist pastor.

Tate began his academic career at Ouachita Baptist College in the summer and fall of 1944. In October of that year Robert Naylor, pastor of the First Baptist Church of Arkadelphia and later president of Southwestern Baptist Theological Seminary, baptized him as a Baptist. He had already been baptized as a Presbyterian at the age of seventeen.

During his last two years as a student at Ouachita, Tate served as pastor of the Zion Baptist Church in his hometown of Washington, preaching every other Sunday. Shortly after having become pastor, a tornado ripped through the town and destroyed the pre-Civil War frame church. The same tornado blew the shingles off his family's home and knocked the chicken house down but did little other damage. For the next year, while the church house was rebuilt, the congregation met in the old county courthouse, which had served as the state capitol building for the

Confederate government of Arkansas after Federal forces occupied Little Rock in 1862.

Tate graduated from Ouachita College in 1947 having compressed four years of college into three by attending summer sessions. He earned a Bachelor of Arts in History but also had enough credits for a major in Bible. Resigning his pastorate in Washington, Arkansas, he journeyed to Louisville, Kentucky, to begin his Bachelor of Divinity at the Southern Baptist Theological Seminary. In 1948 he became pastor of the Goshen Baptist Church in Glen Dean, Kentucky, serving there until January 1956. Glen Dean was the hometown of Julia Moorman who later would become his wife.

Dr. and Mrs. A. C. Kolb of Little Rock provided both financial and spiritual support during Tate's seminary years. Dr. Kolb was a physician who had long been associated with Tate's family. Goshen Baptist Church paid Tate twenty-five dollars per week during his six-and-a-half-year pastorate there. He also secured some part-time work while in seminary but the combined income could not meet his needs. Tate states that without the financial and spiritual support of the Kolbs, he does not know how he could have completed his seminary work. The Kolbs' investment blessed Tate's life and the lives of many others who have benefited from his scholarship and ministry through the years.

In the fall of 1950 Tate completed the Bachelor of Divinity at Southern having been delayed somewhat by ill health in 1949, which culminated in an appendectomy in that September and a slow recovery throughout the remainder of the 1949–1950 academic year. In the summer of 1950 with his seminary work nearly complete, he began to visit more as pastor in Glen Dean. As he visited, some of the community members asked if he would teach grades five through eight in one room of the local two-room schoolhouse in Glen Dean. His future wife's (Julia) aunt taught grades one through four in the other room. Although he had not majored in education, he had taken fourteen hours of education courses at Ouachita as electives and was somewhat qualified to teach. He agreed to teach, but his one-year public school experience convinced Tate that his career did not lie in that direction.

Tate had gotten to know Julia's family while serving as pastor of Goshen Baptist even though they were Methodists. The Methodist church had Sunday school each Sunday but only a monthly worship service. Julia's family would attend Sunday school at the Methodist church and then walk to the Baptist church for morning worship. During his year of public school teaching Tate stayed at the home of Julia's family which provided him the opportunity to get to know the family even better. Friendship and love grew and he and Julia married on August 18, 1956. Earlier that year Julia had completed her Bachelor of Arts at Kentucky Wesleyan College in Owensboro, Kentucky. She would later complete her Master of Arts at the University of Louisville in Louisville, Kentucky, and teach school for many years.

After his year of public school teaching, Tate entered the Doctor of Theology program at Southern Seminary in the fall of 1951. Nearing the completion of his dissertation, he became pastor of Hillcrest Baptist Church in Tulsa, Oklahoma, in 1956. While serving as pastor there, he completed his dissertation entitled "A Study of the Wise Men of Israel in Relation to the Prophets" in 1958 under the direction of Clyde T. Francisco and Eric Rust and earned his Doctor of Theology.[1]

What led Tate to the study of wisdom? Very few others were involved in the field and he believed it was an area where he might fruitfully work and carve out a niche. From 1906 to 1954 not a single dissertation was produced on wisdom literature at the Southern Baptist Theological Seminary. H. Wheeler Robinson opened the field with his lectures delivered from 1942 to 1945 as Speaker's Lecturer at the University of Oxford. Oxford University Press published the lectures as *Inspiration and Revelation in the Old Testament* (1946) and made them available to a wider audience.[2] In 1955 a *Festschrift* presented to H. H. Rowley on his sixty-fifth birthday featured essays on Old Testament wisdom by many of the great scholars of the day. It was published as *Wisdom in Israel and in the Ancient Near East.*[3] Other than these works, little had been done with the wisdom literature with the exception of the Book of Job, which

---

[1]Marvin Embry Tate, Jr., "A Study of the Wise Men of Israel in Relation to the Prophets" (Th.D. diss., Southern Baptist Theological Seminary, 1958) xvi+441 leaves (OCLC #19597321).

[2]Henry Wheeler Robinson (1872–1945), *Inspiration and Revelation in the Old Testament* (Oxford: Clarendon Press, 1946).

[3]*Wisdom in Israel and in the Ancient Near East. Presented to Professor Harold Henry Rowley by the Society for Old Testament Study in Association with the Editorial Board of Vetus Testamentum, in Celebration of his Sixty-fifty Birthday, 24 March 1955,* Supplements to *Vetus Testamentum* 3, ed. Martin Noth and D. Winton Thomas (Leiden: Brill, 1955; 1960).

everyone felt compelled to comment upon. In writing his dissertation the lack of resources for studying Israel's wisdom literature forced Tate to combine wisdom with another subject for which resources would be available. Thus he compared the wise men of Israel to the prophets.

The spring of 1958 when Tate graduated proved to be a difficult time at Southern Seminary. Tensions were high among many of the faculty members regarding work done by them but published under the name of another. Thirteen professors resigned in protest against the administration of President Duke T. McCall. Two of them (Clyde Francisco and John Joseph Owens) later withdrew their resignations but the trustees fired the remaining eleven. Ralph H. Elliott, for whom Tate had been a fellow for a semester in 1955 when Elliott was an instructor, was not one of the thirteen although he was sympathetic to their cause. He decided to take a position at the new Midwestern Baptist Theological Seminary in Kansas City, Missouri, thus avoiding the confrontation between the thirteen and the administration. The exodus of the eleven created a shortage in a variety of fields, including Old Testament. In 1959 Page H. Kelley was asked to return to become a faculty member, which he did, joining Francisco and Owens. Tate became the fourth Old Testament professor in 1960 and Donald Williams the fifth in 1961.

Tate resigned as pastor of Hillcrest Baptist Church in 1959 to become assistant professor of Bible and Religion at Wayland College in Plainview, Texas. After a year teaching there, he was invited to return to Southern Seminary to teach Old Testament Interpretation. He remembers his interview going well until Dale Moody demanded he use the new introduction to the Old Testament written by B. W. Anderson. He responded that he would consider the book but could not promise to use it if there were a better text available. Francisco thought all hope of his being hired was lost since he had taken on Moody but Rust reported later in the evening to both Tate and Francisco that all was well. Tate resisted the dictates of one individual then as he continues to do. His integrity has always led him to seek the best in educating his students rather than blindly following the mandates of others. After he became a faculty member, he worked well with Moody and became one of his admirers. In addition to his integrity, he possesses the ability to refrain from allowing one negative experience to determine an entire relationship.

In 1960 Tate became associate professor of Old Testament Interpretation at Southern Seminary. Rust taught both Old Testament Theology and

Philosophy but in 1971 moved completely to Philosophy, handing over the teaching of Old Testament Theology to Tate. In 1978 Tate became professor of Old Testament Interpretation and then in 1992 the John R. Sampey Professor of Old Testament. He became senior professor in 1995.

During his tenure at Southern, Tate has pursued additional study at a variety of institutions. He studied at Oxford University in 1966–1967 and in Jerusalem in 1974 at the Ecumenical Institute for Advanced Theological Studies. In 1975 he studied at the Institute for Ecumenical and Cultural Research in Collegeville, Minnesota, and in 1980 spent a sabbatical studying primarily in Louisville with time spent in other locales as well.

For years Tate has been active in the Society of Biblical Literature and the National Association of Baptist Professors of Religion, attending national and regional meetings, learning from the presentations, and dialoguing with the presenters. From 1993 to 1994 he served as vice president and president of the Southeast Region of the National Association of Baptist Professors of Religion. He also served two terms on the editorial board of *Perspectives in Religious Studies* which at the time served as an executive board for the NABPR. His involvement indicates his passion for learning.

Tate has always been an avid reader and stored in his mind is a vast and current bibliography on the Old Testament and other subjects. As my dissertation advisor, he always amazed me. My questions and our discussions invariably led to his listing books that I should consult so I could clarify and deepen my thinking. I often wondered how he was able to remain so current. One day I entered the Southern Seminary bookstore and there he stood by the new books display. He confided to me that he would stop by, check out what was new, stand for an hour and read, and then decide whether or not to purchase the book. With his excellent memory, even if he decided not to purchase the volume, he knew its basic thesis and argument. Even now during our relatively infrequent visits, he provides me with a reading list that inevitably strengthens and deepens my own knowledge and helps me convey ideas to my students.

Many of his students appreciated his interest in discoveries and learning beyond the fields of biblical studies and theology. Conversations in his office became opportunities to expand horizons and examine relationships between seemingly unrelated areas. I remember one office conversation in which Tate, an avid reader of science publications, brought up quantum theory as we discussed Old Testament theology. He opened our eyes and minds to the magnificence and complexity of God and His world.

Tate's thoroughness marks all of his courses and lectures. I had the good fortune to be his Garrett Fellow for two semesters, grading for and soaking up knowledge in his Old Testament theology and survey courses. His theology course employed the Ten Commandments as the "center" for understanding Israelite faith and practice. His notes for this and other classes filled numerous transparencies and all of us sat copying information at a furious pace only to have each transparency removed before we had time to transfer every word to our notes. The transparencies contained information distilled for us from all of his reading and thinking. Keen insights and provocative ideas were sprinkled throughout the transparencies indicating the vast amount of effort he had put into the course so we might learn. Many of us often wished he would publish his transparencies. They would have made an excellent, engaging text.

In addition to his scholarship and teaching, Tate remains committed to the local church. He has served as interim pastor at the following churches: Irvington Baptist Church, Irvington, Kentucky, 1956; Cotton Center Baptist Church, Cotton Center, Texas, 1959; Pleasant Grove Baptist Church, Middletown, Kentucky, 1961 and 1967; Sulphur Baptist Church, Sulphur, Kentucky, 1963; Cloverleaf Baptist Church, Louisville, Kentucky, 1966; Maranatha Baptist Church, Indianapolis, Indiana, 1967; Bethlehem Baptist Church, Louisville, Kentucky, 1972; Cecilia Baptist Church, Cecilia, Kentucky, 1976; Zion Baptist Church, Elizabethtown, Kentucky, 1976; and East Audubon Baptist Church, Louisville, Kentucky, 1976. Other churches too numerous to mention have also benefited from his knowledge and faith through his preaching and leading Bible studies. Most of his time in Louisville has found him most actively involved in Buechel Park Baptist Church which he and Julia joined in 1961. At Buechel Park he has served in numerous positions including Sunday school teacher and member of the finance committee and the personnel committee. Julia is also very active and was the second woman deacon Buechel Park Baptist Church ordained. The local church has meant much to Tate through the years and his ministry in the church has blessed the lives of many.

His publications have focused on wisdom literature and Psalms although he has written on the former and latter prophets as well.

Typically he has written for Baptist publications. His writing along with that of other Baptist professors, has demonstrated the depth and breadth of Baptist scholarship to the world.

From 1970 to 1974 he helped with the translation of the New International Version. He and Clyde Francisco were responsible for the first level translation of Exodus, and he assisted with the second level translation of Deuteronomy, Joshua, Chronicles, Esther, Psalms, Ecclesiastes, Isaiah, and Ezekiel. Once or twice he also served on a third level team checking the first and second levels of translation and refining the result.

Family remains at the center of Tate's life. He and Julia are the proud parents of Sarah Nell, Martha Jean, Betsey Lou, Marvin Andrew, and Virginia Ruth, and the grandparents of two. Shortly after I arrived at Southern Seminary in the fall of 1979, Southern's publication *The Tie* featured a "PROFile" on Tate. Most "PROFiles" promoted the latest publications of the featured professor but not Tate's: under "Most Recent Accomplishment" was "having three daughters in college at the same time." Who could not admire such a feat?

Throughout his life Tate has maintained a sense of humor. For some, humor provides a means of escape from present reality. For Tate, humor provides a method of recognizing reality and coping with or changing it. His comments, both humorous and serious, are inevitably based on a penetrating examination of the situation and its internal contradictions and lunacy. His humor places things in proper perspective.

It is too early to talk about Tate's legacy because he is still creating one as he continues to research, guide, and teach; to minister through the local church; and to enjoy and encourage his family. I consider myself extremely fortunate and blessed to have learned from him and worked with him and I am not alone. He has made a positive difference in the lives of many individuals and created an enduring impact on scholarship and teaching, particularly among Baptists.

As I think about Tate's life and character, I am reminded of the traits of the wife of noble character in Proverbs 31:10-31. Her traits of diligent work, generosity, preparation for the future, teaching ability, and love for and recognition by family and friends describe Tate as well. Perhaps a paraphrase of Proverbs 31:26 best describe his impact:

> He speaks with wisdom,
>   and faithful instruction is on his tongue.

Books

"Job." Coauthored by John D. W. Watts and John Joseph Owens. In *Broadman Bible Commentary*, edited by Clifton J. Allen, vol. 4, 22-151. Nashville: Broadman, 1971.

Old Testament 171: A Study of Job. Nashville: Seminary Extension Department of Southern Baptist Seminaries, 1971.

Old Testament 171: A Study of Job, Teacher's Guide. Nashville: Seminary Extension Department of Southern Baptist Seminaries, 1971.

Old Testament 171: A Study of Malachi. Nashville: Seminary Extension Department of Southern Baptist Seminaries, 19--.

"Proverbs." In *Broadman Bible Commentary*, edited by Clifton J. Allen, vol. 5, 1-99. Nashville: Broadman, 1971.

Psalms 51-100. Word Biblical Commentary 20. Dallas: Word, 1990.

"Psalms." In *Mercer Commentary on the Bible*, edited by Watson E. Mills, Richard F. Wilson, et al., 431-526. Macon GA: Mercer University Press, 1995.

From Promise to Exile: The Former Prophets. Macon GA: Smyth & Helwys, 1999.

Articles

"Jeremiah and Social Reform." *Review and Expositor* 58 (1961): 438-51.

"The Deuteronomic Philosophy of History." *Review and Expositor* 61 (1964): 311-19.

"The Old Testament Apocrypha and the Old Testament Canon." *Review and Expositor* 65 (Summer 1968): 339-56.

"King and Messiah in Isaiah of Jerusalem." *Review and Expositor* 65 (Fall 1968): 409.

"The Speeches of Elihu." *Review and Expositor* 68 (Fall 1971): 487-95.

"Tithing: Legalism or Benchmark?" *Review and Expositor* 70 (Spring 1973): 153-61.

"Living within the Limits." *Outreach* 5 (August 1975): 36-37.

"Wisdom, the Evangelist." *Outreach* 5 (September 1975): 34-35.

"The Whirlwind of National Disaster: A Disorganized Society (Hosea 7-10)." *Review and Expositor* 72 (Fall 1975): 449-63.

"The Legal Traditions of the Book of Exodus." *Review and Expositor* 74 (Fall 1977): 483-505.

"Old Testament Theology: The Current Situation." *Review and Expositor* 74 (Summer 1977): 279-300.

"The Oxford Study Edition of the New English Bible." *Review and Expositor* 76 (Summer 1979): 325-39.

"The New International Version: The Old Testament." *Review and Expositor* 78 (Summer 1979): 363-75.

"Promising Paths toward Biblical Theology." *Review and Expositor* 78 (Spring 1981): 169-85.

"Saul: His Life and Times." *Biblical Illustrator* 7 (April 1981): 33.

"David and the Philistines." *Biblical Illustrator* 8 (April 1982): 37.

"War and Peacemaking in the Old Testament." *Review and Expositor* 79 (Fall 1982): 587-96.

"The Interpretation of the Psalms." *Review and Expositor* 81 (Summer 1984): 363-75.

"A Survey of Some Introductions to the Old Testament." *Review and Expositor* 84 (Spring 1987): 315-21.

"Questions for Priests and People in Malachi 1:2-2:16" *Review and Expositor* 84 (Summer 1987): 391-407.

"Kingship" and "Theophany." Coauthored by Carol Stuart Grizzard. In *Mercer Dictionary of the Bible*, edited by Watson E. Mills et al., 490-91, 908. Macon GA: Mercer University Press, 1990.

"Psalm 88." *Review and Expositor* 87 (Winter 1990): 91-95.

"Worship." In *Holman Bible Dictionary*, edited by Trent C. Butler, 1421-22. Nashville: Holman, 1991.

"Satan in the Old Testament." *Review and Expositor* 89 (Fall 1992): 461-74.

"The Comprehensive Nature of Salvation in Biblical Perspective." *Review and Expositor* 91 (Fall 1994): 469-85.

"Eric Rust as a Biblical Theologian." *Perspectives in Religious Studies* 22 (Winter 1995): 429-40.

"A Review of Six Books by Baptist Old Testament Scholars: A Review Essay." *Perspectives in Religious Studies* 23 (Winter 1996): 425-36.

Book Reviews

Psalms: Reading and Studying the Book of Praises by W. H. Bellinger, Jr. *Review and Expositor* 88 (Fall 1991): 455-59.

Psalms by J. Day. *Review and Expositor* 88 (Fall 1991): 455-59.

Introducing the Psalms by Klaus Seybold, translated by R. Graeme Dunphy. *Review and Expositor* 88 (Fall 1991): 455-59.

Psalm 31—Rettung als Paradigma. Eine synchronleserorientierte Analyse by Eberhard Bons. *Biblica* 77 (1996): 553-57.

Chapter 3

A History of the Use and Interpretation of the Psalms [1]

John D. W. Watts[2]

The Use of Psalms as a Book of Hymns for Liturgical Purposes

The Book of Psalms is often called the "hymnbook of the Second Temple." Many of the psalms were already used in the singing of choirs and by individuals during the period of Solomon's Temple. Simply singing them required interpretation. William Holladay has published a special study of the twenty-third Psalm[3] in which he shows how the very recitation of this psalm involves interpretation, beginning with the name for God and continuing through the words "the valley of death" and "preparing my table before my enemies." Everyone who uses this psalm makes decisions about these phrases in the very act of singing or reciting the psalm.[4] The interpretation of the psalms begins in the way they are used in worship, and continues in the way they are translated, the use made of them in preaching, and finally in becoming the subject of intense scholarly reflection and analysis. Each step is shaped by the worship forms and thought forms of the day. Poetry like the psalms is uniquely susceptible to these influences. They are almost chameleon-like in their capacity to reflect the faith of the reader.

---

[1]The most recent and complete treatment of this full subject to which I am much in-debted is William L. Holladay, *The Psalms through Three Thousand Years: Prayerbook of a Cloud of Witnesses* (Minneapolis: Fortress Press, 1993) referred to hereafter as "Holladay." An earlier treatment of value is Rowland Edmund Prothero, *The Psalms in Human Life* (London: Thomas Nelson and Sons, 1903) referred to hereafter as "Prothero."

[2]To Marvin Tate who has taught generations of students at the Southern Baptist Theological Seminary to understand and love the Psalms and Wisdom Literature.

[3]Holladay, 6-14, "The Lord Is My Shepherd, Then and Now" and 359-71 "How the Twenty-third Psalm Became an American Secular Icon."

[4]Prothero makes this point throughout his book.

Editors and collectors of the Psalms[5] interpreted as they grouped them into five books.[6] The collection of the *hallelujah*[7] psalms near the end is an interpretation. The Psalms of Ascents interpret Psalms 120-134 as pilgrim psalms to be sung during the trip to Jerusalem.

Rendtorff[8] sees signs of three stages in the understanding of the significance of the psalms. The strategic positions of the *hallelujah* psalms show that they were to be used for the praise of God. The emphatic position of the royal psalms shows a tendency toward messianic interpretation. The positions of the Torah psalms (1 and 119) indicate that "the psalms have become the word of God" to instruct in the will of God and right conduct.

The noting of occasions in David's life[9] which are appropriate for certain psalms almost makes the Book of Psalms into a *Festschrift* for David, celebrating his renown as instrumentalist, singer, and composer, and his reputation for bringing music into temple worship. These notes or superscriptions also provide a strategy for understanding and using the Psalms. Second Samuel uses the same system in reverse as it inserts psalms into the David story.[10]

The Use of Psalms in Worship

At least some of the psalms were used in the First Temple when worship related to the king and his rule.[11] The royal psalms[12] testify to this.

---

[5]Holladay, 67-91.

[6]Psalms 1-41; 42-72; 73-89; 90-106; 107-50. See Rolf Rendtorff, *The Old Testament: An Introduction* (Philadelphia: Fortress Press, 1983) for further information about groups of Psalms.

[7]Psalms 111–113 and 144–150 begin with this exclamation.

[8]Rendtorff, *The Old Testament*, 249.

[9]Psalms 3, 18, 34, 51, 52, 56, 57, 59, 60, 142.

[10]James W. Watts, *Psalm and Story: Inset Hymns in Hebrew Narrative*, JSOTS 139 (Sheffield: Sheffield Academic Press, 1992) studies the hymns at the point in which they are set in the narrative but notes the relation to those in the book of Psalms. See in his index, p. 238.

[11]See Sigmund Mowinckel, *The Psalms in Israel's Worship*, 2 vols. (New York and Nashville: Abingdon Press, 1962): see n. 61 below.

[12]Like Psalms 2, 72, 89, and 110.

The psalms continued to be sung in Judaism after the Exile when there was no king but the temple still functioned.[13] The Songs of Ascents were particularly applicable for pilgrims to the Holy City on a hill. This was the unifying act for Judaism after the Exile. The Mishnah records[14] that psalms were sung by Levites: on the first day of the week, Sunday, Ps. 24; on Monday Ps. 48; on Tuesday Ps. 82; on Wednesday Ps. 94; on Thursday Ps. 81; on Friday Ps. 93; and on Saturday Ps. 92.

The Talmud, compiled between the third and fifth centuries AD, requires few Psalms in its worship. But in the succeeding centuries Jews have used the Psalms increasingly.[15]

Psalms continued to be used after the destruction of the temple in synagogues (in Hebrew) and in Christian churches (in Greek).[16] They were found to be useful to sing the praise of God who gave the Torah as also for the Father of the Lord Jesus Christ.[17] The early church fathers like Crispin and Crispinian, and Theodore the Martyr show how the Psalms played a role under persecution. Augustine chose Psalm 23 as the "hymn of martyrs."[18] The use of the Psalms is noted in early Christian history in their influence on the home and in family devotions.[19]

Psalms played major roles in early Christian liturgy and continue in the Divine Office (the Roman Catholic liturgy). A psalm is recited or sung in every service. This began with the practice of reciting the entire Psalter within a year. It was then modified to the recitation of significant psalms eight times daily. In the Eastern Orthodox liturgy and divine office (time of prayer), psalms found significant places.[20]

The Psalms have been sung in notes and measures of all the kinds of music that have existed since David's harp brought melody into Hebrew culture. From the Medieval Gregorian chants to the hymns of Luther's Reformation, from the melodies of the Wesleys to the hymns of the Scottish Presbyterians, in all the various periods in the development of

---

[13]G. Henton Davies, "Worship in the OT." *Interpreters Dictionary of the Bible* 4:882.
[14]Mishnah *Tamid* 7:4 and A. Cronbach, "Worship in NT Times." *IDB* 4:896.
[15]L. I. Rabinowitz, "Psalms, Book of," *Encyclopedia Judaica* 13:1323.
[16]Holladay, 113-30.
[17]Holladay, 165-68, 175-79.
[18]Prothero, 23-24.
[19]Prothero, 25-26.
[20]Holladay, 179-84.

music, singing, and hymnology in Christianity[21] and in Judaism, psalms have played dominant roles. The place of the Psalms in current hymnals is prominent. And the "new music" of the twentieth century depends largely for its lyrics on them.

The Didactic Use of Psalms for Theology and Interpretation

Some important themes for the Old Testament are developed in the Psalms more than elsewhere in the Old Testament (or the Bible). Among these are the following.

The Kingship of God and David. Compare Psalms 2, 72, 132, 110. "The Psalms describe Yahweh as the ruler—though he rules through the Davidic king."[22] Psalms 132, 2, 110[23] give insight into early Israelite royal ideology. See also Psalms 89/ Isaiah 40-55.[24] The kingship of God is developed most completely in Psalms 93-100.[25]

Joy in Worship. Psalms 16:11; 27:6; 43:4; 48:2; 51:8,12; 105:43; 137:6 and many other Psalms picture a form of worship in joy and exuberant praise that stands out in the Bible, a very different attitude than that in the sacrificial worship of Leviticus.

The Greatness of God. This theme can be seen in Psalms 21:5; 47:2; 48:1; 57:10; 76:1; 77:13; 86:10; 95:3; 96:4 and at least 15 other occurrences. God's creation of the universe as well as his kingly reign over the heavens and all history is the basis for this understanding.

Penitence and the expectation of total forgiveness in Psalms 51 are the ultimate expressions of a sense of sin and guilt with a hope of total forgiveness and absolution. The intimate personal nature of spiritual experience in Psalm 23[26] pictures for many people the best possible spiritual relation to God.

---

[21]Holladay, 165-68, 174-84.

[22]Compare A. Laato, *A Star is Rising: The Historical Development of the Old Testament Royal Ideology and the Rise of Jewish Messianic Expectations*, ISFCJ 5 (Atlanta: Scholars Press, 1997) 84-95. See also Marvin E. Tate, *Psalms 51-100*, Word Biblical Commentary 20 (Waco TX: Word Books, 1990) 504.

[23]A. Laato, *A Star Is Rising* (Atlanta: Scholars Press, 1997) 84-88.

[24]Ibid., 178.

[25]Only in Isaiah 40–41 is the view of God's creative rule so complete.

[26]Compare Isaiah 57:15.

Psalms in the Writing of the New Testament (Hebrew/Greek)

Nestle's Greek New Testament contains an index of Old Testament references in the New Testament. Of a possible 150, 103 psalms appear in that index, many of them with multiple citations in every part of the New Testament. These references show how closely early Christian worship and thought followed Jewish practices in the synagogue. The Psalms were used to point to Christ as the Messiah, but they were also "Christianized" in that the writers treat them as though they were written for Christian worship. McCann gives an excellent view of the use of the Psalms in the New Testament.[27]

Psalms in the Dead Sea Scrolls

The recent study of the Dead Sea Scrolls has documented the important use of the Psalms by that community.[28] Psalms continued to be written in Judaism. The LXX contains a book of psalms called the *Psalms of Solomon* which are to be dated in the first century BC.[29] The Scrolls contain a number of *hayodot* "thanksgiving hymns" and at least thirty copies of Psalms. Among these are fragments of 115 biblical psalms.[30] There is also a chain of prooftexts including some from psalms.[31]

The Psalms in the Writings of the Christian Church Fathers

The Church Fathers (Greek) document the importance of the Psalms for their period.[32] The letter of *First Clement* (ca. 96 AD) contains forty-nine citations from thirty-two psalms. Psalms 2 and 110 play a role here very much like that in Hebrews. The Psalms are used to speak directly to Christians. *Barnabas* (ca. 130 AD) uses a dozen references drawn from ten psalms. He tends more toward symbolic application: for example, Psalm

---

[27]J. Clinton McCann, "The Book of Psalms" in *The New Interpreter's Bible*, vol. 4, ed. Leander E. Keck et al. (New York: Abingdon, 1996) 672-75.

[28]Holladay, 95-112.

[29]Holladay, 97-98.

[30]James A. Saunders, *The Dead Sea Psalms Scroll* (Ithaca NY: Cornell University Press, 1967) 146-48.

[31]George J. Brooke, *Exegesis at Qumran: 4Q Florlegium in its Jewish Context*, JSOTSup 29 (Sheffield: JSOT Press, 1985).

[32]Holladay, 162-65.

1:3 can refer both to the waters of baptism and to the cross. Other works like the letters of Ignatius of Antioch (ca. 98–117 AD) and Polycarp's *Letter to the Philippians* (ca. 155 AD) do not use the Psalms at all, relying instead on New Testament citations. On the other hand, Justin Martyr used the Psalms extensively in much the way Matthew did. He sees in them predictions of Christ and his death. Irenaeus (second half of second century AD) uses psalms to describe Christian spiritual reality. Marcion (ca. 140 AD) was a literalist and rejected allegorical interpretations. According to Marcion, Psalm 2 spoke not of Christ but of future Jewish hope. Marcionites in the fifth century composed psalms of their own instead of using Davidic psalms.[33] The commentary of Origin (185–254 BC)[34] was one of the first complete interpretations.

Among the Latter Fathers (Latin), Jerome (342–420) wrote a commentary on Psalms using some of the allegory from Alexandria and some of the literal interpretation of Antioch. Theodore of Mopsuestia (350–428)[35] was a representative of the school at Antioch with its literal emphasis. The Psalms were used in times of death. Augustine found comfort from the Psalms in the death of his mother, Monica, through whose prayers his conversion was brought about, and the Penitential Psalms were read at the time of his death.[36]

The Benedictine order spread into England bringing with it the use of psalms in all aspects of its life, its Rule, and its ceremonies.[37] The same was true of other orders.

Medieval Commentaries (Jewish)

The use of the Psalms permeated the life of Christian Europe during the Middle Ages. The ceremonies in the courts of Charlemagne, Gregory, and the other Emperors were filled with references from them. The crusades and religious revivals of St. Bernard and St. Francis were inspired by and shaped by the recitation of psalms.[38]

---

[33]E.C. Blackman, *Marcion and His Influence* (London: SPCK, 1948) 64.
[34]Holladay, 169-71.
[35]Holladay, 171-74.
[36]Prothero quotes from Possidius, his biographer: Prothero, 28.
[37]Prothero, 63.
[38]Prothero, 70-109.

Medieval Jewish scholarship was particularly significant for the interpretation of the Psalms. Three methods developed. First was *derash* or applied meaning. A second was *midrash* or free exposition of the text. A third was *peshat*, the plain meaning, or the meaning in context.[39] Holladay treats the development of these methods[40] and shows how the debate shaped the context of serious biblical study for everyone.

The rabbis had used psalms and other scriptures as springboards for their own thoughts, as the Talmud shows. They were then challenged in the early Middle Ages by Karaites who as biblicists sought the literal interpretation of the texts. Europe was recovering from its long intellectual slumber. Muslim universities had helped bridge the break from earlier Greek philosophy. Arabic linguistic study brought Jewish scholars to study the Hebrew language and to produce grammars and word lists.

Saadiah Gaon (882–942 AD) did significant work on Psalms. He thought of the book as a second Torah, a book revealed by God to David. The Karaites taught that the psalms were like prophetic prayers. Two of them countered Goan: Salmon ben Yeruham (b. ca. 910 AD) and Yefet ben 'Ali (mid-tenth century). Both of them wrote commentaries on Psalms, viewing them as written by David and prophets. The psalms had foretold the destruction of the Temple in 70 AD and the coming salvation of the Jews.

Still a different view of Psalms came from Moses Ibn Giqatilah (early eleventh century). His commentary is only known by quotations in other works. He viewed the psalms as prayers and poems relating to events near the time of their inception.

Abraham Ibn Ezra (1090–1167 AD) wrote two commentaries on Psalms, showing knowledge of earlier works, but returned to the views of the Rabbis that the psalms are inspired poetry.[41] Two others added influential and significant commentaries: Rabbi Solomon ben Isaac (known as Rashi) (1040–1105 AD) and Qimhi (1160–1235). All three pointed Jews toward the "plain meaning of the text."

---

[39]David Weiss Halvini, *Peshat and Derash: Plan and Applied Meaning in Rabinnic Exegesis* (Oxford: Oxford University Press, 1991).

[40]Holladay, 149-52.

[41]Uriel Simon, *Four Approaches to the Book of Psalms: From Saadiah Gaon to Abraham Ibn Ezra* (Albany NY: SUNY Press, 1991).

In Reformation and Puritan Theology (Eighteenth Century)[42]

Wycliffe, Hus, and Jerome of Prague, some of the earliest founders of Reformation thought, all died with words from the Psalms on their lips.[43] Savanarola's was another early voice calling for reform whose spiritual growth was closely related to the reading of psalms. His last writings include meditations on the Psalms 51 and 31.[44]

Martin Luther was deeply influenced by the recitation of psalms required by the Augustinian order. He continued to recite them in Latin well into the Reformation. In 1513–1515 he delivered a series of lectures on the Psalms.[45] Two and three years later his lectures on Romans and Galatians led to convictions that brought his break with Rome.

John Calvin also wrote voluminously on Psalms.[46] In the preface to his commentary he follows Athanasius and Luther in calling the Psalter "An Anatomy of all the parts of the Soul, for there is not an emotion of which any one can be conscious that is not here represented as a mirror. . . . Here the prophets themselves, seeing they are exhibited to us as speaking to God, and laying open all their inmost thoughts and affections, call, or rather draw, each of us to the examination of himself in particular, in order that none of the many infirmities to which we are subject, and of the many vices with which we abound, may remain concealed."[47]

The Psalms were also on the lips of martyrs like Thomas More and John Fisher in the English Reformation as they were also on the pioneer

---

[42]Holladay, 192-217.

[43]Prothero, 112.

[44]Prothero, 116.

[45]A copy of these lectures is available in English translation in *Luther's Works* (St. Louis: Concordia Publishing House; Philadelphia: Fortress Press, 1955–1976). The "First lectures on the Psalms" is found in volumes 10 and 11 (1974 and 1976). The second set is called "Selected Psalms" and is found in volumes 12, 13, and 14 (1955, 1956, and 1958). Compare also Prothero's account, 118-22.

[46]The English translation of his Psalms commentaries (*Calvin's Commentaries: Psalms*, trans. James Anderson [Edinburgh: Calvin Translation Society, 1843–1855; repr.: Grand Rapids: Eerdmans, 1948–1949]) is 2,400 pages long. The Latin version appeared in 1557. The French translation came in 1558.

[47]Calvin, *Psalms* 1. xxxvii.

Roman Catholic missionary Francis Xavier.[48] The Continental Anabaptists and the French Huguenots made use of psalms in their hymnody.[49]

Psalms continued to be of importance in Reformed churches through their use of metrical psalms in congregational worship.[50] This began with Zwingli and his followers but was quickly picked up by Calvin. English translations of the Bible brought with them the use of psalms in English worship. The Puritans found in the Psalms a favorite, which brought the recitation of psalms into the center of public life. "In the love of the Psalter, Anglican and Independent, Cavalier and Roundhead, might be united."[51] John Milton shows the influence of the psalms in virtually all his writings.[52] John Bunyan's work echoes psalms throughout. Oliver Cromwell found in psalms a different inspiration.[53] The *Bay Psalm Book* (Cambridge, Massachusetts, 1640) was the first book published in New England. Hymns based on psalms have continued to be the staple of virtually every hymnbook in America since then. Psalms were central to worship and thought for the Scottish Covenanters and consequently for Presbyterians everywhere.[54]

The Psalms have also been used for a great deal of classical religious music from Gregorian chant to Handel's *Messiah*.[55]

Psalms have played a great role in the developing worldwide missionary movement. As early as the mission to the Indians of John Eliot (1604–1690), David Brainard (1718–1747), and the pioneering work of Henry Martyn (1781–1812) and William Carey (1761–1834), the Psalms played dominant roles in shaping their piety and calling.[56] The same was true for David Livingston and others. But beyond the influence of the psalms on the missionaries and their sermons was the way psalms shaped the hymnody of the developing worldwide church in its many languages, just as it had the hymnody of Lutheran Germany and Calvinist

---

[48]Prothero, 123-30.

[49]Prothero, 215.

[50]Holladay, 198ff.

[51]Prothero, 210-36.

[52]Prothero, 221-24.

[53]Prothero, 228-36.

[54]Prothero, 237-98.

[55]The Psalms account for more Scripture in *The Messiah* than any Old Testament book except Isaiah.

[56]Prothero, 299-308.

Scotland. In each instance, writers and singers interpreted psalms in their own way and for their own use.

In Nineteenth and Twentieth Century Scholarship[57]

The nineteenth century brought the recovery of Hebrew as a language to be studied with scientific tools and care. One of the first fruits in the English-speaking world was the commentary on Psalms by Charles Augustus Briggs.[58] It continued as a standard work for more than fifty years, although Briggs's late dating of many psalms is no longer in favor.[59]

The twentieth century also brought new directions in the study of Psalms and major contemporary commentaries reflect these views. Historical source criticism was not particularly useful for Psalms. Most critical study searched for an author for psalms and it was no longer believed that David had personally written all of them. But the psalms were interpreted in terms of an individual pious author and the circumstances in which he wrote.[60]

Form criticism, which studied psalms in terms of their use in worship, their *Sitz im Leben*, was introduced by Herman Gunkel near the beginning of the twentieth century. This kind of study was made to order for the study of this kind of liturgical literature. Sigmund Mowinckel extended Gunkel's methods but concentrated his work in the early Israelite monarchy and the view of divine kingship in the psalms.[61] Gunkel's views of the forms (genres, *Gattungen*) of the psalms[62] as well as those

---

[57]Holladay, 50-264, 265-71.

[58]Charles August Briggs and Emilie Grace Briggs, *A Critical and Exegetical Commentary on the Book of Psalms*, International Critical Commnetary, 2 vols. (Edinburgh: T. & T. Clark; New York: Charles Scribner's Sons, 1906–1907).

[59]See Prothero, who shows how the Psalms were used in the Christian church through the nineteenth century.

[60]W. H. Bellinger, *Psalms: Reading and Studying the Book of Praises* (Peabody MA: Hendrickson, 1990) 15.

[61]The research is contained in his six-volume report: *Psalmen Studien 1-6* (Oslo: Kristiana, 1921–1924). Sigmund Mowinckel, *Opfersang og Sangoffer* (Oslo: H. Ashehoug, 1951); English translation: *The Psalms in Israel's Worship*, 2 vols., trans. D. R. Ap-Thomas (New York and Nashville: Abingdon, 1962).

[62]Herman Gunkel, *Einleitung in die Psalmen*, completed by Joachim Begrich, 4th ed. (Göttingen: Vandenhoeck & Ruprecht, 1985; 1st ed., 1933); English translation: *Introduc-*

of Mowinckel were reflected most completely in Kraus's commentary.[63] The principle forms included the lament of an individual, thanksgiving songs of an individual, laments of the community, hymns or songs of praise, royal psalms, wisdom or Torah psalms, entrance liturgies, prophetic exhortation, psalms of confidence or trust, and mixed types.

The introduction of rhetorical criticism in response to James Muilenburg's call for the discipline to "move beyond form criticism"[64] brought attention back to literary characteristics which distinguished each piece of superb poetry which constituted the Psalms. Studies in parallelism, repetition, chiasm, the structure of psalms, and the figurative use of language followed.[65]

Mitchell Dahood's three-volume commentary[66] reflects new knowledge of ancient Hebrew gained from the Ugaritic tablets. These tablets from the second millennium BC show poetry that is similar to many psalms and suggests the antiquity of Hebrew poetry in its similarity to other Canaanite poems.

The three volumes of the Word Biblical Commentary[67] present a balanced use of various available methodologies. This is particularly true of Marvin Tate's volume. The *New Interpreter's Bible* "Psalms" commen-

---

tion to Psalms: The Genres of the Religious Lyric of Israel, trans. James D. Nogalski (Macon GA: Mercer University Press, 1998). Gunkel also wrote a commentary: *Die Psalmen*, HKAT, 5th ed. (Göttingen: Vandenhoeck & Ruprecht, 1968; 1st ed., 1929).

[63]Hans-Joachim Kraus, *Psalms 1-59. A Commentary* (Minneapolis: Augsburg, 1988) and *Psalms 60-150. A Commentary* (Minneapolis: Augsburg, 1989). Both were originally published in the Biblischer Kommentar: Altes Testament series (BKAT) in Germany in the 1960s. E. S. Gerstenberger, *Psalms Part I, with an Introduction to Cultic Poetry*, FOTL 14 (Grand Rapids MI: Eerdmans, 1988) culminates the use of form criticism of the Psalms.

[64]James Muilenburg, "Form Criticism and Beyond," *Journal of Biblical Literature* 88 (1969): 4.

[65]Cf. Thomas G. Long, *Preaching and the Literary Forms of the Bible* (Philadelphia: Fortress, 1989) 47.

[66]Mitchell Dahood, *Psalms I, II, III*, AB 16, 17, 17A (Garden City NY: Doubleday, 1966, 1968, and 1970).

[67]Peter C. Craigie, *Psalms 1-50*, Word Biblical Commentary 19 (Waco TX: Word Books, 1983). Marvin E. Tate, *Psalms 51-100*, Word Biblical Commentary 20 (Dallas TX: Word Books, 1990). Leslie C. Allen, *Psalms 101-150*, Word Biblical Commentary 21 (Waco TX: Word Books, 1983).

tary by Clinton McCann promises to be a very influential study at the beginning of the twenty-first century.[68]

The last two decades of the twentieth century in America have been particularly productive in books "interpreting psalms."[69] These works include Walter Brueggemann's analysis of fifty-eight psalms in terms of "orientation, disorientation, and reorientation."[70] An earlier volume treated theological issues found in reading and praying the Psalms.[71]

James L Mays wrote a popular commentary on Psalms[72] and a companion volume[73] to address issues relating to the psalms in liturgy and as Scripture. Patrick D. Miller, Jr.[74] wrote a volume of essays on the interpretation of Psalms with expositions of ten psalms. Carroll Stuhlmueller[75] gives interpretations to psalms using different methods. His concern is always related to the New Testament and to ways the psalms can be used now.

Claus Westermann[76] comments on forty-six psalms, including exegesis and theological concerns. S. E. Gillingham[77] helps readers approach the psalms as poems. Gunkel's great introduction to the forms of the psalms finally has been put into English.[78] Harvey H. Guthrie[79] begins

---

[68]J. Clinton McCann, "The Book of Psalms," *The New Interpreter's Bible*, vol. 4, ed. Leander E. Keck et al. (Nashville: Abingdon Press, 1996) 639-1280.

[69]See McCann's bibliography, ibid., 676-77.

[70]Walter Brueggemann, *The Message of the Psalms: A Theological Commentary* (Minneapolis: Augsburg. 1984).

[71]Walter Brueggemann, *Praying the Psalms* (Winona MN: St. Mary's, 1982).

[72]James L. Mays, *Psalms*, Interpretation (Louisville: John Knox Press, 1994).

[73]James L. Mays, *The Lord Reigns: A Theological Handbook to the Psalms* (Louisville: John Knox Press, 1994).

[74]Patrick D. Miller, Jr., *Interpreting the Psalms* (Philadelphia: Fortress Press, 1986).

[75]Carroll Stuhlmueller, *Psalms 1 and Psalms 2*, Old Testament Message 21 and 22 (Wilmington DE: Glazier, 1983).

[76]Claus Westermann, *The Living Psalms*, trans. R. Porter (Grand Rapids: Eerdmans, 1989).

[77]S. E. Gillingham, *The Poems and Psalms of the Hebrew Bible*, Oxford Bible Series (Oxford: Oxford University Press, 1994).

[78]Hermann Gunkel, *The Psalms: A Form-Critical Introduction*, trans. T. M. Horner, FBBS 19 (Philadelphia: Fortress, 1967).

[79]Harvey H. Guthrie, *Israel's Sacred Songs: A Study of Dominant Themes* (New York: Seabury, 1966).

with form-critical views but uses most of his space to help contemporary readers find that the psalms speak to them.

Hans-Joachim Kraus[80] followed up his massive commentary on the Psalms with his treatment of basic themes in their original settings. He deals with God, the people, the king, the individual, enemies, and Zion. A closing section deals with the way New Testament writers use the psalms. Herbert J. Levine[81] writes of the use of psalms in the conflict of faith and experience—the issue of theodicy—with particular attention to the Holocaust.

James Limburg[82] presents a series of essays on the types of psalms and their application today. J. Clinton McCann[83] accompanied his commentary with his appeal for contemporary reading of Psalms as Scripture which provides instruction about God, humanity, and the faithful life.

Sigmund Mowinckel[84] concentrated on the ancient use of the psalms in worship. These studies lead to conclusions about the nature of Israel's worship. A major feature is the description of "the Enthronement Festival of Yahweh" which he believes was practiced in Jerusalem's temple during the monarchy.

Eugene H. Peterson[85] provides reasons for using the psalms as prayers, as well as a plan for doing so. David J. Pleins[86] is aware of current socioeconomic oppression as he appeals for readers to hear the psalms as "poetry of justice." He treats their theological application for work and worship. Nahum M. Sarna[87] presents nine essays on psalms of different types. He tries to understand them in the context of the ancient

---

[80]Hans-Joachim Kraus, *Theology of the Psalms*, trans. Keith Crim (Minneapolis: Augsburg, 1986).

[81]Herbert J. Levine, *Sing Unto God a New Song: A Contemporary Reading of the Psalms* (Bloomington: Indiana University Press, 1995).

[82]James Limburg, *Psalms for Sojourners* (Minneapolis: Augsburg, 1986).

[83]J. Clinton McCann, *A Theological Introduction to the Book of Psalms: Psalms as Torah* (Nashville: Abingdon, 1994).

[84]Mowinckel, *The Psalms in Israel's Worship*: see nn. 11 and 61 above.

[85]Eugene H. Peterson, *Answering God: The Psalms as Tools for Prayer* (San Francisco: Harper & Row, 1989).

[86]David J. Pleins, *The Psalms: Songs of Tragedy, Hope, and Justice* (Maryknoll NY: Orbis, 1993).

[87]Nahum M. Sarna, *Songs of the Heart: An Introduction to the Book of Psalms* (New York: Schocken, 1993).

Near East, but he also draws on early rabbinic sources, and commentators from medieval times and contemporary Jewish writers.

Mark S. Smith[88] places the psalmists in the temple and employs solar imagery as used in the ancient Near East to explore the experience of the authors. Gerald H. Wilson[89] concentrates on the work of editors who shaped the Psalter. His work has proved to be a decisive influence in turning the attention of interpreters to the final literary form of the book and its contents. Erich Zenger[90] has produced an argument for the Christian use of psalms about enemies. He has tried to be correct in liturgical usage, consistent with good theology. His work sidesteps both Marcionite and anti-Jewish errors.

Psalms in Revival Theology
(The Great Awakening; 19th-20th century)

Christian missionaries of the nineteenth and twentieth centuries took the psalms with them. This insured that they were used extensively in Christian congregations speaking and singing in other than Western languages. Translations which had brought Hebrew lyrics through Greek and Latin to the cultures of the West now took them into the cultures and languages of the world.

Psalms in Current Theologies and Hymnody[91]

The Roman Catholic practice of using a Psalm in every public mass has led to a flourishing of new musical settings for psalms. The chants of the Taizé community, for example, contain many texts from Psalms. A special section in a recent Lutheran book on worship is "The Rediscovery of the Psalter."[92]

---

[88]Mark S. Smith, *Psalms: The Divine Journey* (New York: Paulist, 1987).

[89]Gerald H. Wilson, *The Editing of the Hebrew Psalter*, SBLDS 76 (Chico CA: Scholars Press, 1985).

[90]Erich Zenger, *A God of Vengeance? Understanding the Psalms of Enmity*, trans. Linda M. Maloney (Louisville: Westminster/John Knox, 1995).

[91]Holladay, 271-358.

[92]Philip H. Pfatteicherl and Carlos R. Messerli, eds., *Manual on the Liturgy—Lutheran Book of Worship* (Minneapolis: Augsburg, 1979) 19-21.

Problems in the Interpretation of the Psalms

The use of Psalms in devotion, worship, and theology is not without its problems. Holladay has discussed a number of these[93] including Kabbalistic use of psalms in magic incantation, "censored texts," and problems of translation. He notes issues relating to the use of psalms by Christians, by women, and others. He also notes that the psalms are aware of the reality and location of evil, and that Jesus prayed and discussed the psalms.[94]

The Psalms are probably more influential today than ever before. And the need for careful and thorough interpretation remains as important as ever.

---

[93]Holladay, 287ff.

[94]Psalm 110; Psalm 22:2 (Matt. 27:46 | Mark 27:46); and Psalm 31:6 (Luke 23:46).

Chapter 4

From Psalm to Psalms to Psalter

James D. Nogalski

Introduction

The book of Psalms contains 150 individual units, making it the largest book in the Bible. These 150 psalms continue to be investigated individually. However, relatively recently, people have grown curious about more than the individual psalms. They want to know about the psalter as a whole. Two important dimensions of the whole corpus have caught the attention of Psalms scholars. First, how did we get the book of Psalms as we now have it? Second, what happens if one attempts to read Psalms as a book rather than a vessel containing 150 different psalms? This essay will concentrate on the first dimension to shed some light on the complicated nature of the second. The psalms themselves provide evidence of a lengthy process of collection involving many hands (and potentially many different editorial interests). This lengthy process of collection complicates sweeping generalizations about the shape of the psalter. However, this same evidence indicates that the psalms are not as haphazardly arranged as many people presume at first glance.

Davidic Superscriptions and Authorship

Some students are surprised when they begin advanced Bible study to learn that David did not write all 150 psalms. They are even more surprised to learn that serious scholarly objections have been raised about Davidic authorship of many of the psalms which their Bible clearly calls a "psalm of David" (such as, Psalms 3, 4, 5, etc). These two issues require separate treatment. No matter how one approaches the second question, David did not write all 150 psalms. The tradition of Davidic authorship of Psalms essentially derives from those seventy-four headings or superscriptions that mention David explicitly.[1] More superscriptions mention David than any other person. However, these Davidic superscriptions only appear with about half the psalms. Some of the remaining superscriptions mention other persons (Solomon, Asaph, Ethan, Moses) or groups (the sons of Korah) besides David. Some contain no superscription (such as Psalms 1, 2), or list no names in the superscription (such as Psalms 92, 98, 123, 125). In short, based on the superscriptions alone, one cannot maintain that David authored all 150 psalms.

Why would scholars question the Davidic authorship of those seventy-four psalms which mention David in the superscription? Scholars have questioned Davidic authorship for linguistic, material, and tradition-historical reasons. The Hebrew phrase which mentions David creates *linguistic* difficulties because it consists only of a preposition connected to the name David (*l dawid*). This preposition has the basic meaning "to" or "for" but it can mean numerous things in English depending upon the context in which it is used. In Psalms one can find at least three meanings for this preposition when used with a name. First, the preposition can be used to indicate authorship/ownership, and would be translated "belonging to. . . . " This meaning appears probable in the Korahite psalms (Psalms 42-49, 84-88), where the *l* preposition is used with a group and translated in the sense of "belonging to the sons of Korah." These Korahite psalms also show one should not assume the preposition always refers to authorship since it is difficult to see how a group could author a psalm.

Second, the *l* preposition can indicate the destination of a psalm. This usage appears most frequently in the opening address "for the choir director" that appears fifty-five times in various superscriptions. This phrase uses the same Hebrew preposition as those superscriptions that refer to David, but no one interprets these references as signs of authorship.

---

[1]Many, but not all, psalms contain headings that are popularly interpreted as having something to do with the authorship of the individual psalm. Most psalms contain a heading, or superscription, that designates the beginning of a new psalm. Some contain conclusions, or subscriptions, that mark the end of a psalm. In English Bibles, these superscriptions and subscriptions generally fall outside the verse numbering systems, and are often printed in different typefaces. Some English translations of the Bible do not even print these titles, but they are part of the Hebrew text.

Third, the same preposition can be translated as "dedicated to." This meaning can be readily seen in the conclusion (or subscription) of Psalm 18:51: "(dedicated) to David and to his descendants forever." Here, one can see the preposition plus the name cannot mean authorship since David and his *descendants* could hardly compose the same psalm. Thus, the meaning of the *l* preposition in Psalm headings and conclusions varies. The variation of meanings for the *l* preposition when used with a name require that one look carefully at each reference to David in the superscriptions before translating the phrase.

Several Davidic psalms create *material* difficulties for ascribing them to David. These difficulties arise when the psalm in question refers to realities which did not exist in David's lifetime. For example, at least seventeen "Davidic" psalms refer to the temple, yet the first temple was not built until the time of Solomon, David's son.[2] One could mention other, less obvious examples, but this example illustrates the historical difficulties created by the "Davidic" psalms when one attempts to date all Davidic psalms to the time of David (the tenth century BCE).

Scholars have also raised questions about Davidic authorship of canonical psalms on *tradition-historical* grounds. Two aspects dominate this reasoning: the pseudepigraphic tendencies of ancient Near Eastern literature and the liturgical functions of the psalms. Pseudepigraphic writings were a prominent part of ancient Near Eastern literature. Unlike modern writings, ancient Near Eastern literature rarely focused upon the author's identity. Rather, the *authority* of the writing dominated the concerns of writers and readers. Scribes generally did not include the writer's name with a piece of literature. Older works were updated and modified significantly, but the editors considered their work consistent with the work they were editing, meaning they did not add their own names to the revised work. Over time, this tendency increased, and the literature of postexilic Judah was no exception. Works were increasingly composed

---

[2]"Temple" appears in various forms in "Davidic" psalms: *lkyh* (Psalms 5:8; 11:4; 18:7; 27:4; 29:9; 65:5; 68:30; 138:2; 144:12); "your house" (Psalms 5:8; 26:8; 36:9; 65:5; 69:10; 93:5); "house of YHWH" (Psalms 23:6; 27:4; 122:1, 9; 134:1; 135:2). In addition, despite syntactical difficulties, Psalm 30:1 is sometimes translated as a reference to the temple. The superscription of the Hebrew (MT) should be translated "A psalm. A song at the dedication of the temple [house]. Belonging to David." Some translations, however, have repointed the Hebrew of "house" to a construct and translate it as, " . . . the dedication of the house of David."

and ascribed to the heroes of the past, as is commonly recognized for a significant percentage of the "intertestamental" literature, including works like the Psalms of Solomon, the Prayer of Manasseh, Testaments of the Twelve Patriarchs, 1 Enoch, and 4 Ezra.[3] This practice also occurs in works of the apocrypha like Baruch, the Greek additions to Daniel, and the Greek additions to Esther. Also, biblical and extrabiblical traditions about David and Solomon increasingly associated these two kings with psalms and wisdom literature respectively.

In addition to the pseudepigraphic tendencies of ancient Near Eastern literature, evidence suggests that the superscriptions in psalms reflect an awareness of *liturgical* practices from the first or second temple period. The superscriptions reflect liturgical or worship practices, as one can see from the many references to performance which they contain. Many superscriptions refer to the instruments or the mode of performance used to play the song, even if precise meanings of several technical terms remain obscure.[4] These superscriptions can also mention various worship practices.[5] Finally, many of the superscriptions refer to the "leader." This term is often translated as "choir director" based on the assumption that these psalms were sung in worship settings. Given the nature of these references, scholars of the last century have assumed they imply a functioning temple cult. A temple cult setting would further preclude Davidic authorship since the temple would not have been built in David's time.

The extent to which these and other liturgical references can be associated with practices of the second temple (after 520 BCE) is a more

---

[3]These writings as we have them date to the period between 200 BCE and 100 CE: Testaments of the Twelve Patriarchs (second century BCE); 1 Enoch, and the Prayer of Manasseh (second century BCE to first century CE); the Psalms of Solomon (first century BCE); 4 Ezra (first century CE). For a more complete listing, see *The Old Testament Pseudepigrapha*, 2 vols., ed. James H. Charlesworth (Garden City NY: Doubleday, 1983, 1985).

[4]Several superscriptions mention various types of instruments (Psalms 4, 6, 12, 54, 55, 67, 76, etc.). Other superscriptions refer to some mode of performance (Psalms 5, 7, etc.).

[5]Note references to "prayer" in the superscriptions of Psalms 17, 86, 90, 102, 142. References to "atonement" in Psalms 16, 56-60 refer to ritual acts. The term "song of ascents" (Psalms 120-134, etc.) probably refers to a religious pilgrimage. The plural imperatives used in the Hallelujah psalms (111-113; 146-150) also imply some type of worship setting.

complicated question. Evidence for late dating of certain psalms stems from several lines of reasoning. Innerbiblical citations, along with allusions to the destruction of the temple and/or Jerusalem (such as Psalm 137) make it highly likely that many psalms reflect postexilic settings. In addition, Psalm headings in the ancient versions vary considerably.[6] This variation suggests that the titles of the psalms were not as solidly fixed by the time of the so-called Septuagint (LXX) translations as one would presume if these titles had always been part of the individual psalms.

One final piece of indirect tradition historical evidence should be noted. Thirteen Davidic superscriptions contain more detail than merely the name of David. They refer to events from the life of David, indicating that the *reader* should associate the following psalm with a particular episode in David's life: Psalms 3, 7, 18, 34, 51, 52, 54, 56, 57, 59, 60, 63, 142. All of these superscriptions refer to David in the third person, not the first person. It is probably no accident that *all* but one of the biographical episodes noted in these Davidic superscriptions appear in the narratives of the Deuteronomistic History (DtrH). None of these superscriptions refer to accounts unique to the Chronicler, and only one (Psalm 7:1) refers to an event which *may not* be contained in DtrH.[7] These superscriptions thus reflect a point after which the Davidic traditions of the DtrH had gained authoritative status. These biographical notes invite the reader/hearer of the psalm to recall events from David's life as recorded in texts preserved by the worshiping community.[8]

Making decisions about the date and authorship of individual psalms will always be difficult. The content of the psalms rarely refers directly to particular persons or events that can be pinpointed historically. One will thus encounter honest differences of opinion, and different approach-

---

[6]See Otto Eißfeldt, *The Old Testament: An Introduction*, trans. Peter R. Ackroyd (Oxford: Blackwell, 1974) 451-54; Hermann Gunkel and Joachim Begrich, *Introduction to Psalms. The Genres of the Religious Lyric of Israel*, trans. James D. Nogalski (Macon GA: Mercer University Press, 1998) 349-51.

[7]However, some claim that the reference to "Cush" in 7:1 could intend the Cushite of 2 Samuel 18:21-32. See Siegfried S. Johnson, "Cush," *Anchor Bible Dictionary*, ed. David Noel Freedman et al. (New York: Doubleday, 1992) 1:1219.

[8]See also Brevard S. Childs, "Psalm Titles and Midrashic Exegesis," *Journal of Semitic Studies* 16 (1971): 137-50. Childs convincingly argues that postexilic scribes have created these headings based upon the content of the psalms, not upon traditions of Davidic authorship of the psalms themselves.

es, to the same information. Very few Psalms scholars deny that the psalter contains both preexilic and postexilic psalms. Some scholars will argue that the superscriptions, while they may have been added long after David's lifetime, still reflect credible oral tradition about that particular psalm. These scholars will generally hold open the possibility that several Davidic psalms could come from David, if the psalm contains no strong evidence to the contrary. Other scholars will see the superscriptions as spurious evidence that says more about how the psalms were used than about the person who authored them.

To summarize, the "Davidic" superscriptions of the Psalter provide a complex picture when trying to ascertain information concerning the authorship of individual psalms. These superscriptions confirm that some, though not all, of the psalms were intended to be read as though David had written them. However, these superscriptions also create linguistic, material, and traditiohistorical difficulties for assigning the psalms with "Davidic" superscriptions to the hand of David. A clearer, though still blurry, picture begins to develop when one looks at the superscriptions as one piece of evidence which helps illustrate how the psalter developed over time.

Superscriptions and Psalm Groups

Both "Davidic" and non-Davidic superscriptions provide information which helps explain how individual psalms were transmitted and/or edited over time. In at least two ways the superscriptions shed light upon the complex process of collecting and arranging psalms that eventually led to the book of Psalms as we now have it. The superscriptions, taken as a whole, demonstrate principles of arrangement that can only be explained by the collection and/or editing of individual psalms. The superscriptions also provide strong evidence that the psalter grew in stages as smaller collections of psalms were incorporated into the developing psalter.

The superscriptions provide evidence that the psalms were arranged by someone, since recurring elements often appear in clusters. "Davidic" psalms generally appear in groups, especially in Psalms 3-89. As a result, scholars often refer to the first Davidic psalter (Psalms 3-41) and second Davidic psalter (51-70). However, other recurring psalm headings also appear in batches, whether these headings are grouped by names or other information.

Chart 1. *Groups of Psalms*

Books 1–3	Book 4	Book 5
–2 Davidic collections (3-41, 51-70)	–untitled psalms (91, 93-97, 99, 104-106)	–2 small Davidic collections (108-10, 138-45)
–2 Asaph groups (50, 73-83)	–Moses psalm (90)	–2 hallelujah-psalm collections (111-13, 146-50)
–2 Korahite groups (42-49, 84-85/87-88	–psalm (*of David*? [so LXX], 98)	–2 isolated hallelujah psalms (117, 135) followed by
–untitled (1, 2, 33, 71)	–psalm of thanksgiving (100)	thanksgiving songs (118, 136; cf. 106-107)
–Solomon psalm (72)	–psalm of David (101, 103)	–the songs of ascent (120-134)
	–prayer of the afflicted (102)	

In addition to the Davidic groupings in Psalms 3-89, one finds two groups of Korahite psalms (42-48, 84-88). Each Korahite group contains one psalm (43, 86) that does not mention the sons of Korah in the superscription, but clearly someone has either placed these psalms together or (more likely) incorporated two collections of Korahite psalms into larger collections at different points in time. The Asaph psalms also appear in two batches (50, 73-83), although the first "batch" contains only one psalm.

The chart also shows that the first part of the psalter contains groupings of psalms associated with similar names, but the latter portions of the psalter psalms tend to group psalms by other information. Psalms 120-134 contain the phrase "song of ascents" in the superscription, probably because they were pilgrimage songs. Some psalms are grouped together based on similar introductory matter, not on superscriptions. Psalms 111-113 and 146-150 all begin with the command to "praise YHWH" (*hallelujah*). In addition, many of the psalms show a demonstrable tendency for groupings of technical terms within these larger groups.[9] The names, categories, and phrasing of the opening verses of the Psalms played a role in arranging the psalter.

---

[9]See the chart in Gerald Henry Wilson, *The Editing of the Hebrew Psalter*, SBLDS (Chico CA: Scholars Press, 1985) 238-44. For example, six superscriptions classify the subsequent psalm as a *miktam*, a term generally thought to mean a psalm of atonement. Five of these six appear one after the other (Psalms 56-60) in the second Davidic psalter.

However, not every psalm falls into one of the above-mentioned groupings. Nineteen psalms contain no superscription.[10] Other psalms mention persons who appear only once or twice in Psalm headings. For example, Ethan is mentioned only in Psalm 89:1 and only Psalm 90 mentions Moses in the superscription. Only Psalms 72 and 127 mention Solomon, but they are not grouped together. To begin to understand how small groups of psalms were combined with individual psalms, and how these psalms eventually formed the 150 psalms of the canonical psalter, one must look at several indicators of editorial processes which affected the psalter as it developed. These processes suggest that smaller collections were combined and edited at *various stages*, not all at once.

The Psalter as a Collection of Smaller Collections

Editors who worked on the psalter, like those who worked on other portions of the Hebrew Bible, generally worked anonymously. Earlier generations of scholars tended to ignore or denigrate the role this editorial shaping had upon the whole. Recent scholarship has only begun to investigate the intricate details of this shaping. Much work remains before scholarship reaches a consensus about the motivating factors of this editorial shaping and the effect on the interpreter of reading the entire psalter. Nevertheless, recognition of key indicators of the growth of the corpus represents a solid starting point from which this work can progress. These indicators can be seen in at least three areas which transcend the smaller collections: the Elohistic psalter (Psalms 42-83), Psalms 3-89, and the division of the psalter into five books.

The Elohistic Psalter. Most psalms refer to the deity by using God's name in the form of the tetragrammaton YHWH. This name is typically translated into English as a title, "the LORD," using all-capital or capital and small-capital letters. By contrast, the generic term God (*elohim* in Hebrew) appears far less frequently in most of the psalter. However, one section of the psalter (Psalms 42-83) stands out because it noticeably reverses this tendency. This section of the psalter is known as the Elohistic Psalter because it overwhelmingly prefers the term *elohim* over the name

---

[10]Psalms 1, 2, 10, 33, 43, 71, 91, 93-97, 99, 107, 114, 118, 119, 136, 137.

YHWH.[11] Thus, the frequency of the divine epithets suggests something different occurred in Psalms 42-83 than in other parts of the psalter.

The frequency of *elohim* sets Psalms 42-83 apart from the remainder of the psalter, but two other types of evidence allow one to say with virtual certainty that editors systematically changed most of the references from YHWH to *elohim* in Psalms 42-83.

First, three psalm doublets exist in which one version of a psalm (or section of a psalm) appears inside the Elohistic Psalter and another version exists outside the Elohistic Psalter.[12] All three doublets change references to the deity, including changes from YHWH to *elohim* (for example, compare Psalms 14:2, 4 and 53:2, 4). Second, the Elohistic Psalter contains phrases using *elohim*, which typically appear elsewhere with YHWH. For example, the phrase "God, your God" appears twice in the Elohistic Psalter (45:7; 50:7), but nowhere else in the entire Hebrew Bible. By contrast, the phrase "YHWH, your God" is very common.[13] This unusual phrase, among others, suggests that the name YHWH was programmatically edited to "God" in Psalms 42-83.[14]

Interestingly, the Elohistic Psalter incorporates several small collections and presents a snapshot of one "collection of smaller collections"

---

[11]Statistics may vary slightly from program to program. According to one electronic concordance, the ratio of the occurrence of YHWH to *elohim* outside the Elohistic Psalter is more than 5 to 1 (outside the Elohistic Psalter, YHWH appears 650 times, while *elohim* appears 120 times). However, the ratio of YHWH to *elohim* inside the Elohistic Psalter is less than 1 to 5 (YHWH appears only 45 times in comparison to the 245 occurrences of *elohim*). Statistics taken from *Bible Windows*, ver. 4.0 (Silver Mountain Software).

[12]Ps 14 = Ps 53; Ps 40:13-17 (Heb. 40:14-18) = Ps 70; and Pss 57:7-11 (Heb. 57:8-12) + 60:5-12 (Heb. 60:7-14) = Ps 108.

[13]The phrase "YHWH, your God" is a common phrase in the Hebrew Bible. It appears 432 times, with 78% (278 times) occurring in Deuteronomy and the DtrH (fifty-eight times). The phrase "YHWH, your God" appears only twice in the psalter.

[14]The term "programmatically" is appropriate in spite of the fact that YHWH appears nearly fifty times in the Elohistic Psalter. When one evaluates those places where YHWH (or the abbreviation *Yah*) appears, one finds they generally occur (1) in places where YHWH is addressed directly, making the name YHWH especially appropriate; (2) in places where the YHWH appears as part of divine epithets using more than one word for the deity; (3) in places where YHWH is used in poetic parallelism with a line containing another name for God; and (4) places where the reference to YHWH likely entered the psalm after the Elohistic editing (that is, after the Elohistic Psalter was combined with other collections). See my unpublished paper delivered to the 1995 Southeast regional meeting of the Society of Biblical Literature, "The Use of YHWH in the Elohistic Psalter."

at a stage of the collection process which preceded the final form of the Hebrew text tradition known as the Masoretic Text (MT). The Elohistic Psalter begins with the first Korahite collection (Psalms 42-49) and concludes with the end of the second Asaph grouping (Psalms 73-83). In between, one finds the first Asaph psalm (Psalm 50), the Second Davidic Psalter (51-70), the first of two psalms with Solomonic superscriptions (Psalm 72), and two psalms without superscriptions (43, 71). Most of these psalms seem to have undergone the Elohistic revision.

Psalms 3-89. A subsequent stage of the developing corpus can be isolated with considerable certainty due to editorial patterns and musical notations. As noted above, Psalms 3-89 display common tendencies for arranging psalms. In addition, at least one musical notation suggests that the Elohistic Psalter (Psalms 42-83) was combined at one point with the First Davidic Psalter (3-41) *before* these psalms were joined with Psalms 90-150. The first Davidic Psalter did not undergo an Elohistic redaction.[15] However, the presence of *selah* notations occurs almost exclusively in Psalms 3-89.[16]

No one is certain about the meaning of *selah*, but the best guesses suggest it has something to do with the *performance* of psalms. The most common suggestions are that *selah* either marks a point for a musical interlude or denotes the point for some type of refrain. At any rate, this notation does not occur as programmatically as with the substitution of *elohim*, nor does it occur in a recognizable pattern. In this respect, one would not necessarily speak of a *selah* redaction as with the substitution of *elohim*. Rather, the *selah* notations were probably used by performers at a point when Psalms 3-89 were *transmitted* together. This group of psalms comprises not only the Elohistic Psalter and the First Davidic Psalter, but also the second group of Korahite Psalms (Psalms 84-88) and the psalm of Ethan the Ezrahite (Psalm 89). These psalms also constitute the first three "books" of the psalter.[17]

---

[15]The distribution of YHWH and Elohim in the First Davidic Psalter mirrors the psalter as a whole in that YHWH appears 273 times while Elohim appears only forty-nine times.

[16]The word *selah* appears seventy-one times in the Hebrew book of Psalms, but it appears in only two psalms outside Psalms 3-89. The word *selah* appears in Psalm 140:4, 6, 9; and 143:9. It also appears in the victory hymn of Habakkuk 3. Otherwise all occurrence of this enigmatic notation occur in Psalms 3-89.

[17]In all likelihood, Psalm 2 functioned as the introductory psalm of this collection,

The Five Books of the Psalter. For centuries biblical scholars have noted that the psalter is structured as five "books." One early rabbinic tradition of the *Midraš Tehillim* to Psalm 1:1 states, "Moses gave Israel the five books (of the *tôrâh*) and David gave Israel the five books of the Psalms."[18] This tradition of a fivefold division of the psalter that parallels the five books of the *tôrâh* derives from the use of a series of interrelated doxologies which appear at the end of Psalms 41, 72, 89, and 106. Once noted, these doxologies effectively divide the psalter into five blocks (or "books" to use the traditional language): Psalms 1-41; 42-72; 73-89; 90-106; and 107-150.

The four doxologies are interrelated in style as well as language.

Chart 2. *The Doxologies*

Ps 41:13 (H41:14)	Ps 72:18-19a	Ps 89:52 (H89:53)	Ps 106:48
Blessed be YHWH, the God of Israel, from everlasting to everlasting. Amen and Amen.	Blessed be YHWH God, the God of Israel, who alone works wonders, and blessed be his glorious name forever; and may the whole earth be filled with his glory. Amen and Amen.	"Blessed be YHWH forever. Amen and Amen."	Blessed be YHWH, the God of Israel, from everlasting even to everlasting. And let all the people say, "Amen. Praise YHWH."

Each of the four doxologies begins "blessed be YHWH," and concludes with "amen (and amen)." Each of the four contains at least one

---

prior to the addition of Psalm 1. However, the point at which Psalm 2 entered the corpus raises complex questions. It is often noted that Psalm 2 contains numerous linguistic and thematic parallels to the other royal transitional psalms (72 and 89). Psalm 2:12 also exhibits thematic links to the refuge language of Psalms 3-41. It has also been suggested that 2:10-12 contains editorial links back to Psalm 1. Psalm 2, however, exhibits no sign of the Elohistic shaping (unlike Psalm 72, but like Psalm 89). Could it be that an early form of Psalm 2 introduced Psalms 3-41, and that it continued to play this role for Psalms 3-89 as well? More consideration of the role of Psalm 2 is required before these questions can be answered definitively.

[18]Cited in Klaus Seybold, *Die Psalmen. Eine Einführung* (Stuttgart, 1986) 23. This work also appears in English: *Introducing the Psalms*, trans. R. Graeme Dunphy (Edinburgh: T. & T. Clark, 1986).

reference to perpetuity. This verbal repetition links the doxologies to one another. Nowhere else does the Psalter contain this combination of terms. In fact, the word "amen" appears only in these four places in the entire book of Psalms.

Debate exists regarding whether the doxologies always existed as part of the psalms to which they currently belong. In other words, were these doxologies created when the psalms were composed? Or, were the doxologies added to the end of the psalm by editors who wished to link the psalm books? The similar language suggests that these verses were created for their current function to mark the end of the first four sections of the psalter.[19] These verses share a high percentage of vocabulary which is not that common in the psalter. Also, genre considerations suggest that these doxologies, while often appropriate to the context, are not necessary for the psalms in which they appear. In each case, the preceding verses could have concluded the psalm without damaging that psalm's structure or genre components. Finally, the "amen" refrain of Psalm 106 links the end of book four with the conclusion of the psalter. When one sees the link, one cannot help but wonder if it was intentionally created. The first three doxologies conclude with a dual amen, but Psalm 106:48 deviates from this pattern ("Amen. Praise YHWH."). The purpose of this variation makes sense when one recognizes that it can function as an anticipatory link, or inclusio, to the end of the Hebrew psalter, where the last five psalms all begin with "Praise YHWH" (*hallelu-yah*).

Several signs thus suggest that the doxologies were created to connect books 1-5. However, the purpose of these elements remains controversial. It is not clear whether these connecting elements intended to unify the psalter in anything more than a formal manner. Early traditions draw parallels between the five books of Moses (the *tôrâh*) and the five books of David (the psalter). However, no clear evidence suggests that texts of the psalter mirror texts in the *tôrâh*. No convincing evidence has shown that the psalms were intended to be read with specific texts from the Pentateuch. In fact, the Davidic superscriptions (especially those with biographical notations) argue against this assumption. In short, the doxologies clearly divide the psalter into five books, but the purpose of that division has not been ascertained with any degree of certainty.

---

[19]In addition to the vocabulary links already noted, the term "God of Israel" occurs only six times in the psalter, with three of those occurrences in these doxologies.

Variations of the Psalter and Continuing Transmission

In addition to internal signs of a lengthy collection process, variant text traditions of the psalter provide indubitable evidence that the *final form* of the Hebrew psalter as we now have it was not completely standardized until the first century CE. The Hebrew psalter is not the only *final form* of the book of Psalms. The Hebrew psalter represents the form of the psalter that Jewish and Christian tradition ultimately selected as authoritative, or *canonical*, for their respective communities. However, the LXX and manuscript evidence from the Qumran region (the so-called Dead Sea Scrolls) show that divergent text traditions existed for a long time.

Several editorial items in the LXX Book of Psalms complicate the study of the final form of the Hebrew psalter. The LXX contains different wording in places, divides several psalms differently, and contains one psalm not present in the Hebrew Psalter (MT). Before one can speak about the intention of the final form, one must determine the extent to which the wording of the different versions relates to the final form of the MT book of Psalms.

Two examples can illustrate the problem. The LXX assigns several psalms to David which the MT does not. For example, Psalms 33 and 43 have no superscription in the MT, but the LXX assigns both of these to David. Does this difference represent a scribal omission in the transmission of the MT or an addition by the LXX translators? Most scholars would say it represents a continuation of the tradition of assigning/dedicating psalms to David. However, a decision is difficult because the LXX does not place David's name on every untitled psalm.[20] How does this addition (or omission) affect one's understanding of the final form? A similar problem arises when one looks at the presence of the enigmatic term *selah*. According to the LXX, Psalm 2:2 contains the first example of *selah*, while the first example of the term in the MT appears in Psalm 3:3. Did Psalm 2 originally contain the term, or was it added to the text of the LXX tradition? These examples illustrate a certain degree of fluidity when it comes to the editorial notations of the psalter.

---

[20]For example, Psalms 1 and 2, 146-150 contain no superscription in either the MT or the LXX.

Psalm 151 begins immediately after the blank line at the end of Psalm 134:3.

Variations in the way individual psalms are divided offers a case that is even more intriguing. The psalms of the LXX and the MT are not divided in the same places, meaning that the numbers of the psalms are different throughout much of the psalter in these two versions. Twice the LXX combines two psalms into one, and twice it divides one psalm into two.[21] In addition, the LXX contains an additional Davidic psalm at the end (Psalm 151) which is not in the MT at all.

The manuscript findings in the region around Qumran show that the text of most psalms was fairly well established by the time of the Qumran community (mid-second century BCE to first century CE). However, these

---

[21]The LXX treats Psalms 9-10 and 114-115 (MT) as a single unit while dividing Psalms 116 and 147 into two psalms.

manuscripts also demonstrate conclusively that several variant forms of the psalter circulated together, at least into the first century CE. To be sure, these variations occur most prominently toward the end of the psalter, meaning that much of the psalter had probably attained its current form before the first century. Yet, explanation of this variation must be incorporated into any model of the shape of the psalter as a whole. For example, one Qumran fragment (11QPsa) contains Psalm 134 followed by a Hebrew version of Psalm 151 (LXX).[22]

This manuscript thus places Psalm 151 (LXX) at the end of the songs of ascent (120-134), not after Psalm 150. This manuscript dates to the first century CE, and it raises interesting questions. Does it suggest that an earlier version of the psalter included Psalm 151, or was it inserted later? In either case, why did Psalm 151 not have this position in the "final form" of the MT or the LXX?

All signs indicate the psalter had a lengthy history of collection and editing. Signs of common editing across smaller collections and within earlier developmental stages of the psalter complicate any discussion of the coherence of the whole. However, this history of editing must be taken into account if one wishes to develop a convincing picture of the message of the psalter.

A Meaningful Shape for the Entire Psalter?

Despite the complexity of the task, scholars have begun to ask whether the psalter as a whole (not just the individual psalms) should be read as a conveyor of meaning.[23] Some focus on the impression left by the genres of the psalms.[24] The first part of the psalter contains a preponderance of complaint psalms, while the latter portion contains more positively orien-ted psalms (thanksgiving songs, songs of praise, songs of ascent, etc). Does the change from complaint to praise suggest an organizational prin-

---

[22]This photograph appears in Seybold, *Die Psalmen*, 15.

[23]For example, see the very different approaches of Jerome F. D. Creach, *Yahweh as Refuge and the Editing of the Hebrew Psalter*, JSOTSup 217 (Sheffield: Sheffield Academic Press, 1996); and Nancy L. deClaissé-Walford, *Reading from the Beginning: The Shaping of the Hebrew Psalter* (Macon GA: Mercer University Press, 1997).

[24]Claus Westermann, "Zur Sammlung des Psalters," in *Forschung am Alten Testament* (Munich: Kaiser, 1964) 336-43; Walter Brueggemann, *The Psalms and the Life of Faith* (Minneapolis: Fortress Press, 1995).

ciple at work? Is the deviation purely accidental? Questions like these raise interesting possibilities for research, but as yet no clear answer has surfaced.

Other scholars have noted thematic threads by emphasizing the *tôrâh*, royal psalms, or recurring word clusters. Psalm 1 stresses the need to meditate on the "law of YHWH." This emphasis corresponds to the wording of Psalm 119 (where *tôrâh* appears twenty-five times). Several verbal correspondences cause some scholars to suggest that Psalm 119 once concluded a version of the psalter which began with Psalm 1, prior to the incorporation of the songs of ascent.[25]

The royal psalms and/or allusions to David tend to appear at the transitional points of at least some of the collections.[26] For example, Psalm 2 speaks about YHWH's selection of a king just before the first Davidic collection begins in Psalm 3. The Second Davidic Psalter concludes with a complaint song about old age (Psalm 71) followed immediately by the first psalm with a Solomonic superscription, as though possibly cognizant of the transition from David's death to Solomon's reign. However, a chronological development cannot be documented for the entire psalter.

Word clusters have also been suggested as potential keys for interpreting the whole. For example, Jerome Creach suggests the psalter is organized around the concept of seeking refuge in YHWH.[27] Creach argues that several of these refuge texts reflect editorial work. He makes the case that terms related to this concept show a development in the metaphor of refuge across the psalter. In turn, this development sheds light upon the psalter's literary shaping.

While none of these suggestions can be said to have carried the field, they do represent progress by demonstrating content links that transcend the various collections. They show that no single organizational principle can adequately explain every aspect of Psalms. A comprehensive treatment must explain the psalter's organizational structure. It must also do justice to the individual psalms and the smaller collections of the psalter.

---

[25]Westermann,"Zur Sammlung des Psalters," 338-39; and H. H. Guthrie, *Israel's Sacred Songs: A Study of Dominant Themes* (New York: Seabury Press, 1966) 191. For example, only Psalm 1:1-2 and Psalm 119:1 contain the word combinations of walk, path, and "*tôrâh* of YHWH."

[26]Wilson, *The Editing of the Hebrew Psalter*, 209-14.

[27]Creach, *Yahweh as Refuge and the Editing of the Hebrew Psalter*.

The lack of a single organizing principle further suggests a complex development of the psalter. Some general agreements appear to be gaining acceptance with respect to the major stages of the psalter's development.

General Observations on the Development of the Psalter

Four general observations will summarize some basic agreements concerning the order in which the smaller collections were added to the psalter.

First, common editorial tendencies can be more readily documented in books 1-3 than in books 4-5. One sees editorial agendas in the Elohistic Psalter that are not present elsewhere. One sees more patterns in the arrangement of the superscriptions in the first three books. The overwhelming number of occurrences of *selah* appear in books 1-3. These tendencies suggest that at some point the Elohistic Psalter was combined with the First Davidic Psalter, prior to the addition of books 4-5.

Second, even books 1-3 show signs of a lengthy collection process. One can safely presume, for example, that the psalms of the first Korahite collection (Psalms 42-49) were transmitted together before they were incorporated into the larger collection which became the Elohistic Psalter. One can safely argue that the first Davidic psalter (3-41) and the second Davidic psalter (Psalms 51-70) were transmitted independently for a lengthy time period because the former did not experience the revisions of the Elohistic Psalter while the latter did.

Third, several psalms and/or parts of psalms, may very well have been composed for their current positions, either as *introductions* or *conclusions* to sections of the *developing* corpus. For example, Psalm 72:20 ends book 2 with the editorial notation that "the prayers of David, the son of Jesse are ended." The author of this note must have been aware of its position at the conclusion of the second Davidic psalter, although the point at which it was added remains complicated by various factors.[28] Both Psalm 2 and Psalm 1 may have been composed and/or

---

[28]How does one determine whether this note was composed for the second Davidic psalter or for both Davidic psalters after they were combined? In either case, this note is not aware that additional Davidic psalms appear later in the corpus. Also, how does one evaluate the fact that this verse comes *after* the doxology (72:18-19) which "ends" book two, but precedes the editorial note of 72:20?

placed at the beginning of existing collections as the psalter developed. The placement of these psalms can be explained by their content.[29]

Fourth, the fact that the introductions of book 5 exhibit more cohesion than those in book four suggests different collection principles were operative for these two sections. Book 4 contains a much higher percentage of untitled psalms than the other books, and very few signs of extended collections. Book 5, like books 1–3, contains several relatively lengthy blocks of similar psalms.[30] By contrast, book 4 contains relatively few such groups, as one can quickly see from chart 1 above. Discussion about the cohesion of book 4 centers on thematic links.[31] The different character of book 4 and book 5 suggest they entered the larger corpus at separate points, with book 4 probably preceding book 5. However, this evidence also suggests that book 5 was probably not added in a single stroke.[32]

Research on the shaping of the psalter will continue. The collection of the psalms was a lengthy and complex process. The study of the shaping of the psalter has raised intriguing questions, but has not yet culminated in widespread agreement concerning the extent to which these organizing principles can and/or should affect one's understanding of the message of the Psalter as a whole.

---

[29]See the discussions of these two psalms above.

[30]For example, as the songs of ascent (120-134), two Davidic collections (107-110, 138-145), and two hallelujah psalm collections (111-113, 146-150).

[31]See the discussions in Jerome Creach, "The Shape of Book Four of the Psalter and the Shape of Second Isaiah," *Journal for the Study of the Old Testament* 80 (1998): 63-76; and Erich Zenger, "The Composition of the Fifth Book of Psalms, Psalms 107-145," *Journal for the Study of the Old Testament* 80 (1998): 77-102.

[32]The links between Psalms 1 and 119 are strong, so one cannot rule out that Psalm 119 once ended a version of the psalter. In addition, the manuscript evidence from Qumran at least suggests that Psalms 135-150 did not always immediately follow the songs of ascent in Psalms 120-134.

Chapter 5

The Poetry and Literature of the Psalms

Daniel S. Mynatt

Poetry is used extensively throughout the Hebrew Bible, much more so than is commonly believed by people who stereotype it as a "book of laws." In fact, some books in the Hebrew Bible are exclusively poetry (Psalms, Proverbs, Song of Solomon, Lamentations), while others are almost entirely poetry (Job). Most of the prophetic books are largely recorded in poetry, and even the historical books, which are normally written in narrative prose, occasionally contain a significant poetic section (Exodus 15; Judges 5).

The fundamental building block of Hebrew poetry is the single poetic line, called a stich. The stich is known by other names, such as member, colon, or half-verse, but all of these terms are more ambiguous than the term stich. The verse below, Psalm 26:2, illustrates how stichs function.

Prove me, O LORD, and try me;
    test my heart and mind.[1]

The first "line" of the poem, "Prove me . . . " is the first stich. A stich is simply a single line of poetry emphasizing one thought. Since the "Prove me . . . " stich occurs first, we can designate it Stich A. Obviously, Stich B is the line following, "test my heart. . . . " Taken together, Stich A and B form one verse of poetry, called a bistich.

Stichs are very easy to identify in the New Revised Standard Version (NRSV), and other similar translations, because of the method of indentation used in the poetic sections of the Hebrew Bible. Stich A is always printed against the left margin (along with the verse numbers). Stich B is always indented one level, as in the example above.

---

[1]All scripture references are from the New Revised Standard Version (NRSV) unless otherwise noted.

Occasionally, a stich is longer than can be printed on one line of text. In this case, the stich will be continued on the line below, indented twice. For example, see Psalm 26:3:

> For your steadfast love is before
> > my eyes,
> and I walk in faithfulness to
> > you.

In this case, stich A begins "For your steadfast . . . " and stich B begins "and I walk. . . . " Both stichs have additional words belonging to them, indented just below each stich; "my eyes" is part of stich A, and "you" is part of stich B.

Fortunately, one verse of Hebrew poetry normally corresponds with the numbered verses in our printed Bibles. Unfortunately, however, this is not always the case. For example, see Psalm 28:3:

> Do not drag me away with the wicked,
> > with those who are workers of evil,
> who speak peace with their neighbors,
> > while mischief is in their hearts.

In this case, there are two verses of Hebrew poetry in one numbered verse. The first poetic verse starts with "Do not drag . . . " in stich A, and the second poetic verse starts with "who speak peace" in stich A. Each verse also has a stich B. In the NRSV, this situation is easily detectable, because the first words of stich A in both cases are against the left margin with no indentation.

One bistich verse of Hebrew poetry per one numbered verse in our printed Bibles is the rule, but there are other exceptions. For example, sometimes the poetic structure does not conform at all to traditional verse divisions (23:1-3). At other times, bistichs will be forsaken for tristichs (25:2), in which case the first words of both stich B and stich C will be indented once from the left margin.

Parallelism

What makes poetry poetic? What distinguishes poetry from prose? In English, the most easily recognizable feature of poetry—at least popular poetry—is end rhyme. For example:

> Humpty Dumpty sat on a wall,

Humpty Dumpty had a great fall.

In Hebrew, poetry is distinguished, not by end rhyme (which occurs only rarely), but by the concept of parallelism. Parallelism is the art of balancing one line against another both in form and in content. For example, see Psalm 26:4:

> I do not sit with the worthless,
>   nor do I consort with hypocrites.

This verse contains two poetic lines, stich A and stich B. In form, this verse is said to be "parallel" because stich B balances stich A. Furthermore, each stich contains a single thought, here the reluctance to associate with evildoers. Thus, the thought of stich A is balanced by the parallel thought in stich B. In fact, parallelism is sometimes called "thought rhyme" because one thought echoes another.

Parallelism is a good name for this type of poetic structure because each line is parallel to the other both in form (the arrangement of the lines) and in thought (the content of the lines). Parallelism is the most common, distinctive characteristic in Hebrew poetry, and it was used extensively by other ancient Near Eastern cultures as well.

There are different types of parallelism, distinguished by the relationship between successive stichs in a verse. The most common type of parallelism is Synonymous Parallelism, in which stich B simply repeats the thought of stich A. This is the type of parallelism we have used thus far to illustrate the concept of parallelism. Refer again to Psalm 26:4; both stichs contain the same thought. Thus stich B simply repeats the thought of stich A. See the next verse, Psalm 26:5:

> I hate the company of evildoers,
>   and will not sit with the wicked.

Once again, both stichs make precisely the same point. Thus, stich B is related to stich A by Synonymous Parallelism. Other examples of Synonymous Parallelism are Psalm 35:1, 40:13, and 43:5.

Modern readers in the Western world are often baffled by parallelism. To us repetition is boring, and we are taught in composition classes to avoid it. But to the ancient Hebrew poets, skill and artistry were demonstrated by how cleverly one could develop couplets that make the same point twice in different words.

A second type of parallelism is Antithetic Parallelism, in which the thought expressed by stich B contrasts the thought of stich A. See Psalm 31:6, where the contrast is between trusting in idols and trusting in Yahweh.

> You hate those who pay regard to worthless idols,
>   but I trust in the LORD.

Antithetic Parallelism is especially common in Proverbs (Proverbs 10:1; 20:29), and it can also be found in the teachings of Jesus (Matthew 10:39). In English, stich B frequently begins with the word "but"; however, this is not absolutely necessary (Proverbs 10:20).

A third type of parallelism is Synthetic Parallelism, in which the thought of stich A is carried out or completed in stich B. The structure of the verse is still parallel, but there is no longer any parallelism of thought, since the second stich adds new information to the first. For example, see Psalm 25:16:

> Turn to me and be gracious to me,
>   for I am lonely and afflicted.

In this example, stich B offers a rationale for stich A (see Psalm 28:6 for another example). Stich B may function in various other ways as well, such as closing a conditional sentence (27:10) or giving the result of stich A (30:2). A general (but not foolproof) rule is that if stich A and B make no sense apart from each other, then Synthetic Parallelism is at work.

Other aspects of Hebrew poetry are different versions of the same basic principles. For example, Graduated Parallelism, also known as Climatic Parallelism, describes a verse where stich B repeats stick A, but also adds new information. This device is common in tristichs, where the advance in thought is more readily apparent (24:7, 29:1).[2] Incomplete Parallelism occurs when stich B omits but implies some aspect of stich A, such as a verb (26:9), a noun (30:4), or an adjective (33:12). External Parallelism describes the relationships between poetic verses. The main types of parallelism are the same as described above; however, here they are applied to successive verses. For example, both stichs in Psalm 37:1

---

[2]See Werner Schmidt, *Old Testament Introduction*, trans. Matthew O'Connell (New York: Crossroads, 1984) 300.

and 37:2 are related by Synonymous Parallelism, but the verses themselves are related to one another by Synthetic Parallelism.

Divisions

In its canonical form, the Psalms are divided into five sections, called books (book 1: Psalms 1-41; book 2: 42-72; book 3: 73-89; book 4: 90-106; book 5: 107-150). Each of the first four sections concludes with a benediction or doxology (41:13, 72:19, 89:52, and 106:48). Within each section there is a variety of material, representing differing dates, authors, and literary types. Thus, most modern scholars view the five books as an organizing device imposed on a group of already collected materials, in an attempt to imitate the five books of the Torah.

The existence of repeated Psalms (known as doublets) is strong evidence that the Book of Psalms originated through collections which were at first circulated independently and were subsequently compiled into the larger anthology of our biblical book (14 and 53; 40:13-17 and 70). Traces of these originally independent collections are still apparent. For example, Psalm 72:20 concludes with the notice, "The prayers of David son of Jesse are ended." But there is another collection of the Psalms of David coming after this verse, in Psalms 138-145. The notice makes sense only if we assume that originally one collection of David Psalms ended in 72:20 and the other was not yet adjoined to it.

Subdivisions

The subcollections of Psalms within our canonical book are isolated on the basis of similarities in the superscriptions or other content similarities. Some of the most apparent subcollections are (1) the First Davidic collection (3-41), distinguished by the name "David" occurring in the superscription; (2) the Elohistic Psalter (Ps. 42-83), in which psalms are characterized by the use of Elohim instead of Yahweh, even in phrases where one would expect Yahweh; (3) Pilgrimage Psalms (120-134), also called Psalms of Ascent because of use of that word in the superscription; (4) another Davidic collection (Ps. 138-145); and (5) Hallelujah Psalms (111-118, 146-150), distinguished by the frequent use of the phrase "Praise the Lord" (Hebrew *hallelujah*).

In many English translations, superscriptions are the short annotations between the chapter or psalm number and the first verse ("Psalm 3. *A psalm of David, . . .* "). In most English Bibles, the superscriptions function as unnumbered subtitles for the Psalms. In Hebrew Bibles, the superscription is ordinarily the first verse of the Psalm (followed of course in NJV but also notably in NAB). Thus, in English, Psalm 3 has eight verses, but nine in Hebrew. Only thirty-four psalms in the Hebrew Bible lack a superscription. In the Septuagint, the number of superscriptions is larger. The superscriptions are not original to the composition of the Psalms; they were added later and must be interpreted in that light.

The superscriptions generally contain four types of information: (1) affiliation, (2) interpretive context, (3) musical information, and (4) psalm type. A psalm may have none, one, or more than one of these four parts.

(1) Affiliation is the person or group associated with the psalm. Most affiliations are "of David," which may mean "by David," "to David," or "for David," as well as many other possibilities. An example of group affiliation is "of the Korahites" in Psalms 44-49. The Korahites appear to have been a guild of singers in the Second Temple period (1 Chronicles 9:19, 31; 12:6; 2 Chronicles 20:19).

(2) Interpretive context is historical information given in the superscription by which the Psalm is intended to be understood. For example, Psalm 51 refers to the episode in David's life when he was confronted by Nathan after his affair with Bathsheba (2 Samuel 12). The superscription invites the reader to interpret the psalm in this context. These historical notices, however, are not original to the psalms to which they are attached and may not be reliable for historical purposes. They probably tell us more about manner in which the psalm was interpreted than about the origin of the psalm.

(3) Musical Information refers to the various kinds of musical directions prefacing the psalms. Fifty of the psalms have the superscription "to the leader," presumably the music director. Some of the terms give information regarding the instruments upon which the psalm is to be played (*with stringed instruments*: 4, 6) or the name of the melody (*according to Lilies*: 45, 69). Some terms are simply obscure (*The Sheminith*: 6, 12).

(4) Superscriptions occasionally also identify the psalm type, clearly the case with the *Songs of Ascents* (120-134).

Hermann Gunkel

The pioneer of psalm interpretation in this century was Hermann Gunkel (1862–1932). His insights were so foundational that virtually every modern approach to the psalms has used Gunkel's research as its basis. Gunkel noted the cultic nature of the psalms and argued that the psalms were used in the worship settings of the cult to accompany authentic acts of worship. Thus, his perspective differed from previous scholars in that he argued the psalms were better understood in the context of the cult rather than in the context of when the psalms might be dated.[3]

Gunkel applied form criticism to the psalms, looking for common characteristics in the psalms and then classifying them into types or categories. The presupposition is that not all psalms are alike in type, just as not all hymns in church services are alike. Invitation hymns and call-to-worship hymns are both used for worship, but they are of different types and are used on different occasions. Gunkel then speculated regarding the setting in life for each type of psalm, under the assumption that psalms were written in connection with acts of worship in the temple. In other words, the psalm types could be used to gain new understanding in Israel's worship. For example, the hymns were used at the temple to praise Yahweh and the Royal Psalms were used for coronations, weddings, or other important events for Israel's royalty.

Gunkel developed a list of psalm types based on his original research. Fortunately, Gunkel's major work on the Book of Psalms, which was completed after his death, is now available in English, titled *Introduction to Psalms*.[4] Gunkel isolated five major types: Hymns, Royal Psalms, Communal Laments, Individual Laments, and Individual Thanksgiving Songs. The types are called major because there are several examples of each in the Book of Psalms. Gunkel also identified six smaller types, each of which has less examples in Psalms than the major types, or the examples are incomplete (having been mixed with another type). The smaller types are: Sayings of Blessing and Curse, Pilgrimage Songs, Victory Songs, Communal Thanksgiving Songs, Legends, and Torah Songs. Gunkel also put emphasis on both the liturgical and Wisdom Movement influences in the Psalms.

---

[3]Hermann Gunkel, *An Introduction to the Psalms*, completed by Joachim Begrich, trans. James D. Nogalski (Macon GA: Mercer University Press, 1998) 21. Regarding dating the Psalms, Gunkel comments "we do not consider this problem to be important."

[4]See previous citation for bibliographic information. Prior to 1998, this important work was unavailable in English.

Gunkel's categories formed the basis for most subsequent scholarship in the form criticism of the Book of Psalms, and his list is still very influential. However, later scholars developed other typologies which are more descriptive of the psalms than is Gunkel's list. A very popular typology of psalms is the one used in the introductory article for the psalms in the NRSV *New Oxford Annotated Bible*, which is often a required textbook in biblical studies courses.[5] That list is represented as follows.

1. *Hymns* are general songs of praise to Yahweh. Anderson sees three thematic categories of hymns: Hymns to God who created Israel (100, 111); Hymns to God who created the world (8, 19); and Hymns to the creator and the ruler of history (3, 33).[6] Thus, hymns deal with a very broad and general subject matter, as opposed to, for example, Thanksgiving Psalms, which are in response to God's specific acts of kindness.

Hymns contain three basic elements. First, there is a call to worship or invitation to praise. This is followed by the main section of the psalm which gives the reason for the praise. The reason is frequently introduced by the Hebrew word *ki*, translated "for" or "because." The last section is a recapitulation of the praise to Yahweh. Sometimes the conclusion repeats the call to worship exactly, creating a literary device known as "inclusio" (Psalm 135). Hymns may expand, repeat, or modify these elements in various creative ways, but these three elements are basic to a hymn's form. A good example of a hymn is Psalm 147:

1. 147:1a   Call to Praise
2. 147:1b-6   Motive (*ki* in 1:b)
3. 147:7   Call to Praise
4. 147:8-11   Motive (*ki* is implied in 8)
5. 147:12   Call to Praise
6. 147:13-20b   Motive (*ki* in 13)
7. 147:20c   Recapitulation (an inclusio)

---

[5]Robert C. Dentan, "The Psalms," *The New Oxford Annotated Bible with the Apocry-phal/Deuterocanonical Books. New Revised Standard Version*, ed. Bruce M. Metzger and Roland E. Murphy (New York: Oxford University Press, 1991) 674OT. Dentan's introduction to Psalms is carried over *in toto* (with one brief editorial addition) from *The New Oxford Annotated Bible with the Apocrypha. Revised Standard Version*, expanded edition, ed. Herbert G. May and Bruce M. Metzger (New York: Oxford University Press, 1977) 656.

[6]Bernhard Anderson, *Out of the Depths* (Philadelphia: Westminster, 1983) 138-39.

We can isolate some special subtypes of hymns. These are set apart primarily on thematic grounds rather than on form-critical distinctions; that is, they are grouped together because they address the same topic. The Songs of Zion are hymns which give praise to the place where God dwells, namely Jerusalem, otherwise known as Zion (46, 48). Much of the language in these psalms is concentrated on extolling Jerusalem and everything in it (such as citadels, ramparts, and towers: 48:12-13). Enthronement Songs are psalms that proclaim the royal dominion of God (47, 93, 95-99). Here, much of the language focuses on Yahweh's royal rule and kingship over the earth (47:2).

2. *Laments* could also be called "songs of petition," because in this type of psalm the worshipper is asking Yahweh for something. Laments contain three basic elements: an invocation, a description of the situation that is causing the psalmist distress, and the petition. The key element is the petition, because it functions as an appeal to God for relief from the psalmist's suffering. There are a number of other variable elements in laments, aspects which may or may not occur, with the result that laments can be quite diverse.[7] A good example of a lament is Psalm 13:

1. 13:1-2 Invocation
2. 13:3a Petition
3. 13:3b-4 Description of Distress
4. 13:5 Confession of Trust (a variable element)
5. 13:6 Vow of Praise (a variable element)

Once again, there are different kinds of laments. In community laments, the petition is corporate (44, 58, 74, 79, 80, 83). The difficult situation is something that affects the entire community, such as war or famine. In individual laments, the petition is personal, and the difficult situation frequently results from illness or personal adversaries (3-7, 31). Individual laments are the largest single category of psalms, but this should not be surprising since it is human nature to complain about troubles much more than to give thanks for good fortune (compare the Parable of the Ten Lepers, Luke 10:11-19).

---

[7]For a brief but comprehensive sketch of the variable elements, see Schmidt, *Old Testament Introduction*, 306.

One category of laments are the imprecatory psalms. They are usually individual Laments (35, 58, 59, 69, 70, 109, 137, 140) but can occasionally be community laments (12, 83). In these psalms, the writer cries out to God for vengeance on his enemies as part or all of the petition. They are called "imprecatory" or "curse" psalms because this cry for vengeance usually incorporates some kind of curse on the enemy. Imprecatory psalms are at times very violent: in Psalm 58:6 the psalmist asks God to break the teeth of his enemies. These psalms sometimes pose difficulty for Christians, who view them on the one hand as incompatible with the teachings of Jesus (Matthew 5:43-44), but on the other as being part of inspired Scripture. We should remember, however, that the psalms represent authentic human experience, and anger is part of the human condition.

3. *Songs of Trust* or Trust Psalms are also called Songs of Confidence, because these psalms are affirmations of faith and confidence in God (11, 16, 62, 131). They frequently express the notion of utter dependence on God (16:1-2). Thus, the dominant characteristic of this type of psalm is its theme: an expression of trust in Yahweh.

Songs of Confidence are related to the laments. One variable element among many laments is an expression of confidence or trust that God has heard the lament and will help (3:3-4). In the Trust Psalms, this element has been developed to the point that it is a literary work by itself: the psalmist expresses utter confidence in God's readiness to help. Psalm 23, the Shepherd's Psalm, is probably the most familiar psalm of all, and it belongs to this category.

4. *Thanksgivings* are songs which thank God for something specific, like a healing (30). They are linked by form to the lament, where one of the variable elements includes the worshipper promising praise and thanksgiving once he has been delivered (see Psalm 13:5-6). In thanksgiving psalms the worshipper fulfills that vow by offering a song of thanks to God for his help.

The thanksgiving psalm contains three basic elements. First, there is an introduction in which the worshipper states his intention to give thanks. Second, there is a main section, which in itself is also composed of three parts: (a) a recounting of the distress which caused the petition, (b) the worshipper's cry for help, and (c) an account of Yahweh's deliverance. Last, the thanksgiving psalm concludes with the psalmist offering thanks and praise to God for his gracious act.

As with the laments, there is considerable variety among the thanksgiving psalms. The elements, particularly the three parts of the main section, may be repeated, mixed, or some may be omitted. The logical order of thought is not necessarily followed.

A good example of a thanksgiving psalm is Psalm 30:

1. 30:1-5   Introduction
2. 30:6-12a   Main Section
    a. 30:6-7   Recounting of the Distress
    b. 30:8-10   Cry for Help
    c. 30:11-12a Yahweh's Deliverance
3. 30:12b   Thanks and Praise

There are two types of thanksgiving psalms. In individual thanksgiving psalms, a single individual is doing the thanking (30, 32, 34, 92, 116, 118, 138). In community thanksgiving psalms (124), the people corporately are giving thanks for deliverance from some communal affliction. Many scholars dispute whether this latter category exists or should be blended with another.[8]

5. *Sacred History* psalms recount history so that the story of God's dealings with Israel might be told (78, 105, 106, 135, 136). Christian hymnody has nothing exactly like this with which to compare. These psalms are usually quite lengthy because of their desire to tell large portions of the story of Israel's faith. Some make reference to events that are difficult to identify from our knowledge of the history of Israel (78:9-11).

6. *Royal Psalms* are psalms about the earthly king of Israel (2, 18, 20, 21, 45, 72, 101, 110, 132). Although these psalms are theoretically related to the Davidic dynasty (most have David in the superscription), in reality they provide almost no concrete information. Instead they describe the "ideal ruler" and glorify God upon whom the ruler is dependent.

Royal Psalms vary widely in their form. Their identification as a separate category depends completely on the fact that all of them deal with the earthly king. Psalms 2 and 110 were composed for a coronation. Psalm 45 is a wedding psalm. Psalm 132 is a liturgy celebrating the Davidic dynasty.

7. *Wisdom Psalms* reflect the ideas and vocabulary of the Wisdom Movement, represented by books such as Proverbs, Job, and Ecclesiastes.

---

[8]Schmidt, *Old Testament Introduction*, 308, and Anderson, *Out of the Depths*, 111.

Wisdom Psalms are didactic, teaching psalms. Most are essentially meditations on the good life, giving practical instructions for living successfully. They frequently contrast the ways of the righteous and the wicked (37, 49, 73, 112, 119).

The most famous of all Wisdom Psalms is 119. It is the longest of the psalms, due mainly to its acrostic structure. Each stanza is composed of eight verses, and each verse within the stanza begins with the same letter of the Hebrew alphabet. The psalm uses all twenty-two letters of the alphabet, yielding 176 verses. Thus, Psalm 119 has a lot to say about successful living. Psalm 37 also uses the acrostic structure.

8. Although the majority of the Psalms were used in worship, and many were spoken in public, some are associated with specific festivals, rituals, or other worship experiences and were probably written precisely for some type of cultic ceremony. These are the *Liturgies* or Liturgical Psalms, and they have noticeable liturgical elements, such as litanies. These psalms are like special occasion hymns (Christmas and Easter hymns) because they were in all likelihood related to a specific event or time of the year, but otherwise not often used.

Liturgical Psalms contain excerpts from things said or done during these special rituals or services. Some are judgment speeches made during public worship (50, 82). Psalm 81 is a judgment speech that may have been composed specifically for the Festival of Booths. Others are liturgies for entrance into the temple (15, 24). Another type is Torah liturgies (1, 19:7-14), in which Torah is emphasized. These are much like the Wisdom Psalms in that they have similar themes and try to teach the listener how to live successfully.

9. Mixed types of psalms do not fit clearly into any single category but instead mix elements from two or more categories (36).

The Book of Psalms can be compared to both a hymnbook and a prayer book. It is like a hymnbook in that it contains the songs sung by generations of worshippers in their public liturgy. It is like a prayer book in that the psalms express the wide array of human emotions, from sheer delight to numbing anger. It is no wonder, then, that the Book of Psalms is one of the most beloved books in the Hebrew Bible.

Chapter 6

The Ancient Near Eastern Context
of the Book of Psalms

Joel F. Drinkard, Jr.[*]

Before getting into the heart of the essay some disclaimers are necessary. Old Testament studies in general and Psalms study in particular have had several bouts of "parallelomania" in the past century and a half. Beginning with the discovery of the major cuneiform libraries and the decipherment of cuneiform, numerous attestations of borrowing directly from Akkadian were proposed for Hebrew literature and poetry. The two favored targets were Genesis, especially 1–11, and Psalms. This Pan-Babylonianism was epitomized in the Babel-Bible controversy. Egyptian parallels were also used to support the borrowing of Egyptian ideas, especially of Wisdom Literature and certain Psalms, for example, the *Hymn of Aton* and Psalm 104.

A second round of parallelomania erupted after the discovery of the Canaanite/Ugaritic literature at Ras Shamra. Not only did the Ugaritic material provide us with our first real taste of Canaanite literature and epics, it also gave us another northwest Semitic language related to Hebrew. Ugaritic poetry was found to be quite similar to Hebrew in terms of parallelism. Even numerous word pairs have been noted in Hebrew and in Ugaritic. So the "borrowing" from, or at least close affinity to, Ugaritic by Hebrew became a given. The three-volume commentary of Dahood on Psalms in the Anchor Bible series presented numerous readings based on

[*]Marvin Tate served as my supervisor during the first part of my doctoral program at Southern Baptist Theological Seminary. His interest in Hebrew poetry and Wisdom were well established at that time. His research on Psalms had an early culmination in his volume on Psalms 51-100 for the Word Biblical Commentary. For the last sixteen years he has been both mentor and colleague at Southern Baptist Theological Seminary. He is now revising the three volumes of the Word Biblical Commentary on Psalms. This topic is thus most appropriate for a *Festschrift* dedicated to Marvin Tate. It is in his honor that the following essay is offered.

Ugaritic parallels. More recent scholarship has backed away from many of Dahood's proposals, especially those that involve emending the text.

We must grant that the many parallels pointed out by these scholars have helped us better understand and interpret Psalms. Akkadian, Egyptian, and Ugaritic poetry have enriched our reading of the Book of Psalms. But we must also note that such parallels do not necessarily imply borrowing by one culture from another. Much like the modern world we live in, so also the world of the ancient Near East (ANE) was not a place of isolation. Israel had trade and commerce with each of her neighbors. She also had political contact with each of them. Obviously Israel would be aware of the language and literature of each of their cultures. In addition, Israel's history indicates that she had her origin in the Mesopotamian homeland of Akkadian—that was her heritage according to the Patriarchal/Ancestors Narrative. Israel also described her heritage as including a period of dwelling in Egypt, much of that time spent as an oppressed minority. But Joseph and Moses are both described as living in the highest levels of Egyptian hierarchy.

Even more to the point, Israel was a part of the ANE world. That culture was also her culture. It is not so much that Israel "borrowed' from all her neighbors. It is more the realization that she was part and parcel of that culture. This was her world. What really would have been surprising would have been if Israel did not share cultural commonalities with all her neighbors.

So in this essay we shall not use terms such as "borrowing," but will instead speak of the common ANE background of the Book of Psalms. Before we look at other commonalities, we will look at the structural aspects of poetry—especially parallelism and rhythm/meter. Then we will consider a number of comparative examples from the ANE world to show the commonality. Then we will look at a number of specifics from Ugarit to show the especially close relationship Hebrew shares with Ugaritic. Finally we will look at samples of theological comparisons between Psalms and other ANE cultures. The examples will be taken primarily from hymns, but a similar comparison could be made from laments and penitential psalms.

Poetic Structure

The poetic structure of Hebrew is most often classified as having at least two primary elements, parallelism and rhythm or meter. Parallelism is, by most accounts, the primary characteristic of Hebrew poetry, and is the characteristic easiest to retain in translation. While the exact nature of parallelism is much debated, its existence is universally accepted. I am inclined to agree with Kugel's explanation of parallelism without trying to describe the precise relationship between the individual lines "A, and what is more, B."[1] Such an understanding of parallelism allows one to include the classical types (synonymous, antithetic, synthetic) as well as the numerous nuances of later scholars. Parallelism is a common feature of Semitic poetry and thus is found widely across the ANE. Even the Egyptian language—not a Semitic language—has evidence of parallelism in some of its poetry. In the next section below, we will see examples of parallelism from both Akkadian and Egyptian. Kugel is also helpful in heightening our awareness of repetition or parallelism in prose as well as poetry.

A second element of Hebrew poetry, and especially of the Book of Psalms, is meter or rhythm. If there is debate about parallelism in terms of how to understand it, there is considerably more argument regarding rhythm or meter and its very existence in Hebrew poetry. At least three approaches to rhythm/meter have been proposed: counting stressed or accented syllables, counting all syllables, and counting word units. Among those arguing for counting stressed syllables were Karl Budde, Eduard Sievers, and Sigmund Mowinckel. Several American scholars have been at the forefront of counting syllables, including David Noel Freedman and his students.[2] Freedman has also suggested counting words as a method of determining meter.[3] Other scholars would reject any attempt to identify meter at all. Among these are Kugel[4] and O'Connor.[5] Even Freedman acknowledges that attempts to find one single pattern to

---

[1]James L. Kugel, *The Idea of Biblical Poetry* (New Haven CT: Yale University Press, 1981) 1-58. Note his statement on 58 which he makes in reference to Lowth's three categories: "Biblical parallelism is of one sort, 'A, and what's more, B,' or a hundred sorts; but it is not three."

[2]David Noel Freedman, "Pottery, Poetry, and Prophecy: An Essay on Biblical Poetry," in *Pottery, Poetry, and Prophecy: Studies in Early Hebrew Poetry* (Winona Lake IN: Eisenbrauns,1980) 7.

[3]Freedman, "Pottery, Poetry, and Prophecy," 8.

[4]James L. Kugel, *The Idea of Biblical Poetry* (New Haven CT: Yale University Press, 1981) 297-98.

[5]M. O'Connor, *Hebrew Verse Structure* (Winona Lake IN: Eisenbrauns, 1980) 138.

encompass all Hebrew poetry has failed.[6] Some scholars would use the terms meter and rhythm interchangeably.

Dennis Pardee argues that meter is distinct from rhythm. Meter is defined as a regular and predictable observable recurrence. He argues that this regularity is lacking in both Hebrew and Ugaritic poetry.[7] Thus, according to Pardee, meter is not present in Hebrew or Ugaritic. But one can speak of rhythm in Hebrew poetry as long as one recognizes that the rhythm is not regular or predictable. I tend to agree with Pardee and would say rhythm does exist in Hebrew and Ugaritic poetry. Likewise rhythm also appears to exist in a similar fashion in Akkadian poetry.[8] Nevertheless, in this essay, I will be concerned more with parallelism than rhythm.

Comparisons with Egyptian and Akkadian poetry

Turning now to ANE examples of poetry that may be compared with the Book of Psalms, we may begin with an Egyptian example. In the *Hymn of Aton* we note significant similarity or commonality with the Book of Psalms:

> How manifold it is, what thou hast made!
> They are hidden from the face (of man).
> O sole god, like whom there is no other!
> Thou didst create the world according to thy desire,
> Whilst thou wert alone:
> All men, cattle, and wild beasts,
> Whatever is on earth, going upon (its) feet,
> And what is on high, flying with its wings.[9]

---

[6]Freedman, "Pottery, Poetry, and Prophecy," 6. "No regular, fairly rigid system will work with any large sample without extensive reshaping of individual poems and verses. . . . Many poems do not seem to have clear-cut metrical or strophic patterns and may never yield to this sort of analysis."

[7]Dennis Pardee, "Ugaritic and Hebrew Metrics," in *Ugarit in Retrospect: 50 Years of Ugarit and Ugaritic* ed., Gordon D. Young (Winona Lake IN: Eisenbrauns, 1981) 116.

[8]Charles Gordon Cumming, *The Assyrian and Hebrew Hymns of Praise* (New York: Columbia University Press, 1934) 95.

[9]"The Hymn to the Aton," trans. John A. Wilson, in *The Ancient Near East. An Anthology of Texts and Pictures*, ed. James B. Pritchard (Princeton NJ: Princeton University Press, 1958) 229.

One may compare both the parallelism and the content of this excerpt with Psalm 104:24:

> O LORD, how manifold are your works!
>> In wisdom you have made them all;
>> the earth is full of your creatures.[10]

Note especially the similar words and the same type of parallel structure in the first two lines of the excerpt from the *Hymn of Aton* and the first two lines of Psalm 104:24.

One may also compare with the latter part of the *Hymn of Aton* excerpt with Psalm 8:1a, 3-8:

> [1]O LORD, our Sovereign,
>> how majestic is your name in all the earth!
>
> . . . .
>
> [3]When I look at your heavens, the work of your fingers,
>> the moon and stars that you have established;
> [4]what are human beings that you are mindful of them,
>> mortals that you care for them?
> [5]Yet you have made them a little lower than God,
>> and crowned them with glory and honor.
> [6]You have given them dominion over the works of your hands;
>> you have put all things under their feet,
> [7]all sheep and oxen,
>> and also the beasts of the field,
> [8]the birds of the air, and the fish of the sea,
>> whatever passes along the paths of the seas.

One additional example from Egyptian may be cited. It is from the *Hymn to Amun*:

> Atum, who made the people,
> Who distinguished their natures and made them able to live. . . .
>> *(Hymn to Amun* IV.2-3)[11]

---

[10]Unless otherwise specified, all biblical references are from the New Revised Standard Version (NRSV), and verse numbers for English translations follow the English verse system.

[11]*Near Eastern Religious Texts Relating to the Old Testament*, ed. Walter Beyerlin (Philadelphia: Westminster Press, 1978) 13.

In these examples from the Psalter and the Egyptian hymns, one god is praised as creator of the universe. This god's manifold works in creation are extolled. Parallelism is used in each example. Although the theme is similar, and several phrases are quite close, one need not assume borrowing from one culture by the other.

A comparison may also be made with Akkadian poetry and Hebrew poetry. One may compare the following four excerpts from Akkadian with Psalm 89, concerning the theme of the incomparability of the deity:

> O mighty God, to whom there is no rival
> in the assembly of the great gods.   (*Hymn to Marduk* no. 5)[12]

> O LORD who is like thee, who can be compared to thee;
> Mighty one, who is like thee, who can be compared to thee;
> LORD Nannar who is like thee, who can be compared to thee?
>   (*Hymn to Sin* no. 5)[13]

> What god in heaven or earth can be compared to thee,
> Thou art high over all of them
> Among the gods superior is thy counsel.
>   (*Hymn to Marduk* no. 3)[14]

> Creator of the totality of heaven and earth, art thou O Shamash.
>   (*Hymn to Shamash* no. 7)[15]

Compare Psalm 89:5-8:

> [5]Let the heavens praise your wonders, O LORD,
> your faithfulness in the assembly of the holy ones.
> [6]For who in the skies can be compared to the LORD?
> Who among the heavenly beings is like the LORD,
> [7]a God feared in the council of the holy ones,
> great and awesome above all that are around him?
> [8]O LORD God of hosts, who is as mighty as you, O LORD?
> Your faithfulness surrounds you.

---

[12]Cumming, *The Assyrian and Hebrew Hymns of Praise*, 102.
[13]Cumming, *The Assyrian and Hebrew Hymns of Praise*, 103.
[14]Cumming, *The Assyrian and Hebrew Hymns of Praise*, 103.
[15]Cumming, *The Assyrian and Hebrew Hymns of Praise*, 120.

Note the presence of parallelism in the Akkadian examples above. Especially noteworthy is the similarity between the *Hymn to Marduk* no. 3 and Psalm 89:6.

Not only do these examples show a remarkable degree of similarity in the language and style of the respective poems, they also show a common use of parallelism as a poetic device. And each of these examples reflects a common theme—the incomparability of the deity being praised. Across the ANE world, from Egypt to Mesopotamia, peoples considered their deity as the greatest of all deities and beyond compare. In addition, all of these cultures considered the chief deity to be creator of the universe. Like Hebrew, Akkadian also used the word pair *heaven-earth* to describe the totality of their god's creation. These examples seem to indicate an ANE idea world common to all these cultures.

Comparisons between Hebrew and Ugaritic Poetry

If we can note the common features of Egyptian and Assyrian hymns and the Book of Psalms, we must say that the close comparisons between the Hebrew Psalter and Ugaritic epic poetry are even more remarkable. But this affinity should not be surprising given the relative similarity of the two languages. (Some scholars call them two dialects of a Canaanite or South Canaanite language group.) Although a considerable time gap separates the living language of Ugaritic and the living language of Hebrew (in rough measure, the time from Chaucer to twentieth-century English), the conservative nature of the Hebrew language over a long period of time helped preserve this affinity. In addition, the time gap is less than the gap from the earliest material in the Hebrew Bible to the latest. And the gap is also much less than the gap from the earliest material in the Hebrew Bible and the introduction of the Masoretic pronunciation and accent we depend upon and use as the basis of our rhythmical/metrical constructs.

One common pattern of comparison has been that of word pairs found in Hebrew and Ugaritic. Certainly one would expect more of these word pairs between Ugaritic and Hebrew due simply to the significant overlap in cognate vocabulary. Dahood and his followers have catalogued more than a hundred common word pairs in Hebrew and Ugaritic. But, as Craigie points out, parallel word pairs might be expected to occur in any language which uses parallelism:

[S]imilar word pairs also occur in Akkadian poetry, Egyptian poetry, and in the poetry of certain other languages such as Finnish and Chinese. . . . From this type of data, it might be assumed that in the poetry of any language in which parallelism is used, parallel word pairs will appear, and that a degree of commonality in human experience, and therefore in human poetry, will contribute to common parallel word pairs in the poetry of various languages. If this argument is correct, then one is left with the strong possibility that common word pairs arise independently in various languages.[16]

While caution is in order and the appearance of the same word pair does not necessarily indicate borrowing, one may well assume that a comparison of word pairs is a legitimate way of approaching the Hebrew and Ugaritic idea worlds. The comparison between CAT 1.2 IV.8-9 and Psalm 92:10 (EVV 92:9) is striking. First noted by Ginsberg and given additional insight by Fenton, the parallels are as follows:

Now your enemy, Baal,	*ht.ibk/b`lm*
Now smash your enemy,	*ht.ibk.tmḫs*
Now vanquish your foe .[17]	*ht.tṣmt srtk*[18]

For your enemies, O LORD,	כִּי הִנֵּה אֹיְבֶיךָ יְהוָֹה
for your enemies shall perish;	כִּי־הִנֵּה אֹיְבֶיךָ יֹאבֵדוּ
all evildoers shall be scattered.	[19]יִתְפָּרְדוּ כָּל־פֹּעֲלֵי אָוֶן

Fenton notes the full range of word parallels between the Ugaritic and Hebrew. *ht* ‖ כי הנה; *ibk* ‖ איביך; *b`lm* ‖ יהוה; *tmḫs* ‖ יאבדו. He notes further that the parallelism goes further, that *tṣmt* ‖ יתפרדו are themselves parallel to *tmḫs* ‖ יאבדו; and that *srtk* ‖ כל פעלי און are parallel to *ibk* ‖

---

[16]Peter Craigie, "Ugarit and the Bible," in *Ugarit in Retrospect*, ed. Gordon D. Young (Winona Lake IN: Eisenbrauns, 1981) 105-106.

[17]Unless otherwise specified, all English translations from Ugaritic are taken from *Ugaritic Narrative Poetry*, trans. Mark S. Smith et al., ed. Simon B. Parker, Writings from the Ancient World 9 (Atlanta: Scholars Press, 1997).

[18]Unless otherwise specified, all examples of Ugaritic texts are taken from *The Cuneiform Alphabetic Texts from Ugarit, Ras Ibn Hani, and Other Places (KTU)*, 2nd enl. ed., ed. Manfried Dietrich, Oswald Loretz, and Joaquin Sanmartin (Münster: Ugarit-Verlag, 1995). This work will be referred to in this essay as CAT.

[19]The Hebrew text cited in this essay is *Biblia Hebraica Stuttgartensia*, 4th rev. ed.

אִיבִיךְ. Thus Fenton suggests a parallel structure abc abd d'b'.[20] One should note that although these similarities are striking, there are some differences. In the Psalms passage the enemies/evildoers are plural; in the Ugaritic text they are singular. Also the Ugaritic verbs are second-masculine-singular active verbs: "you smash, you vanquish" with Baal as subject; in Psalms the verbs are third-masculine-plural and the enemies/evildoers are the subjects who act or are acted upon.

Several passages in Psalms depict Yahweh defeating the sea creatures which were personified in the Baal epic. Psalm 74:13 is a good example:

You divided the sea (יָם) by your might;
You broke the heads of the dragons (תַנִּינִים) in the waters.
You crushed the heads of Leviathan (לִוְיָתָן);
You gave him as food for the creatures of the wilderness.

Yamm (Sea), Tunnan (Dragon), and Lotan (Leviathan) were defeated by Baal in the Baal epic. One of the Ugaritic passages that describes this battle is CAT 1.3 III 38-42:

Surely I fought Yamm, the beloved of El,	*lmḫšt.mdd/il ym*
Surely I finished off River, the Great God,	*l klt.nhr.il.rbm/*
Surely I bound Tunnan and destroyed (?) him.	*l Ištbm.tnn.ištm.*lh
I fought the Twisty Serpent,	*mḫšt.bṭn.`qltn/*
The Potentate with Seven Heads.[21]	*šlyt.d.šb`t.rašm*

The repetitions found in the Ugaritic poetry such as the threefold "surely" above, and the earlier example "Now your enemy, now your foe," is also often found in the Book of Psalms. Another example is found in Psalm 29:1-2:

[1]Give to Yahweh, O sons of gods	הָבוּ לַיהוָה בְּנֵי אֵלִים
Give to Yahweh glory and strength	הָבוּ לַיהוָה כָּבוֹד וָעֹז׃
[2]Give to Yahweh the glory (כָּבוֹד) of his name	הָבוּ לַיהוָה כְּבוֹד שְׁמוֹ

---

[20]Terry Fenton, "Nexus and Significance: Is Greater Precision Possible?" *Ugarit and the Bible*, ed. George J. Brooke. Adrian H. W. Curtis, and John F. Healey, (Münster: Ugarit-Verlag, 1994) 72-73.

[21]Parker, ed., *Ugaritic Narrative Poetry*, 111.

Bow down (הִשְׁתַּחֲווּ) to Yahweh
   in the splendor of holiness.   ²²הִשְׁתַּחֲווּ לַיהוָה בְּהַדְרַת־קֹדֶשׁ:

Both parallelism and repetition occur. The name Yahweh occurs four times in the two verses, once in each line. All four lines begin with a plural imperative calling for adoration of Yahweh. The first line tells who are being addressed: the "sons of gods"; the second lines tells what they are to give, "glory and strength"; the third repeats and explains "the glory"; the fourth adds a new element.

The combination of glory/honor and bowing down or prostrating oneself occurs in two lines from the Baal cycle. In Ugaritic, both words (which are cognates with the Hebrew words) are verbs:

At the feet of El she bows down and falls	*lp`n.il.thbr.wtql*
Prostrates herself and honors him	*tšthwy.wtkbdh*
	(CAT 1.4.IV 25-26)²³

Just as the sons of gods or divine beings are called upon to give glory to Yahweh and bow down to him, so also Lady Athirat, Consort of El, bows down and honors El. Yahweh receives the same obeisance and adoration as El.

These examples demonstrate only a few of the commonalities between the Book of Psalms and Ugaritic. They demonstrate that Hebrew and Ugaritic shared a common poetic structure and, more importantly, a common thought world. From these examples, we turn now to consider a comparative study of specific aspects of God as found in the Book of Psalms.

God in the Book of Psalms and in the Ancient Near East

The following examples are chosen to indicate something of the common thought world of the Book of Psalms and the ANE. These are by no means the only motifs that could have been chosen; and certainly these do not begin to cover every instance of these motifs, either from the Book of Psalms or from Ugaritic and Akkadian examples. Nevertheless, they are selected to show a common thought world across a variety of attributes of God.

---

²²My translation.
²³Parker, ed., *Ugaritic Narrative Poetry*, 127.

1. *God as Creator*

Both the Egyptian *Hymn to Aton* and the *Hymn to Amun* described the deity as the creator god.[24] Here we will add additional examples from Egypt, Akkadian, Ugaritic, and the Book of Psalms to indicate how each culture described its chief god(s) as creator.

Two Akkadian examples clearly indicates that the deity, in this case Marduk and Asshur respectively, is creator.

> Heaven and earth are thine,
> The space of heaven and earth is thine.   *(Hymn to Marduk* no. 6)[25]

> Creator of the upper universe, builder of the mountains,
> Creator of the gods, begetter of the goddesses.   *(Hymn to Asshur)*[26]

These two Assyrian examples may be compared with another Egyptian passsage from the Hymn to Amun:

> Jubilation to you, because of all foreign lands,
> > To the height of heaven
> > And the width of earth,
> > And to the depth of the sea!
> The gods are bowing down to your majesty
> > And exalting the power of the one who created them,
>
> . . . .
>
> > who raised the heaven and laid out the earth,
> > who made what is and created what will be
> > > > *(Hymn to Amun* VII, 3-5, 6-7)[27]

This Egyptian passage immediately calls to mind Psalm 95:4-5:

> [4]In his hand are the depths of the earth;
> > the heights of the mountains are his also.
> [5]The sea is his, for he made it,
> > and the dry land, which his hands have formed.

In CAT 1.6 III 10-11, El is given several epithets. He is beneficent and benign (or, compassionate). He is also Creator of creatures:

---

[24]See above, 3-4.

[25]Cumming, *The Assyrian and Hebrew Hymns of Praise*, 120.

[26]Cumming, *The Assyrian and Hebrew Hymns of Praise*, 120.

[27]Beyerlin, ed., *Near Eastern Religious Texts Relating to the Old Testament*, 15.

In the dream of Beneficent El the Ben[ign]   *b ḫxlm.lṭpn.il d pid*
In the vision of the Creator of Creatures[28]   *b ḏrt.bny.bnwt*

Cross translates another phrase containing several epithets of El as follows:

Indeed our creator is eternal   *k qnyn. `l[ ]*
Indeed ageless is he who formed us.[29]   *k drd<r>.d yknn*
                                         (CAT 1.10.III.6)

Similarly, Athirat, consort of El, is called Creatress of the Gods in CAT 1.4 III 25-26:

They entreat Lady [A]thirat of the Sea,   *tmgnn.rbt[.]aṯrt ym*
Beseech the Creatress of the Gods[30]   *tġẓyn.qnyt ilm*

In each of these cultures, the primary deity being worshipped is called the creator. In addition to the passages cited above, the Book of Psalms in numerous other passages worships Yahweh as the creator. One additional passage will have to suffice:

[6]By the word of the LORD the heavens were made,
     and all their host by the breath of his mouth.
[7]He gathered the waters of the sea as in a bottle;
     he put the deeps in storehouses.
[8]Let all the earth fear the LORD;
     let all the inhabitants of the world stand in awe of him.
[9]For he spoke, and it came to be;
     he commanded, and it stood firm.   (Psalm 33:6-9)

2. The Council of the Gods/Divine Council

In the religious thought of Mesopotamia and Canaan, the chief god had a council of gods or divine council who either advised him or who actually made decisions binding on all the gods. In Israel, Yahweh has a similar council of heavenly beings (at times called "the sons of God/gods" בני אלהים) who served as a kind of advisory board to King Yahweh.

---

[28]Parker, *Ugaritic Narrative Poetry*, 157-58.
[29]Frank Moore Cross, *Canaanite Myth and Hebrew Epic* (Cambridge MA: Harvard University Press, 1973) 15.
[30]Parker, ed., *Ugaritic Narrative Poetry*, 125.

Mullen suggests that Egypt also had a "synod of the gods" though it had little or no role in Egyptian religious thought.[31]

In Mesopotamia the decrees of the council of the gods (*puḫur ilani*) were obligatory on all the gods. This role is clearly seen in *Enuma eliš* where the council proclaims Marduk their king and deliverer.[32]

> If I am indeed to be [your avenger],
> To vanquish Ti'amat (and) [to keep you alive],
> Convene the assembly and [proclaim my lot supreme].
> [When you are joyfully seated together] in the Court of Assembly,
> [May I] through the utterance of my mouth [determine the destinies],
>   instead of [you].   (*Enuma eliš*, tablet 3, 116-20)[33]

> Marduk, thou art our avenger;
> To thee we have given kingship over the totality of the whole universe,
> So that when thou sittest in the assembly, thy word shall be exalted.
>   (*Enuma eliš*, tablet 4, 13-15)[34]

Elsewhere the divine council is mentioned in a hymn to Marduk. However, the role of the council in this passage is not clear; what is clear is that Marduk is the greatest god in the council.

> O mighty god to whom there is no rival
>   in the assembly of the great gods.   (*Hymn to Marduk* no.3)[35]

In the Canaanite/Ugaritic understanding of the divine council, El sat as the head of the assembly. He is due deference as creator and father of the gods. The divine council is even called "the assembly of the sons of El," *phr bn ilm* in several passages:

Mightiest Baal [answers(?)],	*y[t]b.aliyn.b`l*
The Cloudrider testifies:	*yt`dd.rkb.`rpt*
" . . . He stood and abased me,	*qm.ydd.w qlṣn*
He arose and spat on me,	*yqm.w ywpṯn*

---

[31]E. Theodore Mullen, Jr., *The Divine Council in Canaanite and Early Hebrew Literature*, Harvard Semitic Monographs 24 (Chico CA: Scholars Press, 1980) 113-14.

[32]Mullen, *The Divine Council in Canaanite and Early Hebrew Literature*, 115.

[33]The translation is from Alexander Heidel, *The Babylonian Genesis*, 2nd ed. (Chicago: University of Chicago Press, 1951) 35.

[34]Ibid., 36-37.

[35]Cumming, *The Assyrian and Hebrew Hymns of Praise*, 104

Amid the ass[em]bly of the sons of El."   *b tk pḫr.bn.ilm.*

(CAT 1.4.III.10-14)[36]

The council is also known as the Assembled Council, *pḫr m'd*. In the following passage, Yamm is challenging the council and El. He sends messengers instructing them to show no deference either to El or to the council, and to demand that Baal be handed over to Yamm.

Then Yamm's messengers arrive,   *aḫr.tmġyn.mlak.ym[.]*
The legation of Judge River.   *t`dt.ṭpt.nhr.*
At El's feet they [do not] bow down,   *l p`n.il l tpl.*
They do not prostrate themselves   *l tšthwy.pḫr.m`d*
    before the Assembled Council.   (CAT 1.2.I.30-31)[37]

Two other phrases which are used in Ugaritic to describe the divine council ("council of El," `dt ilm, and the "circle of El," dr il) appear in contexts which indicate their meaning:

Then the council of 'El arrived   *[aḫ]r.mġy.`dt ilm*
And 'Al'iyan Ba`l spoke:     *[w ]y`n.aliy[n.]b`l*
"Come now, O Kindly One,   *[.t]tb`.l l ṭpn [il.]d pid.*
    'El the Compassionate
Will you not bless Kirta, the Noble,   *l tbrk [krt.]ṭ`*
Will you not strengthen Nu`man, lad of 'El?"     *l tmr.n`mn [ġlm] il*

(CAT 1.15.II.11-16)[38]

The gods offer blessing, they go;   *tbrk.ilm.tity*
The gods go home to their tents   *tity.ilm.l ahlhm*
The circle [assembly] of 'El to their dwellings   *dr il. l mšknthm*

(CAT 1.15.III.17-19)[39]

---

[36]Parker, ed., *Ugaritic Narrative Poetry*, 124. I do note that the transliteration of Smith in Parker sees only a *y[ ]* as the first word of the first line and reconstructs possibly *y`n* as a parallel to *yt`dd*. CAT reads *y[t]b*, "Aliyan Baal sits enthroned."

[37]Parker, ed., *Ugaritic Narrative Poetry*, 100.

[38]The English translation of this passage is that of Mullen, *The Divine Council in Canaanite and Early Hebrew Literature*, 249.

[39]Parker, ed., *Ugaritic Narrative Poetry*, 26. The word "assembly" inserted in the translation is not Greenstein's translation, but a suggestion from Mullen's translation, *The Divine Council in Canaanite and Early Hebrew Literature*, 118. Mullen further notes that *dr*, "assembly" in this line parallels *ilm*, "gods" in the two previous lines.

While other phrases indicating the assembly of the gods do occur in Ugaritic, they lack a context to show their meaning. These phrases include *phr ilm*, "assembly of the gods" (CAT 1.47.29), in a list of gods which has no other context; similarly, *mphrt bn ilm*, "assembly of the sons of El" (CAT 1.65.3), in a list just after *dr bn il*, "circle (assembly) of the sons of El," but again lacking any context.

Clearly in all these Canaanite/Ugaritic passages, El is the chief deity of the divine council to whom all others should give obeisance. Now it should be mentioned that Baal does have an assembly in these texts, as does Ti'amat in Mesopotamian texts. Ti'amat's assembly is that of the monster beings she has created. Baal's assembly is mentioned in a list of sacrifices being offered to various gods, but has no other context.

The Book of Psalms has numerous references to Yahweh at the head of the divine council. The extended passage below from Psalm 89:6-9 (EVV 89:5-8) uses several different phrases to describe the council:

The heavens praise your wonders, O Yahweh,
And your truth in the council of the holy ones (בִּקְהַל קְדֹשִׁים)
For who in the skies can compare to Yahweh?
Who is like Yahweh among the sons of god
(בִּבְנֵי אֵלִים i.e., the gods)?
A dreadful god in the council of the holy ones (בְּסוֹד־קְדֹשִׁים)
Great and terrible above all those around him.
Yahweh, god of (the heavenly) hosts, who is like you
Mighty Yah(weh), your faithful ones surround you.[40]

In this passage, Yahweh is described as incomparable; none of the divine council or heavenly hosts can be compared to him. Another passage, Psalms 82:1 likewise refers to the divine council, using a different phrase:

God has taken his place in the divine council;	אֱלֹהִים נִצָּב בַּעֲדַת־אֵל
in the midst of the gods he holds judgment.	בְּקֶרֶב אֱלֹהִים יִשְׁפֹּט:

Here God brings judgment on the gods of the council. Because of their injustice and lack of understanding, the gods are condemned! In

---

[40]The translation here is that of Mullen, *The Divine Council in Canaanite and Early Hebrew Literature*, 191.

Israel's view even divine beings were subject to God's justice and judgment.

Each of these cultures has a concept of a divine council. Jacobsen[41] has argued that the divine council reflects a primitive democracy in which the assembly of elders met at times of specific need and appointed a leader just to deal with that specific crisis. While that may be the origin of the divine council, in each of the cultures the council appears more as an advisory body for a supreme deity—a Privy Council or Cabinet to advise a king. It is to that role of God as monarch that we now turn.

3. *God as King*

Throughout the ANE the chief god was described as king. In the Akkadian hymns, the chief god is often called the king of heaven and earth:

> Shamash, king of heaven and earth
> governor of things above and below. (*Hymn to Shamash* no.6)[42]

> Marduk, regent of heaven and earth (*Hymn to Marduk* no. 1)[43]

> In powerful sovereignty thou rulest the lands,
> Thou placest on the glittering heavens thy throne. (*Hymn to Sin* no. 2)[44]

In the Canaanite Baal cycle, El is the chief god and head of the divine council. He is regularly called king, as the following texts indicate.

She comes to the mountain of El and enters	*tgly.dd il.w.tbu.*
The tent of the King, the Father of Years.	*qrš.mlk.ab.šnm*
At the feet of El she bows down and falls,	*l p`n il.thbr.w tql*
Prostrates herself and honors him.	*tšthwy.w tkbdnh*
	(CAT 1.6.I.34-38)[45]
[In lament] he cries to Bull El, his Father,	*[an]y[.]l ysh.tr il.abh*

---

[41]Thorkild Jacobsen, "Primitive Democracy in Ancient Mesopotamia," in *Toward the Image of Tammuz and Other Essays on Mesopotamian History and Culture*, ed. W. L. Moran (Cambridge MA: Harvard University Press, 1970) 157-70.

[42]Cumming, *The Assyrian and Hebrew Hymns of Praise*, 146.

[43]Cumming, *The Assyrian and Hebrew Hymns of Praise*, 146.

[44]Cumming, *The Assyrian and Hebrew Hymns of Praise*, 147.

[45]Parker, ed., *Ugaritic Narrative Poetry*, 153

To [E]l, the King who created him   *[i]l.mlk.d yknnh*
                                           (CAT 1.4.IV.47-48)[46]

Yet alongside those texts which speak of El as King, are texts which speak of El removing another god from being king. Apparently El had the authority to name other gods as king, and to remove their kingship. In effect, El was the supreme king, a king of kings, and the other gods were lesser, vassal kings. In a speech addressed to Mot, Shapsh says:

How will Bull El, your Father, hea[r] you?   *ik.al.yšm[`]k.[t]r.il.abk.*
Surely he will remove the support of your throne.   *l.ys`.alt ṯbtk*
Surely he will overturn the seat of your kingship,   *l yhpk.ksa.mlkk*
surely he will break the scepter of your rule.   *lyṯbr.ḫṭ.mṭpṭk*
                                           (CAT 1.6.VI.26-29)[47]

Baal is given kingship by El. The divine council assents to this decision with the following affirmation:

Our king is mightiest Baal   *mlkn.aliy[n.]b`l*
Our ruler with none above him.   *ṯpṭn.w in.d `lnh*
                                    (CAT 1.4.IV.43-44)[48]

Kothar wa-Hasis, the craftsman of the gods, tells Baal to vanquish his foe Yamm and then:

So assume your eternal kingship,   *tqh.mlk.`lmk*
   your everlasting dominion.   *drkt.dt.drdrk*
                                     (CAT 1.2.IV.10)[49]

The passage is quite reminiscent of the statement in Psalm 145:13 concerning Yahweh as King:

Your kingdom is an everlasting kingdom,   מַלְכוּתְךָ מַלְכוּת כָּל־עֹלָמִים
   and your dominion endures
      throughout all generations.   וּמֶמְשַׁלְתְּךָ בְּכָל־דּוֹר וָדוֹר

The same image of Baal as king is found in CAT 1.101.1-4:

---

[46]Parker, ed., *Ugaritic Narrative Poetry*, 128.
[47]Parker, ed., *Ugaritic Narrative Poetry*, 163.
[48]Parker, ed., *Ugaritic Narrative Poetry*, 128.
[49]Parker, ed., *Ugaritic Narrative Poetry*, 103.

Ba'l sits enthroned, (his) mountain like a dais,   *b'l.yṯb.kṯbt.r*
Haddu the shepherd, like the Flood dragon.   *hd.r['y] k mdb.* In the
midst of his mount, Divine Sapan,   *btk.rh.il.spn.*
On the mount of (his) victory.   *b[m] r.tliyt*[50]

This passage may be compared with Psalm 29:10:

The LORD sits enthroned over the flood;   יְהוָה לַמַּבּוּל יָשָׁב
    the LORD sits enthroned as king forever.   וַיֵּשֶׁב יְהוָה מֶלֶךְ לְעוֹלָם׃

The parallels between the Ugaritic passage and the Psalms passage
are obvious, although the context differs. In the Baal epic, Baal has
apparently just defeated Yamm and has returned victorious. He sits enthroned, now secure in his kingship. In Psalm 29, Yahweh, after appear-
ing in the theophany in the thunderstorm, sits enthroned above his
creation.

In another relevant passage concerning kingship, Yahweh is called a
great king; his dwelling place on Mount Zion is described as well:

[1]Great is the LORD and greatly to be praised
        in the city of our God.
His holy mountain, [2]beautiful in elevation,
        is the joy of all the earth,
Mount Zion, in the far north יַרְכְּתֵי צָפוֹן,
        the city of the great King   (Psalm 48:1-2)

The reference to Mount Zion in the far north (or, "in the Heights of
Zaphon") has parallels in the Baal cycle:

Come and I will reveal it   *atm.w ank ibġyh.*
In the midst of my mountain, Divine Sapan,   *b tk. ġry.il.spn*
In the holy mount of my heritage   *b qdš.b ġr.nhlty*
In the beautiful hill of my might.   *b n'm.b gb'.tliyt*
    (CAT 1.3. III 28-31)[51]

---

[50]Both the English and the Ugaritic transcription are taken from Cross, *Canaanite
Myth and Hebrew Epic*, 148-49.
[51]Parker, ed., *Ugaritic Narrative Poetry*, 110.

Each of the ANE cultures described their chief gods as king. As king, the god has a royal palace and a royal city. Israel likewise described Yahweh as we have noted. We offer one additional passage from Psalms:

> ⁶Sing praises to God, sing praises;
>> sing praises to our King, sing praises.
>
> ⁷For God is the king of all the earth;
>> sing praises with a psalm.
>
> ⁸God is king over the nations;
>> God sits on his holy throne.   (Psalm 47:6-8)

4. *God as a Storm Deity*

In every culture of the ANE, at least one god had the attributes of a storm deity. The Assyrians had a storm deity, Ramman, who is described in terms quite similar to that of Yahweh:

The lord in his fury,	the heavens quake before him;
Ramman in his fury,	the earth trembles;
The great mountains	break to pieces before him.
Before his anger,	before his fury,
Before his roaring,	before his thunder;
The gods of heaven	to heaven ascend;
The gods of earth	to earth retire;
To the heights of heaven	they penetrate;
Into the depths of earth	they enter. (*Ramman* no. 1)[52]

This passage in Akkadian may be compared with Psalm 29:3-10, a theophany of God in a thunderstorm:

> ³The voice of the LORD is over the waters;
>> the God of glory thunders,
>> the LORD, over mighty waters.
>
> ⁴The voice of the LORD is powerful;
>> the voice of the LORD is full of majesty.
>
> ⁵The voice of the LORD breaks the cedars;
>> the LORD breaks the cedars of Lebanon.
>
> ⁶He makes Lebanon skip like a calf,
>> and Sirion like a young wild ox.

---

[52]Cumming, *The Assyrian and Hebrew Hymns of Praise*, 88-89

[7]The voice of the LORD flashes forth flames of fire.
[8]The voice of the LORD shakes the wilderness;
    the LORD shakes the wilderness of Kadesh.
[9]The voice of the LORD causes the oaks to whirl,
    and strips the forest bare;
    and in his temple all say, "Glory!"
[10]The LORD sits enthroned over the flood;
    the LORD sits enthroned as king forever.

Baal is clearly a storm deity in the Canaanite epics. He is often described as "the Rider of the (storm) Clouds", *rkb ʿrpt*. In addition many passages speak of him in terms of thunder, lightning, and rain. When Baal is absent, drought is the result; when he comes, he brings the rains and the thunderstorms. I mention only three examples below.

Let the clouds make rain in the summer,	*yr.ʿrpt tmṭr.b qẓ*
the dew lay dew on the grapes.	*ṭl.yṭll l nbm*
Seven years Baal is absent	*šbʿ.šnt ysrk.bʿl*
Eight, the Rider of the Clouds:	*ṯmn.rkb ʿrpt.*
No dew, no downpour,	*bl.ṭl.bl rbb*
No swirling of the deeps,	*bl.šrʿ.thmtm.*
No welcome voice of Baal.	*bl ṭbn.ql.bʿl*
	(CAT 1.19.I.40-46)[53]
Baal opens a break in the clouds	*ypṭḥ bʿl.bdqt[.]ʿrpt*
Baal gives vent to his holy voice.	*qlh.qdš[.]bʿl[.]ytn*
Baal recites the is[sue of (?)] his [li(?)]ps,	*yṯny.bʿl.xṣ[at.]špth*
His ho[ly(?)] voice, the earth [sha(?)]kes,	*qlh.q[dš.]ṯrr.arṣ*
. . . .	
The high places of the Ear[th] shake.	*bmt.a[rṣ] tṯtn*
	(CAT 1.4.VII.27-35)[54]
So now may Baal enrich with his rain	*wnap.ʿdn.mṭrh bʿl*
May he enrich with rich water in a downpour.	*yʿdn.ʿdn.ṯr(!))t.bglt*
And may he give his voice in the clouds,	*wtn.qlh. bʿrpt*
May he flash to the earth lightning .	*šrh. lars. brqm*
	(CAT 1.4.V.6-9)[55]

---

[53]Parker, ed., *Ugaritic Narrative Poetry*, 69.

[54]Parker, ed., *Ugaritic Narrative Poetry*, 136-37.

[55]Parker, ed., *Ugaritic Narrative Poetry*, 129; both the transliteration and translation here are Smith's.

The appearance of Yahweh in a theophany in a thunderstorm was mentioned above. In addition, several passages in Psalms use language similar to the Canaanite/Ugaritic description of Baal as "Rider on the Clouds."

> Sing to God, sing praises to his name;
>> lift up a song to him who rides upon the clouds—
> his name is the LORD—
>> be exultant before him.   (Psalm 68:4)

> O rider in the heavens, the ancient heavens;
>> listen, he sends out his voice, his mighty voice.   (Psalm 68:33)

> you set the beams of your chambers on the waters,
> you make the clouds your chariot,
>> you ride on the wings of the wind,
> you make the winds your messengers,
>> fire and flame your ministers.   (Psalm 104:3-4)

Yahweh, like Baal, comes in the thunderstorms, rides on the winds, rides on the clouds, and uses the clouds as his chariot. His voice is heard in the thunder, his flashing fire is seen in the lightning.

5. God as Wise

Wisdom is another characteristic of deity. The cultures of the ANE attributed wisdom to their chief deity. The Akkadian examples refer to Marduk and Shamash as wise.

> O lord, Bel, thou prince who art mighty in understanding
>> (*Hymn to Marduk* no. 10)[56]

> As for those who speak with the tongue in all countries,
> Thou knowest their plans, their walk thou observest,
> Shamash, wise one, lofty one, thine own counsellor art thou.
>> (*Hymn to Shamash* no. 7)[57]

> O lord that knowest fate, who of thyself art glorious in Sumer,
> Father Enlil, lord of unerring word,

---

[56]Cumming, *The Assyrian and Hebrew Hymns of Praise*, 130.
[57]Cumming, *The Assyrian and Hebrew Hymns of Praise*, 130.

Father Enlil, whose omniscience is self-created
Thou possest all wisdom, perfect in power.   (*Hymn to Marduk* no. 1)[58]

In Ugaritic texts, El is the deity to whom wisdom is ascribed. A part of the attribution of wisdom to El seems to be related to his age, his gray hair, and long beard. Such an attribution may reflect the respected position elders held in those cultures.

Your decree, O El, is wise,	*thmk.il.ḥkm*
You are wise for eternity,	*ḥkmt `m `lm*
A victorious life is your decree	*ḥyt.ḥẓt thmk*
	(CAT 1.4.IV.41-43)[59]

You are great, O El, so very wise;	*rbt.ilm.l ḥkmt*
The gray hair of your beard instructs you,	*šbt.dqnk.l tsrk*
[Your] soft b[eard] down to your chest.	*rḥn{n}t.dt.l irtk*
	(CAT 1.4.V.3-5)[60]

The Book of Psalms also describes the wisdom and understanding of Yahweh:

How great are your works, O LORD!
    Your thoughts are very deep!   (Psalm 92:5)

O LORD, how manifold are your works!
    In wisdom you have made them all;
    the earth is full of your creatures.   (Psalm 104:24)

who alone does great wonders,
    for his steadfast love endures forever;
who by understanding made the heavens,
    for his steadfast love endures forever; . . .   (Psalm 136:4-5)

Great is our Lord, and abundant in power;
    his understanding is beyond measure.   (Psalm 147:5)

---

[58]Cumming, *The Assyrian and Hebrew Hymns of Praise*, 132.
[59]Parker, ed., *Ugaritic Narrative Poetry*, 128.
[60]Parker, ed., *Ugaritic Narrative Poetry*, 129.

6. *God as Just and Merciful*

The deity was understood to be both just and merciful. Justice and mercy together assured the rights of the oppressed and defenseless would be protected. The Egyptian god Amun is described as one

> Who hears the prayer of him who is in captivity (?),
> Merciful to the one who appeals to him,
> Who delivers the fearful man from violence,
> Who judges the weak and the injured.   (*Hymn to Amun*, IV,3-5)[61]

Both Shamash and Marduk are described as merciful in the Akkadian examples below. Shamash also is shown to be just by his actions. Marduk demonstrates his justice by his protection of the defenseless.

> Lord of all creatures,
> Merciful unto the lands art thou.   (*Hymn to Shamash* no. 1)[62]

> Shamash honors the head of the just man;
> Shamash rends the evil man like a thong   (*Hymn to Shamash* no.1)[63]

> [Marduk] the merciful,
> whose turning [i.e., mercy] is near.   (*Hymn to Marduk* no.4)[64]

> Thou liftest up the weak, thou increasest the small;
> Thou raisest up the powerless, thou protectest the weak.
> Marduk, unto the fallen thou grantest mercy;
> Stands under thy protection the weakling. . . .
> thou commandest his raising up.   (*Hymn to Marduk* no. 12)[65]

Using very similar language, Yahweh or God is said to protect the powerless and defenseless in the Book of Psalms:

> Father of orphans and protector of widows
>   is God in his holy habitation.   (Psalm 68:5)

---

[61]Beyerlin, ed., *Near Eastern Religious Texts Relating to the Old Testament*, 14.
[62]Cumming, *The Assyrian and Hebrew Hymns of Praise*, 139.
[63]Cumming, *The Assyrian and Hebrew Hymns of Praise*, 97.
[64]Cumming, *The Assyrian and Hebrew Hymns of Praise*, 139.
[65]Cumming, *The Assyrian and Hebrew Hymns of Praise*, 140.

The LORD watches over the strangers;
> he upholds the orphan and the widow,
> but the way of the wicked he brings to ruin.
The LORD will reign forever,
> your God, O Zion, for all generations.   (Psalm 146:9-10)

In the Ugaritic texts, humans are expected to demonstrate the same justice and mercy toward others as the deity. Dan'el is described as a good man who:

Takes care of the case of the widow,	*ydn dn.almnt*
Defends the need of the orphan.	*ytpt.tpt.ytm*

(CAT 1.17.V. 7-8)[66]

By contrast, Kirta, although king, does not exercise justice and mercy:

You've let your hand fall into vice	*šqlt blt.ydk*
You don't pursue the widow's case	*l tdn dn.almnt*
You don't take up the wretched's claim	*l ttpt tpt.qsr.npš.*
You don't expel the poor's oppressor	*l tdy [[t]]qšm.`l.dl.*
You don't feed the orphan who faces you,	*l pnk l tšlhm.ytm.*
Nor the widow who stands at your back.	*b`d kslk.almnt*

(CAT 1.16.VI. 44-50)[67]

As a consequence, Kirta has now become sick according to the text. The judgment of the deity on Kirta is attributed to his actions, his injustice.

Also in Ugaritic poetry El, as chief god, is often given the epithet "the Compassionate" or, as Smith prefers, "the Beneficent" and "the Benign":

All the while she is servile before Bull El the Beneficent	*t`pp.tr.il.d pid*
Deferential to the Creator of Creatures.	*tġzy.bny.bnwt*

(CAT 1.4.II.10-11)[68]

Then Beneficent El the Benign	*apnk.ltpn.il d pid*
Descends from his seat, sits on the footstool,	*yrd.l ksi.ytb l hdm.*

---

[66]Parker, ed., *Ugaritic Narrative Poetry*, 58.
[67]Parker, ed., *Ugaritic Narrative Poetry*, 41.
[68]Parker, ed., *Ugaritic Narrative Poetry*, 122.

[And] from the footstool, sits on the earth.   *w l.hdm.yṯb l ars.*
(AT 1.5.VI. 11-14)[69]

In the Book of Psalms, Yahweh is also shown to be compassionate. The three examples below indicate Yahweh's compassion and kindness. These examples could be multiplied many times. In one of these examples Yahweh's compassion is paralleled by his goodness.

As a father has compassion for his children,   כְּרַחֵם אָב עַל־בָּנִים
so the LORD has compassion
for those who fear him.   רִחַם יְהוָה עַל־יְרֵאָיו
(Psalms 103:13)

For the LORD will vindicate his people,   כִּי־יָדִין יְהוָה עַמּוֹ
and have compassion on his servants.   וְעַל־עֲבָדָיו יִתְנֶחָם:
(Psalms 135:14)

The LORD is good to all,   טוֹב־יְהוָה לַכֹּל
and his compassion is over
all that he has made.   וְרַחֲמָיו עַל־כָּל־מַעֲשָׂיו:
(Psalms 145:9)

Conclusions

What conclusions may be drawn from this comparative study? First, there was a common thought world in the ANE, which the Book of Psalms shares with Israel's neighbors. All the cultures studied used a common mode of expression, repetition or parallelism, to express their ideas. This style of parallelism is found in the epic poetry of Ugaritic as well as the hymnic material from Akkadian and Hebrew.

More importantly, the cultures also assigned similar attributes of their respective deities. The comparison of what they said is more striking than the technique of how they said it. Each of the attributes mentioned in this essay has a remarkable degree of similarity of expression across the ancient Near East: their gods are described as creator, king, head of the divine council, wise, just, and merciful. Most cultures have a storm god as a chief god. The attributes of the god held in common could have been multiplied many times, but space prohibits exploring additional ones. We

---

[69]Parker, ed., *Ugaritic Narrative Poetry*, 149.

might observe such attributes as the glory of the deity, the deity as savior/deliverer, the deity as protector/defender, the deity as warrior, the deity as judge, and so forth.

Further, a comparison could be made of human attributes, or of the concepts of nature in these cultures. This study could have included laments as well as primarily hymnic materials (and epic material for Ugaritic). In a word, this essay has only scratched the surface of comparisons between the Book of Psalms and its ANE context.

However, even from this limited study, I conclude that the Book of Psalms reflects the ANE context that Israel shared with its neighbors. The Psalmists did not borrow or copy from those cultures; they simply were products of and inheritors of a common tradition.

The commonalities of expression, many times even the use of cognate words, shows that for the ancient Near East there was in a sense a "global community," or to borrow a different phrase "it's [i.e., it was] a small world after all."

Chapter 7

The Canonical Shape of the Psalms

Nancy L. deClaissé-Walford

Scholars traditionally have approached the Book of Psalms, the Psalter, as a collection of laments and hymns of ancient Israel, preserved and handed down to us in a somewhat random order. We select and use psalms—like Psalm 23 or Psalm 42 or Psalm 145—with little or no concern for the psalms surrounding them. Why shouldn't we? After all, each psalm is a self-contained unit, two-thirds of them with a title,[1] and with a beginning, a middle, and an end. We don't need to read Psalm 22 to understand Psalm 23, or Psalm 146 to understand Psalm 145. Each psalm has an individual message.

But during the past twenty years, a different way to look at the text, called the canonical approach, has encouraged readers to reexamine the "shape" of the Psalter and ask questions about the possibility of a deliberate rather than random ordering of the psalms within the book. Is it possible to read the whole Book of Psalms as we read the prose books of the Old Testament, as a connected narrative with its own beginning, middle, and end? J. Clinton McCann, Jr., in a collection of essays titled *The Shape and Shaping of the Psalter*, suggests that scholars are increasingly aware that "the purposeful placement of psalms within the collection seems to have given the final form of the whole Psalter a function and message greater than the sum of its parts."[2] Clues about the ordering of the psalms are evidenced throughout the book. In this essay, I will examine those clues—what I like to call footprints, footprints of the community which shaped the Book of Psalms into the form in which it is preserved in the Old Testament.

---

[1]Psalm titles are called "superscriptions." Of the 150 psalms in the Book of Psalms, 102 have such superscriptions or titles.

[2]J. Clinton McCann, Jr., ed., *The Shape and Shaping of the Psalter*, JSOTSup 159 (Sheffield UK: JSOT Press, 1993) 7.

From the time of the Enlightenment until the mid-twentieth century, scholars who studied the biblical text gave the majority of their time to the disciplines of textual, source, form, and redactional criticism. Hermann Gunkel and his student Sigmund Mowinckel devoted a good portion of their careers to the critical study of the Book of Psalms. Gunkel applied the form-critical method to the psalms, categorizing each psalm by its form and type (*Gattung*) and then attempting to discover the particular setting in the life of ancient Israel (*Sitz im Leben*) in which such a form might have been composed and used.[3] Sigmund Mowinckel built on the work of Gunkel and tried to discover where each psalm in the Psalter would have been used in the cultic worship of ancient Israel.[4] Gunkel and Mowinckel understood the psalms as individual compositions; they wrote nothing about the "shape" of the Psalter as a book or a story.

The canonical approach to the text of the Old Testament was championed by Brevard S. Childs. In a 1976 essay titled "Reflections on the Modern Study of the Psalms," and in his 1979 *Introduction to the Old Testament as Scripture*, Childs encourages scholars to move away from dissecting the text of the Old Testament, and move toward examining it in the form in which it was preserved for us, as a whole.[5] Childs maintains, in fact, that it is largely useless to study the text of the Old Testament as Gunkel and Mowinckel had done. The Israelite editors who compiled and transmitted the text of the Old Testament deliberately obscured the underlying layers of tradition—the settings in the life and in the worship of ancient Israel—in a process Childs calls "actualization." The editors' purpose was to keep the text from "being moored in the past" and to make it relevant to successive generations of readers and hearers. Childs writes:

---

[3]See Hermann Gunkel, *The Psalms: A Form-Critical Introduction*, trans. Thomas M. Horner, Facet Books Biblical Series 19, ed. John Reumann (Philadelphia: Fortress Press, 1967).

[4]See Sigmund Mowinckel, *The Psalms in Israel's Worship*, 2 vols., trans. D. R. Ap-Thomas (Nashville: Abingdon Press, 1962).

[5]Brevard S. Childs, "Reflections on the Modern Study of the Psalms," in *Magnalia Dei: The Mighty Acts of God*, ed. F. M. Cross et al. (Garden City NY: Doubleday, 1976) 377-88, and *Introduction to the Old Testament as Scripture* (Philadelphia: Fortress Press, 1979).

The psalms are transmitted as the sacred psalms of David, but they testify to all the common troubles and joys of ordinary human life in which all persons participate. . . . Through the mouth of David, the man, they become a personal word from God in each individual situation.[6]

Another scholar, James A. Sanders, shares Brevard Childs' interest in studying the final form of the text of the Old Testament. But Sanders disagrees with Childs' assertion that it is useless to try to understand the underlying layers of traditions which make up a text. Sanders maintains that biblical texts are grounded in specific historical settings, that those settings can be discovered, and that they are important for understanding the canonical shape of the texts. But he maintains that scholars have looked in the wrong places for the historical settings of the texts of the Old Testament. Hermann Gunkel tried to discover the original oral setting for each psalm, and Sigmund Mowinckel studied the cultic settings. But Sanders is concerned with communities of faith.[7]

Each psalm may have been composed by an individual, perhaps in an oral setting. And each psalm may have been used in ancient Israel's worship experience. But each psalm in the Psalter was remembered, valued, and repeated within the ancient Israelite community of faith. Communities found value in the texts of which the Old Testament was composed, or those texts would not have been preserved. Sanders writes:

The text cannot be attributed to any discreet genius, such as author or editor or redactor, in the past. It can only be attributed to the ancient communities which continued to find value in the received traditions and scriptures, generation after generation, passing them on for the value they had found in them.[8]

Sanders goes on to say that communities find value in texts when those texts provide answers to two basic existential questions: "Who are we?" and "What are we to do?"[9] The ancient Israelites repeatedly asked these

---

[6]Childs, *Introduction to the Old Testament as Scripture*, 521.

[7]James A. Sanders, *Canon and Community: A Guide to Canonical Criticism*, Guides to Biblical Scholarship, ed. Gene M. Tucker (Philadelphia: Fortress Press, 1984) and *From Sacred Story to Sacred Text* (Philadelphia: Fortress Press, 1987).

[8]Sanders, *Canon and Community*, 29.

[9]James A. Sanders, *Torah and Canon* (Philadelphia: Fortress Press, 1972) xv.

questions of, and found answers in, their traditions—the stories and texts which they passed on from generation to generation. And each generation took meaning from the stories and passed that meaning along to the next generation—subtly updating the stories and texts within their own context.

At some point in the history of ancient Israel, the community wrote down their authoritative traditions in a precise form and order and passed them on unchanged. The texts were fixed; Childs' process of "actualization" was complete. The Torah—Genesis, Exodus, Leviticus, Numbers, and Deuteronomy—was probably the first portion of the Old Testament to be placed in a fixed format. Next came the Prophets—Joshua, Judges, Samuel, Kings, Isaiah, Jeremiah, Ezekiel, and the Twelve. And then the Writings, which includes the Book of Psalms. We know little about the process by which the traditions of ancient Israel moved from a fluid to a fixed method of transmission, but we do know that the process of fixing the text of the Old Testament was completed sometime after the beginning of the Common Era.[10]

The text of the Old Testament is made up of materials that were recited, handed down, edited, and preserved over the course of thousands of years of ancient Israel's history. The Psalter is no exception. The psalms, the songs of which the book is composed, come from a variety of times and places. The superscriptions and contents of the psalms give the reader some clues about their composition. Seventy-four of the psalms in our Psalter are ascribed to David; two are ascribed to Solomon; twenty-five to Korah, Asaph, Ethan, and Heman, described in 1 Chronicles 15:16-19 and 2 Chronicles 20:19 as musicians in David's and Solomon's courts; and one to Moses. Psalms 120–134 are identified in their superscriptions as "Songs of Ascents," and thirty-six psalms have no superscription at all. Some psalms, such as Psalms 3 and 48, come from early in the life of ancient Israel; some, such as Psalms 1 and 137, seem clearly to be from Israel's later life. Scholars talk about different "types" of psalms: individual laments like 4, 5 and 16; community laments like 58, 60, and 123; general hymns like 100, 134, and 150; trust psalms like 23 and 131; and royal psalms like 2 and 72. Lament psalms dominate in

---

[10]For a full discussion of the process, see Nancy L. deClaissé-Walford, *Reading from the Beginning: The Shaping of the Hebrew Psalter* (Macon GA: Mercer University Press, 1997) 105-18.

books 1, 2, and 3 of the Psalter, while the reader finds more hymns in books 4 and 5.[11]

But why these 150 psalms and why in this particular order? Why is Psalm 1 the first psalm in the Psalter? Why is Psalm 72 placed seventy-second? And why does Psalm 150 close the collection? If we agree that the ordering of the psalms in the Psalter was purposeful and that we can read the book canonically as a coherent whole, then we may ask what influenced the particular ancient Israelite community which shaped the Book of Psalms into its final form to order the psalms as they did. We are not the first to ask the question. The Midrash on Psalm 3 states:

> As to the exact order of David's Psalms, Scripture says elsewhere: *Man knoweth not the order thereof* (Job 28:13). R. Eleazar taught: The sections of Scripture are not arranged in their proper order. For if they were arranged in their proper order, and any man so read them, he would be able to resurrect the dead and perform other miracles. For this reason the proper order of the sections of Scripture is hidden from mortals and is known only to the Holy One, blessed be He, who said, *"Who, as I, can read and declare it, and set it in order?"* (Isa 44:7).
>
> When R. Joshua ben Levi sought to arrange the Psalms in their proper order, a heavenly voice came forth and commanded: "Do not rouse that which slumbers!"[12]

Perhaps Rabbi ben Levi is wiser than we are, but we will rouse the slumbering book and ask it to shed some light on our questions about its shape and form. And perhaps we will learn from its story.

The Book of Psalms most likely did not achieve the "shape" in which we have it in our Old Testament until late in the postexilic period, perhaps as late as the first century of the common era.[13] What do we know

---

[11]In books 1, 2, and 3, fifty-two of the eighty-nine psalms are laments and twenty-four are hymns. In books 4 and 5, fifteen of the sixty-one psalms are laments and thirty-seven are laments.

[12]William G. Braude, *The Midrash on Psalms*, vol. 1 (New Haven CT: Yale University Press, 1959) 49-50.

[13]The Dead Sea discoveries and the Septuagint indicate that a number of "editions" of psalm collections circulated in ancient Israel. More than thirty fragments of psalms scrolls have been discovered at Qumran, among them two significant finds in caves 4 and 11. The fragment from cave 4 contains portions of Psalms 6-69, which are, for the most part, in the same order as the psalms in the Hebrew Bible/Old Testament Book of Psalms. The fragment from cave 11 contains thirty-nine canonical psalms with other poetry mixed

about the religious, social, and political situation of the postexilic community, the community which shaped the story of our Psalter? A brief history will be helpful.

In 597 BCE, the army of the Babylonian Empire carried Jehoiachin, the king of Judah, and many of his subjects into exile (2 Kings 25). A decade later, the army sacked Jerusalem and destroyed the temple; the nation of Israel, ruled by the Davidic kingdom, was at an end. But within fifty years, the Babylonian Empire was badly deteriorated, with a number of socioeconomic, religious, and political problems. In 539, Babylon fell to Cyrus II, leader of the Persian Empire. In the following year, Cyrus issued an edict in which he declared that he was reestablishing all of the sanctuaries of the people that had been captured by the Babylonians and returning the exiled people to their homelands.[14]

Sometime after 538 BCE a group of Jewish exiles made their way from Babylon to Jerusalem to begin the process of rebuilding Jerusalem and the temple. By 515, the temple was standing once again and functioning as a cult center (Ezra 6:15-16).

The Persian empire allowed the Jews to rebuild their temple and resume their religious practices. Temple and cult were restored, but the nation-state of ancient Israel with a Davidic king at its head was not. Except for a brief time of independence during the second and first centuries BCE, the people lived continuously as vassals, first to the Persians, then to the Greeks, and then to the Romans, throughout the period of the second temple. Under the same circumstances, many nation-

---

in. The order of the psalms on this scroll is Psalms 101-103, 109, 118, 104, 147, 105, 146, 148, 121-132, 119, 135-136, 145, 154 (attested elsewhere only in the Syriac Bible—a prayer for deliverance), 139, 137, 138, Sirach 51:13-30 (an apostrophe to Zion), Psalms 93, 141, 133, 144, 155 (also only in the Syriac Bible), 142, 143, 149-150 (a hymn to the creator), 2 Sam. 23:7 (a prose statement about David's compositions), Psalms 140, 134, and 151 (in most Greek translations but in Hebrew only in cave 11).

In the Septuagint tradition—the Greek translation of the Hebrew Bible—the psalms are in the same order as they are in the Christian Old Testament, but Psalms 9 and 10 are grouped as a single psalm, as are Psalms 114 and 115. An additional psalm (151) appears at the end of the book. And the superscriptions are longer and occur with more psalms than in the Christian Old Testament. See deClaissé-Walford, *Reading from the Beginning*, 15-20.

[14]James B. Pritchard, ed., *Ancient Near Eastern Texts Relating to the Old Testament*, 3rd ed. (Princeton NJ: Princeton University Press, 1969) 316. The Book of Ezra includes two portions of the restoration policy of Cyrus, in 1:2-4 and 6:3-5.

states in the ancient Near East simply disappeared from history. But ancient Israel did not. The postexilic community strove to find a new structure for existence and identity which went beyond traditional ancient Near Eastern concepts of nationhood. King and court could no longer be the center and grounding of national life; temple and cult had to assume that position—with YHWH, not David, as king over a new "religious nation" of Israel.

Postexilic Israel redefined "nationhood" and found a way to remain a separate and identifiable entity even among the vast empires of that day. How? Why did Israel survive when nations all around did not? Israel survived because the people asked the questions "Who are we?" and "What are we to do?" of their traditional and cultic literature, and then interpreted and shaped that literature into a document that answered those vexing questions. That document was the Hebrew Bible. And the people found in the texts of that document, which included the Psalter, a hermeneutical rationale for identity and survival.

We may read the Book of Psalms, then, as a contributing part of the story of the survival of ancient Israel. What is the Psalter's story? It celebrates the reigns of David and Solomon in books 1 and 2; laments the dark days of oppression during the divided kingdoms and the Babylonian exile in book 3; and looks forward to and rejoices in Israel's restoration to the land and in the reign of YHWH as king in books 4 and 5.[15]

We will begin with an exploration of book 1 (Psalms 1-41). Thirty-nine of the forty-one psalms in book 1 of the Psalter are, according to their superscriptions, "psalms of David."[16] Readers of this collection of

---

[15]The five divisions of the Psalter is an early tradition in Judaism. The Psalms scrolls from Qumran are divided into five books. The *Midrash Tehillim*, which contains very early material, such as the sayings of Rabbis Hillel and Shammai (ca. first century BCE), states in the commentary to Psalm 1:

> As Moses gave five books of laws to Israel, so David gave five books of Psalms to Israel, the book of psalms entitled *Blessed is the man* (Psalm 1:1), the book entitled *For the leader: Maschil* (Psalm 42:1), the book, *A Psalm of Asaph* (Psalm 73:1), the book *A Prayer of Moses* (Psalm 90:1), and the book *Let the Redeemed of the Lord say* (Psalm 107:2).

See James A. Sanders, *The Dead Sea Psalms Scroll* (Ithaca NY: Cornell University Press, 1967) and William G. Braude, *The Midrash on Psalms*, vol. 1 (New Haven CT: Yale University Press, 1959).

[16]Psalm 10 has no superscription, but it is strongly linked to Psalm 9. Psalm 33, also

psalms encounter David in all facets of his life. We read David's heartfelt laments:

> O YHWH, how my adversaries have increased!
> Many are rising up against me,
> Many are saying of my being,
> "There is no deliverance for him in God." (Psalm 3:1-2)[17]

> How long, O YHWH? Will you forget me forever?
> How long will you hide your face from me?
> How long shall I take counsel in my own being?
> How long will my enemy be exalted over me?   (7:1-2)

> Be not far from me, for distress is near;
> For there is none to help.
> Many bulls have surrounded me;
> Strong bulls of Bashan have encircled me.
> They open wide their mouth at me,
> As a ravening and a roaring lion.
> I am poured out like water,
> And all my bones are out of joint;
> My heart is like wax;
> It is melted within me.   (22:11-14)

We read David's equally stirring praises:

> I love you, O YHWH, my strength.
> YHWH is my rock and my fortress and my deliverer,
> My God, my rock, in whom I take refuge;
> My shield and the horn of my salvation, my stronghold. (18:1-2)

> YHWH is my shepherd,
> I shall not want.
> He makes me lie down in green pastures;
> He leads me beside restful waters.
> He restores my being.   (23:1-3)

We read David's awe at the God who created the world and humankind:

> When I see your heavens, the works of your fingers,
> The moon and the stars, which you have put in place;

---

untitled, has solid linguistic links to Psalm 32.

[17]All translations of the biblical text are my own unless otherwise indicated.

What is humanity that you remember us? . . .
Yet you have made us a little lower than God,
And you crown us with glory and majesty!   (8:3-5)

The heavens are telling of the glory of God;
And their expanse is declaring the work of his hands.   (19:1)

In Psalms 3–41, we encounter David the king and David the human being, with all his victories and strengths, all his shortcomings and flaws.

But the Psalter does not begin with a "psalm of David." Before the collection of Davidic Psalms 3-41 are two psalms without superscriptions. Psalm 1 is categorized as a wisdom psalm. It begins with the Hebrew word אַשְׁרֵי *'ashrê*, translated as "happy" or "blessed": "*'ashrê*—happy—is the person" who does such and such but does not do such and such and who "delights in" and "meditates on the Torah of YHWH day and night." Therefore, we enter the story of the Psalter through the voice of wisdom. To find wisdom, to be *'ashrê* or "happy," enter the story; delight in it; meditate on it.

Psalm 2, which also has no superscription, is said to be a "royal" psalm. Form critics categorize the royal psalms not by literary type, such as "lament" or "praise," but by subject matter, the person of the king. In its "original" setting in the life in ancient Israel, Psalm 2, probably especially verses 7-8, would have been recited at a coronation ceremony of a Davidic king in Jerusalem:

I will indeed tell of the decree of the LORD:
He said to me, "You are my son.
Today I have begotten you.
Ask of me, and I will surely give the nations as your inheritance,
And the end of the earth as your possession."   (2:7-8)

But in Psalm 2, it is YHWH, not a Davidic king, who sits on the throne. Kingship *is* important, but the enthroned one is YHWH (v.4).[18] The Psalm closes with the same word with which Psalm 1 begins, *'ashrê*. "Happy are those who take refuge in Him!" The *'ashrê* in 2:12 connects Psalm 2 with Psalm 1 as an introduction to the story of the Psalter. Enter the

---

[18]For a full discussion of the text of Psalm 2, especially verses 10-12, see deClaissé-Walford, *Reading from the Beginning*, 43-48.

story of the Psalter; read about this God named YHWH who now will be our king; delight in it; meditate on it.

The psalms of David in book 1 are followed in book 2 (Psalms 42–72) by a collection of Psalms of the Sons of Korah (Psalms 42–49). According to the Books of Chronicles, the sons of Korah were temple keepers and temple singers during the reigns of David and Solomon.[19] As we read this portion of the story of the Psalter, our focus is still on the Davidic dynasty, but David himself is not as prominent in book 2 as in book 1. Of the thirty-one psalms in book 2, only eighteen are attributed to David. It is interesting, however, that the eighteen are grouped together at the end of book 2 (Psalms 51–65, 68–70) and eight of them (Psalms 51, 52, 54, 56, 57, 59, 60, and 63) have superscriptions that place the psalms with specific events in the life of David.[20] The superscription of Psalm 51 says it is

> For the choir director. A Psalm of David, when Nathan the prophet came to him after he had gone in to Bathsheba.

The superscription addresses Psalm 56

> For the choir director; according to *Jonath elem rehokim.* A Mikhtam of David, when the Philistines seized him in Gath.

And the superscription of Psalm 57 states that it is

> For the choir director; set to *Al-tashheth.* A Mikhtam for David, when he fled from Saul in the cave.

Psalm 71 originally had no superscription, but in a number of Bible translations and in many commentaries it is variously entitled "A prayer for old age" (KJV), "Prayer of an old man for deliverance" (ASV), "An old man's cry to God" (IB), "I will hope continually" (NIB), and so forth. In verses 6-9, we read:

> By you I have been sustained from birth;

---

[19]See, for example, 1 Chronicles 6:31-38 and 9:19. For a full discussion, see Michael Goulder, *The Psalms of the Sons of Korah,* JSOTSup 20 (Sheffield UK: JSOT Press, 1982).

[20]Thirteen psalms in the Psalter locate themselves, in their superscriptions, in particular historical settings in the life of David: Psalms 3, 7, 18, 34, 51, 52, 54, 56, 57, 59, 60, 63, and 142.

You are the one who took me from my mother's womb;
My praise is continually of you.
I have become a marvel to many;
For you are my strong refuge.
My mouth is filled with your praise,
And with your glory all day long.
Do not cast me off in the time of old age;
Do not forsake me when my strength fails.   (71:6-9)

In its position after eighteen psalms attributed to David, Psalm 71 might be read as the words of an aging David at the end of his reign.[21]

Psalm 72 is one of only two psalms in the Psalter attributed to Solomon.[22] H.-J. Kraus describes Psalm 72 as a collection of wishes and prayers for the well-being of the king, likely used at a royal enthronement ceremony in Jerusalem.[23] Brevard Childs suggests that the canonical placement of Psalm 72, that is, its place within the story of the Psalter, indicates strongly that the psalm "is 'for' Solomon, offered by David."[24] Thus we may hear David say:

Give the king your judgments, O God,
And your righteousness to the king's son.
May he judge your people with righteousness,
And your afflicted with justice.   (72:1-2)

Psalm 72 ends with the words "The prayers of David son of Jesse are ended" (v. 20).

Book 2 is a moving and poignant segment of the story of the Psalter. It opens with King David in the background and the temple singers at the forefront. David comes forward again in Psalms 51–65 and 68–70, but the reader is constantly reminded of the humanness of the great king (Psalm 51—Bathsheba, Psalm 56—the Philistines, Psalm 57—hiding from Saul). Book 2 ends with abrupt finality: "the words of David, son of Jesse, are ended" (Psalms 72:20).

---

[21]See 1 Kings 1:1–2:11.

[22]The other is Psalm 127, one of the Psalms of Ascents.

[23]H.-J. Kraus, *Psalms 60-150: A Commentary*, trans. H. C. Oswald (Minneapolis: Augsburg Publishing House, 1989) 76-77.

[24]Childs, *Introduction to the Old Testament as Scripture*, 516.

"A Psalm of Asaph" opens book 3 (Psalms 73–89) of the Psalter. Like the sons of Korah, Asaph was, according to the Books of Chronicles, a temple singer during the reigns of David and Solomon.[25] Fifteen of the seventeen psalms in book 3 are attributed to Asaph and the sons of Korah. Only one psalm, Psalm 86, is attributed to David. With the close of Psalm 72, David moves to the background. The focus is now on David's descendants, who will determine the future of ancient Israel.

Along with Psalm 1, Psalm 73 is classified as a wisdom psalm. In Psalm 73 the psalmist looks at the world around and sees the wicked (the רְשָׁעִים *rᵉshʿîm*) prospering while the righteous (the צַדִּיקִם *sadîqîm*) are suffering, and questions whether conventional theology and mores still hold true in life.[26] There seems to be no reasoned connection between righteousness and reward, wickedness and punishment. The psalmist writes:

> As for me, my feet came close to stumbling,
> My steps had almost slipped.
> For I was envious of the arrogant
> As I saw the prosperity of the wicked.
> For there are no pains in their death,
> And their belly is fat.
> They are not in trouble like other people,
> Nor are they plagued like humankind. . . .
> They mock and speak in wickedness of oppression;
> They speak from on high.
> They have set their mouth against the heavens,
> And their tongue parades through the earth.   (73:2-5, 8-9)

---

[25]First Chronicles 6:39 and 25:1, 2 and 2 Chronicles 5:12 state that Asaph is the brother of Heman, the son Berechiah, a descendant of Levi through Gershom, and part of one of the great families or guilds of musicians and singers in preexilic Israel. See Harry P. Nasuti, *Tradition History and the Psalms of Asaph*, SBLDS 88 (Atlanta: Scholars Press, 1988).

[26]Humankind in the ancient Near East believed in a basic moral governance of the universe. Act and consequence were connected in daily life. Thus, the good prospered and the wicked perished. Sages, wisdom teachers, and writers taught that there was a fundamental order in the world which could be discerned by experience, that the gods had established the order, and that all of humankind was bound by the rules governing that order. For a detailed treatment, see *The Sage in Israel and the Ancient Near East*, ed. John G. Gammie and Leo G. Perdue (Winona Lake IN: Eisenbrauns, 1990).

Psalm 73 opens a new chapter in the story of the life of ancient Israel. Walter Brueggemann maintains that Psalm 73 was purposefully placed at a "fault line" in the story of the Psalter. David's reign is over and Solomon's reign will end with the nation of Israel divided into two rival kingdoms who will be in constant conflict with one another and with the nations around them.[27]

The psalms of David in books 1 and 2 of the Psalter evoke a nostalgia for the days of David's kingdom, but even in David's day all was not well. Observe the great number of laments of David in books 1 and 2 and remember Psalms 51, 56, and 57. And now, in book 3, which recounts the period of the divided kingdom, more troubles are facing the people of ancient Israel—Egypt, Assyria, Babylon, internal court intrigue.

Book 3 ends with an overwhelming cry of lament. Psalm 89 is classi-fied as a royal psalm—like Psalm 2—but it is very different from the other royal psalms. It begins with words of praise to the LORD:

The heavens are yours, the earth also is yours;
The world and all it contains, you have founded them.
The north and the south, you have created them;
Tabor and Hermon shout for joy at your name.
You have an arm with strength;
Your hand is mighty, your right hand is exalted.
Righteousness and justice are the foundation of your throne;
Steadfast love and truth go before you.   (89:11-14)

But the psalm ends with questions and darkness and despair:

But you have cast off and rejected,
You have been full of wrath against your anointed.
You have spurned the covenant of your servant;
You have profaned his crown in the dust. . . .
How long, O LORD?
Will you hide yourself forever?
Will your wrath burn like fire? . . .
Where are your former steadfast loves, O LORD,
Which you swore to David in your faithfulness? (38-39, 46, 49)

---

[27]Walter Brueggemann, "Bounded by Obedience and Praise: The Psalms as Canon," *JSOT* 50 (1991): 82-83. And see 1 Kgs 11–14.

Psalm 89 powerfully expresses the gap between ancient Israel's under-standing of the promises and ways of God and the actualities of their history. The ancient Israelites were the chosen people of YHWH who once had a king and a temple and who had once lived in their own land. But those days ended with the destruction of Jerusalem and the exile. What now is Israel to do?

Book 4 of the Psalter (Psalms 90–106) opens with Psalm 90, the only psalm in the book ascribed to "Moses, the man of God." It begins:

> LORD, you have been our dwelling place in all generations.
> Before the mountains were born
> Or you gave birth to the earth and world,
> Even from everlasting to everlasting, you are God.   (90:1-2)

And it ends:

> Do return, O LORD, how long will it be?
> And be sorry for your servants.
> O satisfy us in the morning with your steadfast love,
> That we may sing for you and be glad all our days.   (90:13-14)

The words of Psalm 90 are placed on the lips of Moses, the man of God, the only human being whom God knew "face to face" (Deut 34:10). The whole of book 4 is, in fact, dominated by the person of Moses. Out-side book 4, Moses is mentioned only once in the Psalter (77:21). In book 4, he is referred to seven times (90:1; 99:6; 103:7; 105:26; 106:16, 23, 32). Moses represents a unique and special time in the history of ancient Israel, a time before the Davidic covenant, before the monarchy, before the judges, before the settlement in the land. By placing a psalm of Moses at the beginning of book 4, the shaping community reminds the reader that long before the time of David and Solomon, the temple in Jerusalem, and the nation of ancient Israel, YHWH met Moses at a bush in the wilderness, delivered a people from oppression and slavery, and pro-vided and cared for them in the wilderness.

In the middle of book 4, the reader encounters a group of psalms known as "the kingship of YHWH" psalms. In Psalms 93–99, the reader encounters the kingly YHWH, reigning in glory and strength over the people of Israel and over all the earth:

> The LORD reigns, he is clothed with majesty;
> The LORD has clothed and girded himself with strength;

Indeed, the world is firmly established, it will not be moved.
Your throne is established from of old;
You are everlasting. (93:1-2)

Say among the nations, "The LORD reigns;
Indeed, the world is firmly established, it will not be moved;
He will judge the peoples with uprightness. (96:10)

The LORD reigns, let the people tremble;
He is enthroned above the cherubim, let the earth shake! (99:1)

YHWH—not a king of the Davidic line—led the Israelites out of Egypt, through the wilderness, and into the promised land during the time of Moses. And YHWH—not a king of the Davidic line—will once again lead the people out of bondage, through their ordeals, and into their promised inheritance. Go back to an earlier time in your history; remember what YHWH did for the Israelites in the exodus and in the wilderness. And celebrate YHWH's good reign.

Book 4 ends, fittingly, with two psalms that recount the history of ancient Israel during the time of YHWH's reign over the people—Psalms 105 and 106. In Psalm 105, we read about the exodus from Egypt:

Then the LORD brought them out with silver and gold,
And among the tribes there was not one who stumbled.
Egypt was glad when they departed,
For the dread of them had fallen upon them.
He spread a cloud for covering,
And fire to illumine by night.
They asked, and he brought quail,
And satisfied them with the bread of heaven.
He opened the rock and water flowed out;
It ran in the dry places like a river. (105:37-41)

Psalm 106 also speaks of the exodus from Egypt:

The Israelites quickly forgot the LORD's works;
They did not wait for his counsel,
But craved intensely in the wilderness,
And put God to the test in the desert. . . .
They made a calf in Horeb
And worshiped a molten image.
Thus they exchanged their glory
For the image of an ox that eats grass.

They forgot God their deliverer,
Who had done great things in Egypt. (106:13-14, 19-21)

Psalms 105 and 106 are both recountings of the history of ancient Israel, but what very different stories they tell. Book 4 reminds the ancient Israelite community that YHWH was and, indeed, is the deliverer, the protector, and the provider of ancient Israel—YHWH is king. Remember. YHWH did marvelous things for Israel in the past. But Israel was disobedient and unfaithful, despite YHWH's goodness. In the present situation, it is up to Israel to obey or to disobey—to repeat the mistakes of the past or to remember and prosper.

Psalm 106 ends with a petition to YHWH:

Save us, O LORD our God,
And gather us from among the nations,
To give thanks to your holy name
And boast in your praise.   (106:47)

Book 5 of the Psalter (Psalms 107-150) opens with words which were undoubtedly placed at its beginning in answer to the request of the people at the end of book 4:

O give thanks to the LORD, for he is good,
For his steadfast love is everlasting.
Let the redeemed of the LORD say so,
Whom he has redeemed from the hand of the adversary
And gathered from the lands,
From the east and from the west,
From the north and from the south.   (107:1-3)

The psalm goes on, in verses 4-32, to tell the stories of four groups of people—wanderers, prisoners, sick persons, and shipwrecked sailors—whom YHWH redeems from various perils. In the last part of the psalm, verses 33-43, the psalmist celebrates the goodness of YHWH who dictates the use of the land (vv. 33-35), allows hungry citizens to establish a city, sow fields, plant vineyards, and gather a harvest (vv. 36-37), provides for increase in population and goods (v. 38), gives protection against enemies (vv. 39-40), and sustains the needy (v. 41). The future of the upright is secure and the unrighteousness are left speechless (v. 42). These verses describe YHWH performing the traditional duties of a king in the ancient Near Eastern world out of which the Israelites came. In Psalm 107, YHWH, not David or an heir of David's line, is the deliverer of the people, and YHWH performs the kingly functions. Psalm 107 ends with the words:

> Who is wise? Let him give heed to these things;
> And consider the steadfast love of the LORD. (107:42)

And then the reader encounters an interesting phenomenon. Psalms 108, 109, and 110 are "psalms of David." And in book 5, fifteen psalms are attributed to David, the greatest number encountered since book 2.[28] Psalm 108, interestingly, juxtaposes two psalms which appear earlier in the Psalter—Psalms 57 and 60. Psalms 57 and 60 are located in book 2 in a group of psalms which identify themselves in their superscriptions with specific events in the life of David. The superscription to Psalm 57 says it is a "mikhtam"[29] of David when he hid from Saul in a cave.[30] The superscription of Psalm 60 states that it is a mikhtam of David when he struggled with Aram-naharaim and Aram-zobah, and when he smote— through Joab—twelve thousand of Edom in the Valley of Salt.[31]

In Psalm 108, elements of Psalms 57 and 60 combine first to praise YHWH for deliverance (108:1-5, from 57:7-11) and then to petition YHWH for ongoing deliverance (108:6-13, from 60:5-12). Another psalm surely could have expressed the same confidence in YHWH; another psalm could have petitioned YHWH's intervention and deliverance. But the community which shaped the Psalter took two well-remembered psalms ("mikhtams") about specific incidents in the life of David and appropriated them to the new life situation of postexilic Israel. The postexilic community, like David, had cause to praise YHWH for their deliverance from exile. But they, like David, continued to need YHWH's intervention in their life. In Psalm 108, "a psalm of David," David wisely acknowledges YHWH's ability to deliver and sustain.

---

[28]In book 5, Psalms 108, 109, 110, 122, 124, 131, 133, and 138-45 are attributed to David. In books 1 and 2, fifty-seven of the seventy-two psalms are connected with David. In books 3 and 4, however, only three psalms of David occur.

[29]The meaning of "mikhtam," which designates Psalms 16 and 56-60, is uncertain. But the Septuagint translates as στηλογραφί α *stālographia*, an "inscription on a tablet," suggesting a valuable composition worthy of engraving in stone or metal, that is, worthy of preservation, remembrance.

[30]The incident to which the superscription refers may be that in 1 Sam. 22:1 or in 24:1-3.

[31]See 2 Sam. 8.

Psalm 145, the last psalm of David in book 5, is a psalm of praise. In it, we read:

> I will extol you, my God, O king;
> And I will bless your name forever and ever. . . .
> All your works will give thanks to you, O LORD,
> And your godly ones shall bless you.
> They shall speak of the glory of your kingdom,
> And talk of your power;
> To make known to all humanity your mighty acts,
> And the glory of the majesty of your kingdom.
> Your kingdom is an everlasting kingdom,
> And your dominion endures throughout all generations.
>
> (145:1-2, 10-13)

The significant presence of David in book 5 of the Psalter gives a strong message to the postexilic community. David, who is no longer king over ancient Israel, David, who has no hope of any of his heirs ever again being king over ancient Israel, David acknowledges God as sovereign, as king. If David, to whom any hope of fulfillment of the promises given by God seems forever lost, if David can praise YHWH the king, then all Israel can and must do the same.

What then is the canonical shape of the Psalter? Enter the story, along with King David, through the lens of wisdom. Read the story, delight in it, and meditate on it. Ask of these verses those vexing questions of identity: "Who are we?" and "What are we to do?" And in the end, along with David, praise YHWH as king over a new community, a new people called Israel, who will survive. "Let everything that has breath praise the LORD! Hallelujah!" (150:6).

Chapter 8

Portraits of Faith:
The Scope of Theology in the Psalms

William H. Bellinger, Jr.

Introduction

What is a psalm? The essays in this volume reflect some of the answers
to that question.[1] Psalms are cultic songs and artful poems; they are part
of a broader ancient Near Eastern phenomenon. Biblical psalms are also
embedded in a canon of Scripture. The Book of Psalms is the most read
and used of all the books in the Old Testament. These texts have influenced many people through the centuries, but the continuing influence of
the Psalter is probably not so much about its background in the ancient
Near East or ancient Israel's worship or poetry as it is the ability of these
songs to relate to every conceivable human experience, whether joy or
sorrow or all circumstances in between. For this reason, readers through
the centuries have been able to relate to the Psalms and learn much of
prayer and faith from them.

One way of articulating this perspective on the Psalms is to describe
these texts as pilgrimage songs of faith. The ancient Israelites went on
pilgrimage to worship in the temple in Jerusalem. The Psalms are the
songs they sang on that pilgrimage. The songs expressed their faith and
spoke to their faith. In a broader sense, life is a pilgrimage or journey,
and we can view the Psalms as the songs the community sings while
moving through the life of faith. Bringing faith to expression helps a
person define and fathom the faith. The Psalms are public expressions of
faith, portraits of faith, and so at base theological.

---

[1]I am pleased to dedicate this essay to Professor Marvin E. Tate. His contributions
to the study of the Psalms are important and often emphasize the theological.

The Psalms are at the heart of biblical theology, for they seek to make theological sense out of experience.[2] Sometimes experience squares with an inherited faith and praise comes forth. Sometimes experience challenges faith and questioning comes forth. The Psalms meditate upon life from the perspective of faith. Indeed, Hans-Joachim Kraus has characterized the content of the Psalms as "a biblical theology in miniature."[3] James Mays begins his theological handbook on the Psalms with this simple but profound sentence: "The psalms are scripture and liturgy."[4] As Scripture and as liturgy, the Psalms use theological language. They speak of God and of God's relationship with persons. Scripture is a word from God; liturgy is a word spoken to God. Most interpreters would agree that the Psalter is at core theological and yet scholars have found difficulty in speaking of the theology of the Psalms. The book is not organized in a systematic way around theological concepts. It is rather a collection of hymns, prayers, and poems. The collection's tie to experience and diversity of material make articulating its theology a complicated task.

Any introduction to the Psalms would be inadequate, however, without attention to this biblical book's theological emphases. Thus, in this essay, I seek to introduce the reader to the primary theological themes in the Psalter. This essay is in no sense exhaustive but rather introduces topics for readers to pursue. We begin with some basic perspectives on the Psalter and on theology and then survey theological topics that arise from studying the prayer, praise, and instruction of the Psalms.

Preliminary Considerations

Scholarship on the Psalms has concentrated on classifying the types of psalms and on understanding the background of the psalms in ancient Israel's worship.[5] More recent scholarship has moved to questions of the

---

[2]W. H. Bellinger, Jr., *Psalms: Reading and Studying the Book of Praises* (Peabody MA: Hendrickson Publishers, 1990) 135.

[3]Hans-Joachim Kraus, *Theology of the Psalms*, trans. Keith Crim (Minneapolis: Augsburg Publishing House, 1986) 12. Kraus's volume is a good example of a theological work that is dominated by historical-critical issues.

[4]James L. Mays, *The Lord Reigns: A Theological Handbook to the Psalms* (Louisville KY: Westminster John Knox Press, 1994) ix.

[5]On critical issues in the study of the Psalms, see Bernhard W. Anderson, *Out of the Depths: The Psalms Speak for Us Today*, rev. ed. (Philadelphia: Westminster Press, 1983); Bellinger, *Psalms*; J. Day, *Psalms*, Old Testament Guides, ed. R. N. Whybray (Sheffield:

canonical shape of the Book of Psalms and to close readings of its Hebrew poetry.[6]

Hebrew Poetry. Poetry is a complex and demanding form of writing, and the poetry of the Psalter calls for the careful attention of readers and involves readers in the drama being portrayed. The poetry uses various features such as parallel structures—a kind of echo effect—various images and figures of speech, repetition, sound play, and the urgent form of direct address to God to create and communicate its message. The message carries powerful theological freight.

> The Psalms are of course poems written out of deep and often passionate faith. What I am proposing is that the poetic medium made it possible to articulate the emotional freight, the moral consequences, the altered perception of the world that flowed from this monotheistic belief, in compact verbal structures that could in some instances seem simplicity itself.[7]

Structures of intensification characterize the poetry in the Psalms. The poetry seems to have movement or sequence toward a culmination and thus produces a narrative development.[8] The poetic language forms persuasive prayer and as such has powerful impact on readers, creating a vision of life in relationship with the living God. The poetry engages life and excites the imagination, an important task for envisioning and structuring life as God's people.

A Confession of Faith. These poetic prayers have also been characterized as Israel's sung creed, a confession of faith supremely representative of the Hebrew Scriptures.[9] The content of the Old Testament is reflected

---

JSOT Press, 1992); Patrick D. Miller, Jr., *Interpreting the Psalms* (Philadelphia: Fortress Press, 1986); Klaus Seybold, *Introducing the Psalms*, trans. R. Graeme Dunphy (Edinburgh: T. & T. Clark, 1990). Also helpful is the April 1992 issue of *Interpretation: A Journal of Bible and Theology* (46/2) entitled "The Book of Psalms."

[6]On Hebrew poetry, see Robert Alter, *The Art of Biblical Poetry* (New York: Basic Books, 1985) and James L. Kugel, *The Idea of Biblical Poetry: Parallelism and Its History* (New Haven/London: Yale University Press, 1981).

[7]Alter, *Art of Biblical Poetry*, 113.

[8]See Robert Alter, "The Characteristics of Ancient Hebrew Poetry," in *The Literary Guide to the Bible*, ed. Robert Alter and Frank Kermode (Cambridge MA: Harvard University Press, 1987) 620.

[9]G. W. Anderson, "Israel's Creed: Sung Not Signed," *SJT* 16 (1963) 277-85.

here: history and kingship, prophecy as judgment and instruction, celebration of torah, and wisdom. The Psalter includes the various voices of the Hebrew Scriptures and the range of difficulties in constructing an Old Testament theology. The theological themes of ancient Israel are in the Psalms: "election and covenant, rejection and restoration, *Heilsgeschichte*, creation, and providence, the way of life and the way of death."[10] The Psalter contains a diversity of poems but is held together as the confession of faith from a worshiping community, as prayer and praise confessing faith in the living God. "This is how, over the centuries, Israel did confess God."[11] The Psalter is a confessional document, confessing faith in the living God and thus our title "Portraits of Faith." It is of fundamental importance to see that this confession of faith comes from a context of worship.

What Is Theology? Before delineating theological themes in the Psalter, I should give some indication of what I mean by theology. The broad perspective gives some starting points. Theology is the search for what the Psalter, in this case, affirms about God in relation to humanity and for the implications of that.[12] Theology has to do with utterances about God, claims about God. It is also important to explore how the Psalter selects and organizes its confessions about God and God's involvement in the world. The Hebrew Scriptures primarily speak of the initiative on the divine side. So I begin with divine initiative and human response.

Basic Perspectives. It might be helpful to summarize briefly basic perspectives on the Psalter before exploring its theological scope. The Psalms are pilgrimage songs of faith for the life of faith. They relate to all of that life; Calvin's phrase "An Anatomy of all the Parts of the Soul" is particularly apt for the Psalter.[13] The Church is a pilgrimage community and so the Psalter forms an appropriate faith resource for the communi-

---

[10]Anderson, "Israel's Creed," 284.

[11]Anderson, "Israel's Creed," 284.

[12]See Rolf P. Knierim, *The Task of Old Testament Theology: Substance, Method, and Cases* (Grand Rapids MI: Eerdmans, 1995) 78-79; Ben C. Ollenburger, "Old Testament Theology: A Discourse on Method," in *Biblical Theology: Problems and Perspectives. In Honor of J. Christiaan Beker*, ed. Steven J. Kraftchick, Charles D. Myers, Jr., and Ben C. Ollenburger (Nashville: Abingdon, 1995) 81-103.

[13]See William L. Holladay, *The Psalms through Three Thousand Years: Prayerbook of a Cloud of Witnesses* (Minneapolis: Fortress Press, 1993) 196.

ty. Pilgrims of faith find themselves in the Psalms and pray these texts.[14] The Psalter is both prayer book and hymnbook relating to both prayer and worship.

Consider now three important theological perspectives in the Psalter, with attention to the major types of psalms.

Covenant Theology

When we begin with the question of how God is involved in the world, one of the significant answers in the Psalter is that God comes to deliver. Several of the psalms recount the history of God's delivering the people. Psalm 105, for example, begins with the ancestral promise and goes on through the entry into the land under the call to remember the wonderful works God has done (v. 5). Psalms 68, 114, and 135 recall the deliverance from Egypt.

> Our God is a God of salvation,
>   and to GOD, the Lord, belongs escape from death.   (68:20)[15]

The thanksgiving psalms from both individuals and the community also give praise and thanksgiving to God for delivering from a particular crisis. Psalms 30, 34, 107, and 118 are representative examples.

> Then they cried to the LORD in their trouble,
>   and he delivered them from their distress. (107:6)

> O taste and see that the LORD is good;
>   happy are those who take refuge in him.[16] (34:8)

In addition, the lament psalms, the most numerous type of psalm, presuppose such a theological perspective. These texts exhibit a human cry deriving from need, but they cry to the God who comes to deliver. These psalms also require an adjustment of the thesis of divine initiative and human response; there is human initiative in these texts. Psalms 6, 13, and 44 illustrate these cries.

---

[14]For examples, see Anderson, *Out of the Depths*, 13-19.

[15]Biblical quotations are from the NRSV.

[16]On the significant note of refuge in God, see Jerome F. D. Creach, *Yahweh as Refuge and the Editing of the Hebrew Psalter*, JSOTSup (Sheffield: JSOT Press, 1996).

Turn, O LORD, save my life;
    deliver me for the sake of your steadfast love. (6:4)

The dialogical nature of the lament and thanksgiving psalms shows that ancient Israel's worship was connected to the rest of life. The affirmation that God comes to deliver was often severely tested in life. The dialogue is part of Israel's sung creed, and the portrait of God as the one who comes to deliver is basic for the theological perspective undergirding these psalms. God comes to deliver and initiates a covenant relationship with the community of ancient Israel. The dialogue in the Psalter is part of the community's response to God's initiative.[17] Three strategically placed psalms (1, 19, and 119) also speak of torah, the covenant avenue of response to the God who delivers.[18]

Prayer in the Psalter. Prayers for help are numerous in the Psalter. They arise from the context of covenant theology and its dialogue with human experience. Claus Westermann has suggested that there are two fundamental psalm categories, those of plea and praise.[19] Spirituality or the life of faith in the Psalter moves between these poles of plea and praise, and the direction of movement is from the basic human cry of plea to that of praise. We should explore the theological dimensions of these prayers. The pleas are prayers for help or laments.

The Psalter's prayers for help exhibit a typical literary pattern. The prayer is addressed to the God who delivers, describes a crisis and pleads for this God to deliver. The vast majority of these laments come to a positive conclusion with some kind of indication that God does not leave

---

[17]Gerhard von Rad, *Old Testament Theology*, 2 vols, trans. D. M. G. Stalker (New York/Evanston: Harper & Row, 1962–1965) 1:355-418, treats the Psalms as ancient Israel's response to God. That emphasis is entirely appropriate. We have noted that it is also appropriate to describe the Psalms in terms of confession of faith.

[18]See the helpful essay by James L. Mays, "The Place of the Torah Psalms in the Psalter," in *The Lord Reigns*, 128-35.

[19]Claus Westermann, *Praise and Lament in the Psalms*, trans. Ceith R. Crim and Richard N. Soulen (Atlanta: John Knox, 1981); Westermann, *The Living Psalms*, trans. J. R. Porter (Edinburgh: T. & T. Clark, 1989); Westermann, *The Psalms: Structure, Content, and Message*, trans. Ralph D. Gehrke (Minneapolis: Augsburg, 1980). The classic work on the types of psalms is Hermann Gunkel, *Introduction to the Psalms: The Genres of the Religious Lyric of Israel*, completed by Joachim Begrich, trans. James D. Nogalski, Mercer Library of Biblical Studies 2 (Macon GA: Mercer University Press, 1998).

the one praying alone and in distress but comes to deliver. There is an expression of certainty that God hears, an expression of confidence or thanksgiving or praise or a vow of praise. Psalm 13 provides a good example.

- Invocation, v. 1
   How long, O Lord? Will you forget me forever?
      How long will you hide your face from me?
- Complaint, v. 2
   How long must I bear pain in my soul,
      and have sorrow in my heart all day long?
   How long shall my enemy be exalted over me?
- Petition, vv. 3-4
   Consider and answer me, O Lord my God!
      Give light to my eyes, or I will sleep the sleep of death;
   and my enemy will say, "I have prevailed";
      my foes will rejoice because I am shaken.
- Conclusion, vv. 5-6
   But I trusted in your steadfast love;
      my heart shall rejoice in your salvation.
   I will sing to the Lord,
      because he has dealt bountifully with me.[20]

The language of these psalms is covenant language. In the tradition of Sinai, God establishes a relationship with the community of ancient Israel and calls them to hear the instruction of God and live accordingly. In the lament psalms, the faith community calls to God, asking God to hear and deliver from the trouble at hand. These psalms are part of the honest covenant dialogue of faith. These ancient prayers call for God to bring to pass the promised deliverance, and most of the laments see a hopeful conclusion to the crisis. These psalms thus offer a powerful model for prayer in the midst of crisis, addressing God and describing the crisis and then persuasively crying for help, all in the context of the honest dialogue of faith and the life of prayer in worship.

---

[20]The literary patterns of laments or of other types of psalms should not be applied in any rigid way. Not all lament psalms have all of these elements and not always in this configuration. As a description, the pattern can, however, be helpful to readers of the psalms.

Psalm 61 provides another example as the speaker calls to God from the edge of life (vv. 1-2) and seeks God's refuge and shelter.

> Lead me to the rock
>> that is higher than I;
> for you are my refuge,
>> a strong tower against the enemy.
> Let me abide in your tent forever;
>> find refuge under the shelter of your wings.   (61:2b-4)

Again, the psalm concludes with a hopeful view.[21] Psalm 79 is an example of a cry spoken by the community after the destruction of the temple by the Babylonians has caused great crisis in ancient Israel. The cry is for the covenant God to deliver.

Psalm 88 provides a particularly powerful example of a lament. It is a lament in the extreme, a prayer at the limit of life.[22] The speaker is gripped by the power of Sheol, the realm of death, full of troubles (vv. 1-7), and, what is more, it is God who has brought about this crisis (vv. 8-12). The speaker fervently cries out to God from the experience of being overwhelmed by crisis (vv. 13-18). Unlike most lament psalms, Psalm 88 ends without a word of hope, still in the midst of darkness.

> Your wrath has swept over me;
>> your dread assaults destroy me.
> They surround me like a flood all day long;
>> from all sides they close in on me.
> You have caused friend and neighbor to shun me;
>> my companions are in darkness.   (88:16-18)

This psalm is a painful and accusing cry. The experience is oppressive for the speaker, and yet the words are still intently prayed to the God who can help (v. 1).

The theological implications of these prayers in the Psalter are quite noticeable. First, these psalms provide a model of the honest dialogue of faith. These prayers countenance no idealistic view of life as it ought to

---

[21]See W. H. Bellinger, Jr., *A Hermeneutic of Curiosity and Readings of Psalm 61*, Studies in Old Testament Interpretation 1 (Macon GA: Mercer University Press, 1995).

[22]See Walter Brueggemann's insightful exposition of the psalm in *The Message of the Psalms: A Theological Commentary*, Augsburg Old Testament Studies (Minneapolis: Augsburg, 1984) 78-81.

be, but realistically speak to God from the very depths of life as it is. Prayer in contemporary communities of faith is often staid and predictable. Contemporary believers can gain much in noticing the honesty, sometimes brutal honesty, of these laments.[23]

Second, the prayers in the Psalter are trying to make sense out of experience. The faith community ancient Israel has affirmed from the Exodus experience that their God is the God who delivers. What the lamenters are now experiencing in life challenges that affirmation. Their experience is not deliverance but trouble and woe. Where is the deliverance God promises? Where is the God who comes to deliver? Much of the Old Testament calls for ancient Israel to hear, to listen to, to obey the living God. The lament psalms record the other side of the covenant dialogue. In these texts, ancient Israel demands that God hear. Ancient Israel's covenant faith promises that God comes to deliver and in these psalms the community challenges God to fulfill the promise. The community seeks to put together faith and the reality of life. In these psalms, that conflict comes to honest and persistent expression.[24]

Third, these psalms constitute bold acts of faith in the face of daunting trouble and woe. For many contemporary believers, the honesty of these prayers will be puzzling or even alarming. Some persons of faith may pray such honest prayers in private, but the notion that such prayers are public prayers for worship issues a challenge to the whole of the contemporary church. We live in a culture that seeks to deny pain and death, but the psalmists saw long before there was what we know as therapy that the way to loving enemies is through—and not around—hostility. The way to abiding joy is *through* depression; the way to genuine hope is *through* fear. Going around the anguish and pain does not lead forward. Denial leads to holding grudges, to more fear, to wounds that fester and cause further turmoil. Acts of denial are not acts of faith. Rather,

---

[23]It is in this context of prayer in the Psalter that readers can consider the psalms with elements of vengeance in them (e.g., Psalms 109; 137). See W. H. Bellinger, Jr., *The Testimony of Poets and Sages: The Psalms and Wisdom Literature*, All the Bible (Macon GA: Smyth & Helwys, 1998) 36-38; Erich Zenger, *A God of Vengeance? Understanding the Psalms of Divine Wrath*, trans. Linda M. Maloney (Louisville: Westminster/John Knox Press, 1996).

[24]The Psalter includes psalms in which the speaker seeks God's forgiveness (Pss 51; 130), but most of the laments see the responsibility for the crisis with God rather than with the lamenter. See Miller, *Interpreting the Psalms*, 4-11.

speaking boldly to the One who can act, asking God to embrace the pain—that is an act of faith. The lament psalms are bold, freeing, and encouraging acts of faith.[25]

Fourth, these texts portray an image of God as the One who accepts these questioning and challenging prayers. The cry is "how long?" but it is not just a cry; it is a cry *to* someone, to the living God. What defines people of faith is persistent speaking to God.[26] Speaking to God in this honest way is both a liberating and frightening act. The prayers in the Psalter leave intact the portrait of God as the God who delivers and articulate the realistic pain that is part of the pilgrimage of faith in that God. God does not leave the lamenter alone but responds, comes, embraces the pain. God is the God who delivers and these psalms beg that it be so. Having honestly spoken to God, the lament calls upon readers to trust this God who embraces the pain.[27] The Psalms are a school of prayer. These laments teach us much about speaking to God and then call for the real adventure of trust even in the midst of trouble.[28]

Praise in the Psalms. Our discussion of prayer in the Psalter has hovered around the pole of plea in Westermann's suggestion. The positive conclusions of most of the psalms of plea suggest, however, that those pleas are on the way toward the other end of the spectrum, the pole of praise. The laments cry out to God and often conclude hopefully, perhaps with a promise of praise. The psalms of thanksgiving fulfill that promise after God has delivered from the crisis. These psalms constitute for Westermann narrative or declarative praise, one of the two types of praise.[29] That is, they narrate the story of how God has come to deliver or they declare testimony to the congregation. The Hebrew term often

---

[25]See Walter Brueggemann, "The Costly Loss of Lament," in *The Psalms and the Life of Faith*, ed. Patrick D. Miller (Minneapolis: Fortress Press, 1995) 98-111. This volume of Brueggemann's essays on the Psalms includes a number of studies important for our topic.

[26]Brueggemann, *Message of the Psalms*, 80-81.

[27]Walter Brueggemann, *Theology of the Old Testament: Testimony, Dispute, Advocacy* (Minneapolis: Fortress Press, 1997) has brought to the fore the tension between divine sovereignty and divine vulnerability.

[28]We might describe the Psalter as praise in the presence and absence of God. See Samuel E. Balentine, *The Hidden God: The Hiding of the Face of God in the Old Testament*, Oxford Theological Monographs (Oxford: Oxford University Press, 1983).

[29]Westermann, *Praise and Lament*, 15-35.

associated with thanksgiving, תודה, comes from an etymology associated with confessing what God has done.

These psalms of narrative praise also have a typical literary pattern. Psalm 30 illustrates the structure.

- Introduction
   The opening section announces the intent to give praise and thanksgiving to God (vv. 1-5).
- Narrative
   The body of the text describes the crisis (vv. 6-7), the prayer for help (vv. 8-10), and the deliverance (v. 11).
- Conclusion
   The psalm ends with a renewed promise of praise (v. 12).

God has delivered the speaker from the power of death (Sheol) and invites the congregation to hear the story and take courage from it.

> For his anger is but for a moment;
>   his favor is for a lifetime.
> Weeping may linger for the night,
>   but joy comes with the morning. (v. 5)

The speaker tells the story of how all was well and then life fell apart. In the midst of his trouble, the speaker cried to God for help, for the opportunity to continue to bear witness to God's faithfulness. In the concluding verses of the psalm, readers see that God has delivered.

> You have turned for me my mourning into dancing;
>   you have taken off my sackcloth
>   and clothed me with joy. (v. 11)

The psalm then renews the promise of praise and thanksgiving. Psalm 30 uses powerful images to narrate deliverance from a particular crisis. Such narrative songs of praise provide a link between the poles of plea and praise in the Psalter and show the prayers of the Psalter on the way to praise. That connection is a word of hope for the faith community reading the psalms.

The narrative psalms of praise are related to the texts typically described as hymns, Westermann's descriptive psalms of praise. These texts describe God and offer praise in more general terms. The descriptive psalms of praise also have a typical pattern. Psalm 117 illustrates.

- Introduction—Call to Praise
  Praise the LORD, all you nations!
      Extol him, all you peoples! (v. 1)
- Body—Reason for Praising God
  For great is his steadfast love toward us,
      and the faithfulness of the LORD endures for ever. (v. 2ab)
- Conclusion—Renewed Call to Praise
  Praise the Lord! (v. 2c)

The conclusion often repeats the introduction. Central to this basic pattern is the call to praise followed by a reason for praising God. The hymns of praise give various reasons for praising God. In Psalm 117 the reason is tied to the persistence of God's unchanging love and trustworthiness.

Psalm 105 follows a similar structure and recounts the history of God's delivering the people. By recounting this history in the context of praise, the community bears witness to God's involvement in the world. They are called to "remember" God's wonderful works, that is, to rehearse or relive the history so it becomes real and significant for the contemporary congregation. As the narrative psalms of praise speak of God's delivering from a particular crisis, the historical-descriptive psalms of praise, such as Psalm 105, describe the history of God's delivering the people. That history provides reason for praising God. Psalm 105 recounts the history from the ancestors through the bondage experience in Egypt and the Exodus, the wilderness wanderings, and the entry into the land of promise. The descriptive hymns of praise grow out of the basic impulse of "hallelujah," the call to praise the living God and then give a reason for the praise. The psalm articulates praise to God and addresses the community with the call to praise and supports that call with reason(s).

The theological implications of this brief treatment of praise in the Psalms are significant. First, praise of God in the Psalms is substantive. With the call to praise comes a reason. There is a depth and richness to the praise in the Psalms.[30]

Second, how does one offer praise to God? The Psalms tell the story of how God has been present and how God has delivered. In contempo-

---

[30]Walter Brueggemann, *Israel's Praise: Doxology against Idolatry and Ideology* (Philadelphia: Fortress Press, 1988) provides a notable treatment of the psalms of praise.

rary communities of faith and in the contemporary media, brief calls to praise uttered with great emotion often pass for the praise of God, but the praise of God in the Psalms begins with a *call* to praise that is followed by a substantial reason or reasons for the community to offer praise. The psalm confesses not a glitzy emotionalism but the great acts and blessing of God.

Third, the praise of God in the Psalms is honest and unfettered. The full-throated praise of God engages the whole person. It weds emotion and reason. Some would prefer bland propriety, but the Psalter calls for the uninhibited praise of the God who delivers. In this way, the psalms of praise are like the laments: they are honest. Indeed, the praise of God is hollow without the accompanying prayer of the psalms of plea. Without lament, praise becomes but a guarantee of things as they are, leaving God serenely irrelevant in heaven. That is the image of the Baals the prophets often attacked. Such a God is a distant, faintly recognizable God who is addressed only with kind and gentle words and is limited to the "nice" parts of life. Many contemporary communities of faith propagate a vision of just such a God, but that God is foreign to the Hebrew Psalter. The covenant God of the Psalms is passionately involved in life and history. The prayer and praise of the Psalter call readers to regain vibrancy in prayer and praise that intersects life and worship and in that experience to pursue trust in God.

This excursus into the prayer and praise of the Psalms has redefined covenant for Old Testament readers. Covenant theology centers on the relationship between God and community and the honest dialogue of faith in worship that is central to that relationship. The Psalms make it clear that the dialogue has two sides. God acts and speaks; and in the Psalms we read ancient Israel's passionate speech acts, calling readers into this covenant relationship and portraying a God who accepts and encourages and participates fully in this dialogue, the God who delivers.[31]

Walter Brueggemann has described the cycle of prayer and praise in a somewhat different way.[32] He speaks of psalms of orientation, disorien-

---

[31]I have not attended to the issue of what "deliverance" means. Suffice it to say that deliverance can be of the sudden, miraculous type or of the type enacted by a community of faith. God can also enable people to endure crises. The key is not to limit the way in which one expects God to act.

[32]Brueggemann, *Message of the Psalms*; Brueggemann, *Praying the Psalms* (Winona

tation, and new orientation. In the psalms of orientation, all is right with the world. The encounter with trouble and woe brings about the psalms of disorientation. In the psalms of new orientation, hope for life has surfaced again with a new awareness and vitality. In this articulation of prayer and praise in the Psalter, the language of the text and the experiences of life are also intimately intertwined.[33]

Creation Theology

The Psalms portray God as the one who blesses in life. God is praised as Creator and King, the trustworthy God who is present to bless. Psalms 29, 97, and 104 illustrate.

> The LORD sits enthroned over the flood;
>   the LORD sits enthroned as king forever.   (29:10)

> O LORD, how manifold are your works!
>   In wisdom you have made them all;
>   the earth is full of your creatures.   (104:24)

And wisdom comes from this God as guidance for human response.[34] Here God is not so much the one who comes to deliver as the one who is constantly present to enable the community to grow and prosper in the world, to experience the health of vital living.

> Happy are the people to whom such blessings fall;
>   happy are the people whose God is the LORD.   (144:15)

MN: Saint Mary's Press/Christian Brothers Publications, 1982); Brueggemann, "Psalms and the Life of Faith: A Suggested Typology of Function," in *Psalms and the Life of Faith*, 3-32.

[33]For yet another description of the Psalms as covenant poetry, see Harold Fisch, *Poetry with a Purpose: Biblical Poetics and Interpretation*, Indiana Studies in Biblical Literature (Bloomington/Indianapolis: Indiana University Press, 1988) 104-35.

[34]It is striking that the three primary psalms (Psalms 1, 19, and 119) meditating on torah, the avenue of response to the covenant God, reflect the perspective of creation theology. Wisdom gives guidance for life as God created it to be lived. The organizing categories I use cannot be applied rigidly in order to separate the psalms. The various perspectives are related.

The choice of the Davidic line of kings, celebrated in the Royal Psalms, is one such blessing. The righteous king is a channel of blessing (Psalms 72, 132).

This creation theology is especially strong in the hymns of praise. Psalms 8 and 19, among others, praise God as the creator.

> The heavens are telling the glory of God;
>   and the firmament proclaims his handiwork.   (19:1)

The enthronement psalms (47, 93, 95-99) celebrate the creator's continuing rule over creation as King.

> The LORD is king, he is robed in majesty;
>   the LORD is robed, he is girded with strength.
> He has established the world; it shall never be moved.   (93:1)

This God is present in Zion with the faith community.

> How lovely is your dwelling place,
>   O LORD of hosts!   (84:1)

Life comes from the divine presence there (Psalms 46, 84, 87, 122). This God is worthy of trust (Psalms 23, 91, 121).

Prophetic Theology

The Psalms also portray God as the one who speaks to the people in liturgical instruction, as in Psalms 15 and 24 which utter qualifications for worship.

> O LORD, who may abide in your tent?
>   Who may dwell on your holy hill?
> Those who walk blamelessly, and do what is right,
>   and speak the truth from their heart;
> who do not slander with their tongue,
>   and do no evil to their friends,
>   nor take up a reproach against their neighbors. (15:1-3)

The emphasis on social ethics is a notable prophetic word that reflects the Old Testament concern for the relationship between worship and life.

God also in the Psalter speaks in prophetic warnings such as in Psalm 50.

"Hear, O my people, and I will speak,
   O Israel, I will testify against you.
   I am God, your God." (50:7)

The people are to order life rightly under God (vv. 4-15). The latter part of Psalm 50 (vv. 16-23) remonstrates with the wicked.

In Psalm 82 even the idols are called to create justice. Also note the prophetic word in Psalm 95. This emphasis is a kind of prophetic theology; the Old Testament prophets echo these themes. God speaks a word of prophetic warning, thus calling the people to repent and live in loyal relationship with God.

O that my people would listen to me,
   that Israel would walk in my ways! (81:13)

Praise and exhortation interact in these texts. God here takes the initiative by speaking and calling for a faithful response. To the beginning reader, this perspective is not so pervasive in the Psalter, but a prophetic perspective undergirds much of the book and is important for the Old Testament.[35]

Conclusion

Our look at major theological themes in the Psalter has been organized around theological perspectives, ways of God's involvement in the life of the worshiping community. We have explored covenant theology in which God acts to deliver the people and calls for response by way of torah. Here we mapped out the emphases of prayer and praise in the Psalms. We also considered creation theology in which God is present to bless and provides wisdom as a means of structuring life in response. And we explored prophetic theology in which God speaks and calls for loyalty, often necessitating repentance in response. The categories are categories important for the whole of the Old Testament.[36] I have

---

[35]It may well be that the prophets cut their teeth on such theology in ancient Israel's worship as reflected in the Psalms.

[36]See W. H. Bellinger, Jr., "The Psalms as a Place to Begin for Old Testament Theology," paper presented at the Psalms and Practice Conference at Austin (TX) Presbyterian Theological Seminary, May 1999. On the categories, see Claus Westermann, *Elements of Old Testament Theology*, trans. Douglas W. Stott (Atlanta: John Knox Press,

attempted to take into account the major types of psalms and their poetic expression in this theological formulation. One could, of course, take a variety of approaches in exploring the Psalter's theology. One could pursue a central theme[37] or consider other theological images. While approaches may well differ, much of the same ground would be covered.

I noted earlier that recent scholarship has attended to the canonical shape of the Psalter.[38] If we were to follow this impulse, the shape of our theological treatment would look somewhat different.[39] The shaping of the Psalter emphasized by Wilson and deClaissè-Walford emphasizes the king-ship of God as the central motif. Hope also bubbles to the surface in a canonical approach to the Psalms.[40] The Psalter moves from individual laments that dominate its first half to community songs of praise which dominate its second half.[41] Theological issues also move to the surface.[42] The shapers of the Psalter emphasized the connections between text and life experience, just as our treatment has suggested. Similar issues come to the fore with the various approaches.

A final comment is in order. Theology at its best is not an abstract enterprise apart from life. Theology rather is intertwined with life experi-ence. The adaptability of the Psalter for contemporary life experiences is one of the bases of the continuing popularity of the book. What is a psalm? A psalm is a portrait of faith. Its images and stories about God's involvement in the world still bring life for communities of readers. It is

---

1982); Westermann, *What Does the Old Testament Say About God?* ed. F. W. Golka (Altanta: John Knox Press, 1979).

[37]James Luther Mays, *Psalms*, Interpretation: A Bible Commentary for Teaching and Preaching (Louisville: John Knox Press, 1994) 29-36.

[38]On the approach, see Gerald Henry Wilson, *The Editing of the Hebrew Psalter*, SBLDS (Chico CA: Scholars Press, 1985); Nancy L. deClaissè-Walford, *Reading from the Beginning: The Shaping of the Hebrew Psalter* (Macon GA: Mercer University Press, 1997); J. Clinton McCann, Jr., *A Theological Introduction to the Psalms: The Psalms as Torah* (Nashville: Abingdon Press, 1993); McCann, ed., *The Shape and Shaping of the Psalter*, JSOTSup (Sheffield: JSOT Press, 1993).

[39]For an example, see J. Clinton McCann, Jr., "Psalms," *The New Interpreter's Bible*, vol. 4 (Nashville: Abingdon Press, 1996) 666-72.

[40]See Brevard S. Childs, *Introduction to the Old Testament as Scripture* (Philadelphia: Fortress Press, 1979) 511-23.

[41]See Westermann, *Praise and Lament*, 250-58.

[42]Walter Brueggemann, "Bounded by Obedience and Praise: The Psalms as Canon," in *Psalms and the Life of Faith*, 189-213.

finally the interaction between the language of these texts and the life of a worshiping community that makes the theology vibrant and viable. Only when we realize that do we see the full impact of the Psalter; only then does its concluding summons become a fitting word from God.

> Let everything that breathes praise the LORD!
> Praise the LORD!   (150:6)

Chapter 9

An Introduction
to the History of Interpretation

M. Pierce Matheney, Jr.[*]

This selective review will follow a definition of "Wisdom Literature" restricted to three books of the Hebrew canon as defined by the Reformers, namely, Job, Proverbs, and Qoheleth (or Ecclesiastes). Moreover, it will be necessary to restrict the emphasis because of the amount of material relevant to the passages that relate to the key personification of Wisdom in Proverbs 8, especially verses 22-31, and the others in Proverbs 1:20-31 and chapter 9, where Lady Wisdom speaks. Job 28 and limited portions of Qoheleth will be related to these passages.

The Old Testament canons of Roman Catholicism and Eastern Orthodoxy are more inclusive by virtue of the so-called apocryphal books, notably including the Wisdom of Jesus ben Sirach and the Wisdom of Solomon. These will be treated according to Jerome's preference as deuterocanonical or secondarily canonical and to them must be added the so-called pseudepigraphical literature of the first two centuries BCE and CE. The stories of Tobit (esp. 4:5-19) and Judith (esp. 8:4-8, 28-31) have some wisdom themes, and Baruch (esp. 3:9–4:4) has a great poem on wisdom, relating to Job 28 and Sirach 24.

---

[*]Marvin Tate, my mentor and friend to whom this essay is dedicated, is the last surviving member of my doctoral committee at Southern Seminary. He has been more than a friend over the years. I remember a conversation with him more than a decade ago. I had been studying various locations of Mt. Sinai, and Marvin just reminded me about my presuppositions: "You know we identify Sinai and Horeb, but we don't really know they were the same mountain." I want to assure my friend of a lifetime I am still finding out more about what I don't know. A further personal word of thanks and a joy to acknowledge is due to the superb help of librarian Craig Kubic and his capable and helpful staff at Midwestern Seminary Library without whose constant attention to detail I would never have been able to prepare this essay.

Wisdom in Deuterocanonical and Pseudepigraphical Literature

Jesus ben Sirach was the most pious and zealous scribe-sage since Ezra, and though his wisdom book was traditional in its reliance on Proverbs and other canonical scriptures, he rationalized wisdom by identifying it with Torah, and historicized it by concluding his long book (chapters 44–50) with a

HYMN IN HONOR OF OUR ANCESTORS
Let us now sing the praises of famous men. . . .   (Sirach 44:1)[1]

The list of patriarchs, kings, and prophets that follows in Sirach 44–50 indicates that Sirach, writing in Hebrew before 180 BCE did what his Greek-translator grandson claimed in the prologue—"So my grandfather Jesus, who had devoted himself especially to the reading of the Law and the Prophets and the other books of our ancestors . . . "—and provided an important date in the formation of the Hebrew canon. Whereas the canonical books of Job, Proverbs, and Qoheleth have been noted as lacking interest in Israel's history, Sirach closed this gap.[2]

Sirach begins his instruction with a strong reminder of Job 28 and Proverbs 8:

All wisdom is from the Lord,
    and with him it remains forever. . . .
Wisdom was created before all other things,
    and prudent understanding from eternity.   (Sirach 1:1, 4)

Then he proceeded to piously identify wisdom with the fear of the Lord:

To fear the Lord is the beginning of wisdom.   (Sirach 1:14a)[3]

Crenshaw cites Hellenistic influence for Sirach's pride of authorship, departing from the anonymity or pseudonomity of other collections.[4] This

---

[1]The title occurs in the text of 44:1 in some Greek versions and appears as a section title in NRSV (but not RSV). English quotations are from the NRSV unless indicated otherwise.

[2]As does also the Wisdom of Solomon 10-19 in a somewhat different fashion.

[3]Cf. Prov. 1:7; 9:10a; Job 28:2a; Psalm 111:10a

[4]Sirach 50:27 is his signature. Compare his proud job description of his scribal calling in Sirach 38:34b-39:11. See James L. Crenshaw, "Introduction, Commentary, and Reflections on the Wisdom of Ben Sira," in *The New Interpreter's Bible*, vol. 5 (Nashville:

sign of a new epoch unfortunately prevented Sirach's work from being accepted in the Hebrew canon.[5] Other Hellenistic cultural influences from Theognis, the Stoics, Isis aretalogies, *The Instruction* of Papyrus Insinger, and the *Satire on Trades* have been alleged, but Sirach owes much more to biblical influences.[6]

The key text for Sirach's view of Lady Wisdom is the poem in chapter 24 entitled "THE PRAISE OF WISDOM."[7] The poem proper (vv. 1-22) draws freely from Proverbs 8:1-36, Job 28, and Proverbs 1:20-33.[8] Wisdom's claim to creation from the mouth of God like a mist covering the earth (v. 3) echoes both Genesis 1:2 and 2:6 combined.[9] Wisdom identifies her throne as "a pillar of cloud" reminiscent of that which accompanied Israel's exodus and wilderness wandering (v. 4; compare Exodus 13:21-22). She traversed all of creation seeking a resting place, until God the Creator chose for her Jacob/Israel (vv. 5-8). In the "holy tent" on Zion, in beloved Jerusalem, Lady Wisdom ministers before the Lord (vv. 9-12).[10] Wisdom's abundant growth in the land flourishes like a garden of Eden with abundant plants and trees, and in the midst are spices and herbal ingredients related to the anointing oil and incense used in worship (vv. 13-17).[11] Wisdom then offers her invitation to those who

---

Abingdon Press, 1997) 624-25.

[5]Martin Hengel, "The Scriptures and their Interpretation in Second Temple Judaism" JSOTSup 166, ed. David J. A. Clines et al. (Sheffield: JSOT Press, 1994) 164.

[6]Crenshaw, "Ben Sira," 625; cf. John G. Snaith, "Ecclesiasticus, a Tract for the Times," in *Wisdom in Ancient Israel* (Cambridge: Cambridge University Press, 1995) 174-75.

[7]The heading occurs in some Greek versions, and so also in the NRSV (but not RSV).

[8]Crenshaw, "Ben Sira," 757. A detailed analysis of this interrelation and interpretation is given by Sheppard as one of his case studies of wisdom hermeneutic: Gerald T. Sheppard, *Wisdom as a Hermeneutical Construct: A Study in the Sapientializing of the Old Testament* (Berlin: Walter de Gruyter, 1980) 19-71.

[9]Sheppard, *Wisdom*, 22-27; Crenshaw, "Ben Sira," 757, sees only Gen. 1:2.

[10]Crenshaw "Ben Sira," 627-28, combines Sirach's strong interest in priesthood and temple cult with his refusal to believe in eternal life (17:27-28) to label him a proto-Sadducee.

[11]Cf. Exodus 30:23-38. See Sheppard, *Wisdom*, 52-60, with appropriate reference to prophetic texts such as Hosea 14:5-8; Ezekiel 47:1-12; perhaps less appropriate is comparison to vegetation images in Song of Songs 4-6, though Song of Solomon certainly belongs in a broader definition of Wisdom Literature.

hunger and thirst after her banquet, and who will obey and work with her precepts to avoid shame and sin (vv. 19-22).[12]

The riddle of the poetry is suddenly given a specific identification: Lady Wisdom is the "book of the covenant," the Torah that Moses commanded (v. 23). This is not the first reference to the Law in Sirach. The poem on the search for wisdom in 6:18-37 concludes in a similar way.[13] The abundance of wisdom available through covenant Torah is like the rivers flowing in primordial times from Eden, overflowing like the sea, deeper than the abyss (vv. 25-27, 29).[14] Sirach alludes to the attempt of the first humans in Eden to know wisdom as falling short of the mark (v. 28). The rivers not only relate to the water of life which flows from disciplined study of Torah but perhaps to the boundaries of the promised land—the Nile, Jordan, and Euphrates—where Lady Wisdom now resides and ministers.[15] Sirach concludes chapter 24 by claiming to be a channel of prophetic and wisdom instruction for seekers of wisdom (vv. 30-34).

A related poem on Wisdom is found in the deuterocanonical Book of Baruch 3:9–4:4. It is closely related to Job 28 as well as a saying about Torah in Deuteronomy 30:12-13. The Job passage is not a personification of Lady Wisdom, but poses a significant question:

> But where shall wisdom be found?
> And where is the place of understanding?   (Job 28:12)

One cannot mine it like precious metals or gems (compare Job 28:1) for

> Mortals do not know the way to it,
> and it is not found in the land of the living.   (Job 28:13)

---

[12]Verese 18, which portrays Wisdom as "eternal mother," is not in all the manuscripts and reads like an addition. Cf. Prov. 9:1-6, and in the prophets, Isaiah 55:1-2.

[13]Cf. 15:1; 19:20; and 23:27; and see Alexander A. Dilella, "The Search for Wisdom in Ben Sira," in *The Psalms and Other Studies on the Old Testament*, ed. Jack C. Knight and Lawrence A. Sinclair (Nashotah WI: Nashotah House Seminary, 1990) 188-90. Sheppard, *Wisdom*, 60-61, compares the poem to a riddle for which the citation of Deut. 33:4 in v. 23 is the answer.

[14]Cf. Genesis 2:10-14, to which Sirach added the rivers Jordan and the Nile: all the major rivers with which Israelites were acquainted, according to Crenshaw, "Ben Sira," 158.

[15]Sheppard, *Wisdom*, 68-71, referring to Gen. 15:18 and Deut. 1:6-8.

Stephan Geller who understands Job 28 as a key to the interpretation of the whole book of Job says v. 13 is an astounding statement to readers of Proverbs and other more optimistic wisdom traditions.[16]

Places of deep mystery, Job 28 continues, the deep and the sea say, "It is not in me" (v. 14). It cannot be bought with precious metals or jewels (vv. 15-19). The question then persists:

> Where then does wisdom come from?
> And where is the place of understanding?   (v. 20)

It is hidden from living and flying creatures (v. 21). Abaddon and Death have only a rumor of it (v. 22).

The poem then reaches a turning point with

> God understands the way to it,
> and he knows its place.   (v. 23)

God sees the universe because he weighed out the wind and measured out the waters, rain, and thunderbolt (vv. 24-26).

> . . . then he saw it and declared it,
> he established it, and searched it out.   (v. 27)

God imparts only a limited working knowledge of pragmatic wisdom to humans:

> Truly, the fear of the Lord, that is wisdom,
> and to depart from evil is understanding.   (v. 28)[17]

The question in Baruch is why Israel is in Babylonian exile (3:9-11). The answer is

> You have forsaken the fountain of wisdom. . . .
> Learn where there is wisdom. . . .   (3:12-14)

But the Job questions reoccurs:

---

[16]Stephan A. Geller, " 'Where Is Wisdom': A Literary Study of Job 28 in Its Settings," in *Judaic Perspectives on Ancient Israel*, ed. Jacob Neusner, Baruch A. Levine, and Ernest S. Frerichs, with Caroline McCracken-Flesher (Philadelphia: Fortress Press, 1987) 156-88.

[17]Not a gloss, but a deliberate echo of Job 1:1, 8.

> Who has found her place?
>> And who has entered her storehouses?   (v. 15)

Rich rulers have sported with creatures and hoarded their wealth, but are gone to Hades (3:16-19). Their descendants have not found knowledge. Various nations, supposedly wise, have not learned the way (3:20-23). In the land, the ancient giants were not chosen to remain, but persisted without wisdom in their folly (3:24-25).[18] Searchers for wisdom have not gone to heaven to bring her down, or gone overseas to find and buy her (3:29-30).[19] "No one knows the way" except the creator God "who knows all things," to whom none can be compared. He found the way to knowledge by his understanding and gave her to Jacob/Israel, "whom he loved" (3:31-36). Then the poem personifies Lady Wisdom:

> Afterward she appeared on earth
>> and lived with humankind.   (3:37)

In agreement with Sirach, Baruch identifies wisdom with Torah:

> She is the book of the commandments of God,
>> the law that endures forever.   (4:1a)

Then Baruch states the consequences of one's relationship with Wisdom:

> All who hold her fast will live,
>> and those who forsake her will die.   (4:1b)

So Baruch appeals for Jacob to repent and take her (that is, Wisdom/Torah) and walk toward her shining light, and ends with a benediction on those who know what is pleasing to God:

---

[18]Sheppard, *Wisdom*, 84-90, discusses interpretations of the Nephilim in Gen. 6:1-4 and the pre-Israelite giants of Canaan in Num. 13:28, 31; 14:12; and Deut., 1:28 whose descendants Philistines used as warriors (2 Sam. 21:10). That God did not choose these Sheppard gets from Deut. 4:37. J. Edward Wright, "Baruch, the Ideal Sage," in *Go to the Land I Will Show You*, ed. Joseph E. Colson and Victor H. Matthews (Winona Lake IN: Eisenbraums, 1996) 193-210, explained how Baruch grew in the LXX of Jeremiah to become Jeremiah's successor and the reputed author of apocryphal and pseudepigraphical works.

[19]Cf. Deut. 30:12-13 regarding the accessibility of the Torah.

Turn, O Jacob, and take her;
    walk toward the shining of her light. . . .
Happy are we, O Israel,
    for we know what is pleasing to God. (4:2-4)

The climax of deuterocanonical personification of Lady Wisdom is in the Wisdom of Solomon. Though Solomon is never named in the book, it is clear that the "I" who speaks in 6:22–9:18 is the idealized monarch of 1 Kings 3–4.[20] The teaching of the Book of Wisdom has some interesting implications for the way in which the Diaspora—the Hellenized Judaism of Alexandria in the first century BCE—appropriated earlier wisdom traditions. This "Solomon" addresses earthly rulers in a diatribe to seek a wisdom equated with justice (1:1-16). The wicked rulers perceive life in ways strangely reminiscent of Qoheleth (2:1-9).[21] But God's gift of immortality presented as proof of God's ultimate justice (2:23; 3:1-9; 5:15-16) answers the question of Job 14:13-17, for which Job 19:25-27 had provided some temporary "hope against hope," and overcomes Qoheleth's gentle skepticism regarding anything past this earthly life (Eccl. 9:10).[22]

The Wisdom of Solomon preliminarily characterizes Lady Wisdom as making herself known to those who desire her, not only sitting at the gate but seeking worthy learners (6:12-16). Using a Stoic form of logic, the beginning of wisdom moves from desire for instruction to love of Lady Wisdom, and love moves to the keeping of her laws, which assures of immortality, which brings one near to God: "so the desire for wisdom

---

[20]Actually all of the "book of the acts of Solomon" in 1 Kings 3–11 is a flattering portrait, but the second appearance at Gibeon has a warning speech in 1 Kings 9:6-9, and the judgments in 1 Kings 11 indicate the Deuteronomistic shaping of the annals to prepare for what follows; cf. M. Pierce Matheney, Jr. "Introduction to 1–2 Kings" and "Commentary on 1 Kings," in *The Broadman Bible Commentary*, vol. 3 (Nashville: Broadman Press, 1970) 147-48, 166-94.

[21]John Thigh, "In Praise of the Wisdom of Solomon," *Brecknell Review: Mappings of the Biblical Terrain: The Bible as Text*, ed. Vincent L. Tollers and John Maier (Lewisburg PA: Backnell University Press, 1990) 316-17, but the consequence in 2:10-11 is not like Qoheleth.

[22]Also the teaching of Proverbs and the Old Testament as a whole, except for Isa. 26:19; Pss. 73:23-24; and most clearly Dan. 12:23. Cf. Roland E. Murphy, *The Tree of Life: An Exploration of Biblical Wisdom Literature*, Anchor Bible Reference Library (New York: Doubleday, 1990) 83-96.

leads to a kingdom" (6:17-20). Monarchs are urged to honor wisdom as "Solomon" begins to tell his story of how he obtained wisdom as a gift from God (chapters 7–9) with a brief introduction:

> I will tell you what wisdom is and how she came to be,
> and I will hide no secrets from you,
> but I will trace her course from the beginning of creation.   (6:22ab)

"Solomon" first confesses his humanity. Moving from conception to birth to his first breath and first cry, Solomon stress his own humanity. He does this in humility to show that kings are one with the human condition of their subjects (7:1-6).[23] He was already king, but he prayed for wisdom and understanding, "and the spirit of wisdom came to me" (7:7; cf. 1 Kings 3:9). He explains he valued her above gems, gold, silver, health, beauty, light, or other goods he might have prayed for, only to discover that all good things came along with wisdom who turned out to be "their mother" (7:8-12). He prays to God to be able to impart what God so freely gave:

> unerring knowledge of what exists,
> to know the structure of the world and the activity of the elements;
> the beginning and end and middle of times,
> the alternations of the solstices and the change of the seasons,
> the cycles of the year and the constellations of the stars,
> the natures of animals and the tempers of wild animals,
> the powers of spirits and the thoughts of human beings,
> the varieties of plants and the virtues of roots.   (7:15-20)[24]

"Solomon" learned everything about wisdom. Her spirit is then described (7:22b-23) with twenty-one qualities (= three times seven or "perfect"), the first set of seven pointing to the nobility and transparency of wisdom, the second set pointing to the moral good associated with wisdom, and the third set pointing to wisdom's indomitable relationship

---

[23]See Murphy, *Tree of Life*, 142; cf. Michael Kolarcik, "Introduction, Commentary, and Reflections on the Book of Wisdom," in *The New Interpreter's Bible*, vol. 5 (Nashville: Abingdon Press, 1997) 496-97.

[24]See Murphy, *Tree of Life*, 142-43; Kolarcik, *Wisdom*, 502-503. This list adds Hellenistic philosophy and the science of the day to the Solomonic extraordinary wisdom and knowledge reputed of his writings in 1 Kings 4:29-34, and perhaps even including healing and magical arts for which he is known in Josephus, *Antiquities of the Jews* 8.2.5.

to humanity. The "fashioner" (*technitis*, cf. "master worker," Prov. 8:20) wisdom taught him this.[25] She is mobile and pervasive because of her pureness.

The next five metaphors at the heart of the poem relate Lady Wisdom to God:

> For she is a breath of the power of God,
> and a pure emanation of the glory of the Almighty. . . .
> For she is a reflection of eternal light,
> a spotless mirror of the working of God,
> and an image of his goodness.   (7:25-26)[26]

Summing up the description, she can do all things, renew all things, pass into holy souls to make them friends of God and prophets. She outshines heavenly luminaries, for God loves the person who lives with wisdom, whose reach is cosmic as she orders all things well (7:27–8:1; cf. 7:14).[27]

Then "Solomon" narrates his love for Lady Wisdom. He desires her for his bride, enamored of her beauty and intimacy with the God who loves her, for she is initiate in the knowledge of God, associate in his works, active cause of all things, fashioner of what exists (8:2-6). Her teaching of righteousness consists of the four cardinal virtues mentioned by Plato and the Stoics: self-control, which moderates the use of pleasure; prudence, which discerns the means for ends; justice, which determines what belongs to each; and courage, which gives strength to surmount difficulties and trials.[28] The wide experience of wisdom includes things of old, things to come, turns of speech, solutions of riddles, foreknowledge of signs and wonders, the outcome of seasons and times, so that "Solomon" determines to marry her (8:8-9).[29]

---

[25]Murphy, *Tree of Life*, 143; Kolarcik, *Wisdom*, 503.

[26]Kolarcik, *Wisdom*, 504; cf. Murphy, *Tree of Life*, 143-44, who points out this goes beyond the "begetting" of Prov. 8:22-25 or "coming from the mouth of the Most High" in Sir. 24:3 to define not just the origin of Lady Wisdom, but the intimacy of her relationship with God.

[27]Kolarcik, *Wisdom*, 448, sums up this unfathomable description of Lady Wisdom: "The author has gone as far as possible in the personification of God's wisdom without creating a separate entity as an intermediate being between human beings and God." Murphy, *Tree of Life*, 144.

[28]Kolarcik, *Wisdom*, 510.

[29]Kolarcik, *Wisdom*, 509-10, says of this love affair:

As a result of this relationship with Lady Wisdom, "Solomon" receives success, honor from all,[30] the gift of immortality, governing, rest, and joy (8:10-16). Recapping the essential features of this reflection on Lady Wisdom, and determining to get her for himself, "Solomon" reflects back on his gifts as a child, a preexistent good soul having entered an undefiled body,[31] and he discerns that only God could give this precious gift to him, so he appeals wholeheartedly to God (7:17-21). Following his impassioned prayer for Wisdom to have dominion over all creatures and the created world, "Solomon" prays, "give me the wisdom that sits by your throne" (9:4).[32] "Solomon" is asking in humility as a servant with little understanding without the wisdom that comes only from God (9:5-6). Not only has God chosen him king, but has commanded him to build the temple on the holy mountain and an altar, a copy of the holy tent that God ordered from the beginning (9:7-8).[33]

Not only is Lady Wisdom with God from creation, but she understands what is pleasing in God's sight and right according to his commandments. So the Book of Wisdom knows and agrees with Sirach 24:23 and Baruch 4:1, identifying Torah with divine wisdom. Once again "Solomon" prays for God to send Lady Wisdom from his heavenly abode beside his throne to labor and guard his works and judgments as he inherits David's throne (9:9-12).

The metaphor of human sexual love to connote the passionate pursuit of values or faithfulness to God has its precursors in the Song of Songs and in the extensive metaphor of Israel's being the bride of God (Isa. 62:4-5; Hos.2:14-23). With its reputed connection with Solomon and this spiritual (allegorical) meaning of God's love for Israel, or Solomon's love for Lady Wisdom, it is no wonder that the rabbis at Jabneh overcame their reluctance to include Song of Songs in the Hebrew canon. Also, this accounts for a rather unique history of its interpretation about which we have no more space to speak.

[30]Cf. Job 29:1-13; or the husband of the good wife, Prov. 31:23.

[31]A Greek way of summing up 7:1-6.

[32]Kolarcik, *Wisdom*, 515-16. Creation by the word and dominion is reminiscent of Gen. 1; creation by wisdom, of Prov. 8. The prayer of Solomon in the vision at Gibeon on which this expands is 1 Kings 3:5-15; cf. 2 Chron. 1:7-12.

[33]Kolarcik, *Wisdom*, 517, cites the plan which David gave Solomon (1 Chron. 28:11-19; "plan" is *tabnit*, the same word Exod. 25:9 uses for God's plan for the tabernacle). Sirach had wisdom ministering in the holy tent in Zion (24:10). Of course the earthly microcosm of a tent/temple reflects a heavenly macrocosm (Isa. 66:1; Psalm 11:4). There is no need to speak of a Platonic concept here.

At this point, "Solomon" asks who can know God's counsel or will (cf. Job 28:12, 20; Baruch 3)? People do not know by their reasoning or designs, for their perishable bodies weigh down the soul and hamper the mind. If we don't know everything on earth, who can trace out the heavens (9:13-16)?[34]

Summing up the prayer concern at the end, "Solomon" asks:

Who has learned your counsel
unless you have given wisdom
and sent your Holy Spirit from on high?
And thus the paths of those on earth were set right
and people were taught what pleases you
and were saved by wisdom.   (9:17-18)

Not only is the gift of wisdom identified here with God's "holy spirit" (as earlier with his "word," 9:1-2), but the agent of creation becomes that of salvation. This theme dominates the next chapter, as wisdom saves those from Adam to Moses, whom she guided with the holy people across the Red Sea, inspiring praise of God.[35]

In the pseudepigraphal writings, the most important reference to a personified wisdom is in 1 Enoch about Lady Wisdom searching for a dwelling (cf. Sirach 24:7):

Wisdom could not find a place in which she could dwell,
but a place was found (for her) in the heavens.
Then Wisdom went out to dwell with the children of the people,
but she found no dwelling place.
(So) Wisdom returned to her place
and she settled permanently among the angels. (1 Enoch 42:1-2)[36]

---

[34]Kolarcik, *Wisdom*, 517-18, who cites Eccl. 7:24. This reminds the reader also of the impossible questions God asks Job in Job 38:4-38, mentioning wisdom within, v. 36, as well as above, v. 37.

[35]Wisdom used the holy prophet (Moses, unnamed) to guide their wilderness journey, withstand enemies, and give them water from the rock when they were thirsty and called on God. Wisdom 11:5–19:22 is a historical meditation on the plagues in the contest between Israel and Egypt in which God rather than Lady Wisdom becomes subject.

[36]"1 (Ethiopic Apocalypse of) Enoch," trans. E. Isaac, in *The Old Testament Pseudepigrapha*, vol. 1, *Apocalyptic Literature and Testaments*, ed. James H. Charlesworth (Garden City NY: Doubleday, 1983) 33.

In the next verse, however, a personified iniquity comes and dwells with them. First Enoch is apocalyptic literature, so the view of Lady Wisdom here is a revelatory wisdom as in the canonical book of Daniel. The context in 1 Enoch is a set of visions about "my Elect One . . . the Son of Man" (45:3; 46:3) who in the context of fountains of wisdom (48:1) was given a name, "the Chosen One" (48:6). In the climactic passage

> wisdom flows like water. . . . The Elect One stands before the Lord of the Spirits. . . . In him dwells the spirit of wisdom, the spirit which gives thoughtfulness, the spirit of knowledge and strength, the spirit of those who have fallen asleep in righteousness. (49:1-3)[37]

Argall's important study of wisdom in 1 Enoch probably overstates its similarity with Sirach, but is a useful summary of wisdom in 1 Enoch.[38] Nicklesburg comments on the key passage:

> The little wisdom poem in ch. 42 suggests a parody on Sirach 24 and Baruch 3:9–4:4. Wisdom does not dwell in Israel; unrighteousness drove her back to heaven a pithy and telling summary of the apocalyptic worldview.[39]

Other pseudepigraphical works that relate to wisdom, though not to the personification of Lady Wisdom, are Fourth Maccabees (1:15-19),

---

[37]*The Old Testament Pseudepigrapha*, ed. Charlesworth, 1:34-36. Helmer Ringgren, *Word and Wisdom: Studies in the Hypostatization of Divine Qualities and Functions in the Ancient Near East* (Lund: Hakan Ohlssons Boktryckeri, 1947) 120-22, compares passages on the withdrawal of Wisdom from 4 Ezra 5:9b-10 and 2 Baruch 48:36, and says 1 Enoch 42:1-2 is "characteristic of the pessimistic view of the apocalyptic writers regarding the wickedness of this world."

[38]Randal A. Argall, "Reflections on 1 Enoch and Sirach: A Comparative Literary and Conceptual Analysis of the Themes of Revelation, Creation, and Judgment," in *Society of Biblical Literature 1995 Seminar Papers*, ed. Eagenett Lovering, Jr. (Atlanta: Scholars Press, 1995) 337-51. As evidence that "Enoch's testament is presented as Wisdom," Argall cites 1 Enoch 5:8, which points to 82:1-2, and a visit to the Tree of Wisdom in 1 Enoch 32. In the Epistle, wisdom is prominent in 1 Enoch 92:1; 93:10; 98:9–99:10; and 104:9–105:2.

[39]George W. E. Nickelsburg, *Jewish Literature between the Bible and the Mishnah* (Philadelphia: Fortress Press, 1981) 216. Nickelsburg is of the opinion that 1 Enoch 37–71, the Parables of Enoch, are a later addition to the 1 Enoch literature from early first century CE (see 150-51, 221-23).

(the Sentences of) Pseudo-Phocylides (129-31), and the Sentences of the Syriac Menander (II.27-33).[40]

Wisdom in Early Jewish Interpretation

There are some wisdom texts at Qumran, though little has been written on the subject.[41] When the term "wisdom" occurs in the Qumran sectarian writings, it is not personified as it sometimes is in Proverbs and Sirach.[42] The closest these writings come to personification is in the Damascus Document:

> God loves knowledge. Wisdom and understanding He has before Him, and prudence and knowledge serve Him. Patience and much forgiveness are with Him towards those who turn from transgression.[43]

Scroll 4Q185 expresses wisdom as universal gift. It is similar to sections of Proverbs 19 and Sirach in that wisdom is personified as a woman who is to be honorably courted and who will reward the one who does so. Van der Woude translates:

> Fr]om Him goes forth knowledge unto every people. Happy is the man to whom she has been given. . . . For the Lord has given Her to Israel and as a noble dowry He has endowed Her. . . . He who holds Her in honor says: Let one take Her as a possession and she will suffice him [and gi]ve what she yields. For with Her is [length of da]ys, fatness of bone, joy of heart. . . . Happy is the man who wins Her. . . . He will give Her as a possession to his offspring.[44]

Scroll 4Q525 is a series of beatitudes which identifies Torah as wisdom:

---

[40]*The Old Testament Pseudepigrapha*, vol. 2, *Expansions of the "Old Testament" and Legends, Wisdom and Philosophical Literature, Prayers, Psalms, and Odes, Fragments of Lost Judeo-Hellenistic Works*, ed. James H. Charlesworth (New York: Doubleday, 1985) 545, 579, 593, respectively. For translation comparison, 4 Maccabees of course is also included in the expanded RSV and now in NRSV.

[41]A. S. van der Woude, "Wisdom at Qumran," in *Wisdom in Ancient Israel*, ed. John Day et al. (Cambridge: Cambridge University Press, 1995) 244-56.

[42]Thomas J. Tobin, "4Q185 and Jewish Wisdom Literature," in *Of Scribes and Scrolls: Studies on the Hebrew Bible, Intertestamental Judaism, and Christian Origins*, ed. Harold W. Altridge et al. (New York: University Press of America, 1990) 145-52.

[43]CD 2:3-5, as in Tobin, "4Q185 and Jewish Wisdom Literature," 149.

[44]Van der Woude, "Wisdom at Qumran," 248; cf. Tobin "4Q185," 148.

Ble[ssed] are they who rejoice in Her, who do not chatter in a foolish way. Blessed are they who seek Her with clean hands, who do not look for Her with a deceitful [heart]. Blessed is the man who reaches Wisdom and walks in the Law of the Most High.[45]

The purpose of the gift of wisdom is in 11QPs (Syriac II):

For to make known the glory of the Lord is Wisdom given, and to recount his many deeds she is made known to man. . . . From the gates of the righteous her voice is, from the assembly of the pious her song. When they eat with satiety she is mentioned. . . . How far from the godless is her word, from all haughty men to know her.[46]

Passionate devotion to Wisdom is represented by a wisdom Psalm the first four verses of which are a version of Sirach 51:13-17. This poem refers to Lady Wisdom as a nurse, a tutor, and a lover passionately desired by the young author.[47]

Finally, one must mention a large wisdom catechism at Qumran called Sapiential Work A (4Q41) of which there are seven fragmentary copies.[48] It consists of wisdom sayings, often in proverbial form, providing practical admonition for life in family and society through a biblically based creation ethic. For instance, it uses wisdom texts, such as Proverbs 6:15, and cites Job 28:20-28 and Isaiah 40:12 describing how God measured out the universe as a basis for his future testing and judging of humankind.[49]

Philo Judaeus of Alexandria is a key figure for understanding wisdom in Hellenistic Judaism.[50] A good example of Philo's appropriation of the wisdom tradition appears in his comments on Proverbs 8:27-30.

---

[45]Van der Woude, "Wisdom at Qumran," 250.

[46]Van der Woude, "Wisdom at Qumran," 252; cf. *The Old Testament Pseudepigrapha*, ed. Charlesworth, 2:618-19.

[47]Van der Woude, "Wisdom at Qumran," 253.

[48]Torlief Elgrin, "Wisdom, Revelation, and Eschatology in an Early Essene Writing," in *SBL 1995 Seminar Papers*, 441-63. Manuscripts are 1Q26, and from cave 4, 4Q415, 416, 417, 418a, 418b, 423.

[49]Elgrin, "Wisdom, Revelation, and Eschatology," 441-47.

[50]Ulrich Wilckens, σοφί α, σοφό ς, σοφί ζω, in *Theological Dictionary of the New Testament*, vol. 7, ed. Gerhard Friedrich, trans. and ed. Geoffrey W. Bromiley (Grand Rapids: Eerdmans, 1971) 500-501.

Now "father and mother" is a phrase which can bear different meanings. For instance we should rightly say and without further question that the Architect who made this universe was at the same time the father of what was thus born, whilst its mother was the knowledge possessed by its Maker. With His knowledge God had union, not as men have it, and begat created being. And knowledge having received the divine seed, when her travail was consummated bore . . . the only beloved Son who is apprehended by the senses, the world which we see. Thus in the pages of one of the inspired company, wisdom is represented as speaking of herself after this manner: "God obtained me first of all works and founded me before the ages" (Prov. viii.22). True, for it was necessary that all that came to the birth of creation should be younger than the mother and nurse of all.[51]

Much work has been writtten concerning wisdom as a cosmic principle in Philo, particularly the way he relates Logos to Sophia.[52] The best discussion is in Jean Laporte's treatment of preexisting wisdom in Philo, which also relates to tabernacle, law, and Eden (cf. Sirach 24).[53]

It is difficult to get a handle on the topic of wisdom in rabbinic teaching. *Pirke Avoth* is a tractate of the Mishnah which consists of wise sayings of the fathers, and speaks to the reader as individuals.[54] Among the sayings of Rabban Gamalial, son of Rabbi Judah the Patriarch, occurs:

Lots of Torah, lots of life; lots of discipleship, lots of wisdom; lots of counsel, lots of understanding; lots of righteousness, lots of peace.[55]

There is a balance between learning and doing, for when Rabbi Hannina ben Dosa says:

---

[51]Philo, *De Ebrietate* 30-31, trans. F. H. Colson and G. H. Whitaker, in *The Loeb Classical Library*, vol. 3, ed. T. E. Page et al. (London: William Hemingway, 1939) 333, 335.

[52]Ringgren, *Word and Wisdom*, 124-25.

[53]Jean Laporte, "Philo in the Tradition of Wisdom," in *Aspects of Wisdom in Judaism and Early Christianity*, ed. Robert L. Wilken (Notre Dame IN: University of Notre Dame Press, 1975) 103-39, esp. 114-19. The essays in this volume provide a helpful analysis of the history of interpretation for Wisdom Literature.

[54]Jacob Neusner, *Torah from our Sages: Pirke Avot* (Chappequa NY: Rossell Books, 1984) 10, 14-15.

[55]Neusner, *Pirke Avoth* 2:7 (65). This suggests that Wisdom is equated with Torah, as practiced by the disciple (cf. Sirach 24; Baruch 4:1).

For anyone whose fear of sin takes precedence over his wisdom, his wisdom will endure. And for anyone whose wisdom takes precedence over his fear of sin, his wisdom will not endure. He would say: Anyone whose deeds are more than his wisdom—his wisdom will endure. And anyone whose wisdom is more than his deeds his wisdom will not endure.[56]

At the end of the sayings is a list of five things of which the Holy One took possession. The first is Torah, for which the proof text is Proverbs 8:22:

What is the source which proves that Torah [is God's possession]? As it is written "The Lord took possession of me [Torah] at the very outset, the first of His works of old."[57]

The most thorough discussion of the rabbis and wisdom is Fischel's long treatise on the Westernization of Midrash.[58] Fischel notes that the relationship of wisdom to Hellenistic and Roman cultures is the result of the openness of the wisdom tradition, from its early days, to international influence.[59]

Wisdom in the New Testament

Gospels. In the gospels, Matthew, or the material Matthew shares with Luke (which some scholars call Q) seems to be the source for teaching about Jesus as a wisdom teacher.[60] The one who hears his teachings and does them is "like a wise man" (7:24). The judgment of the Queen of Sheba who came to listen to Solomon's wisdom will be against Jesus' generation for "one greater than Solomon is here" (12:42 NIV). In the diverse reactions of the crowd to John the Baptist and Jesus, both of whom are seen in Q as wisdom teachers, the last sentence is "Yet wisdom is vindicated by her deeds" (11:19b).[61]

---

[56]Neusner, *Pirke Avoth* 3:9 (106-107).

[57]Neusner, *Pirke Avoth* 10:10 (202). Lady Wisdom's speech is attributed to Torah!

[58]Henry A. Fischel, "The Transformation of Wisdom into the World of Midrash," in *Aspects of Wisdom* (see n. 58, above), 67-101.

[59]Fischel, "The Transformation of Wisdom," 87.

[60]Betty Jane Lillie, "Matthew's Wisdom Theology: Old Things and New," in *Proceedings of the Eastern Great Lakes and Midwest Bible Societies* 9 (1989): 124-37.

[61]Luke 7:35b has "children" for "deeds." Cf. James M. Robinson, "Jesus as Sophos

The rejection of Jesus (and John) by this generation is seen in Q as typical of all Israel's history now focused in current Judaism.[62] Jesus refers to the death of John and his own upcoming crucifixion, putting them in the line of "prophets, sages, and scribes" (Matthew 23:34) rejected and killed by the current generation. Perhaps Jesus speaks as a rejected wisdom teacher in his lament over Jerusalem that follows.[63] The climactic passage on Jesus as wisdom teacher, who then speaks as Wisdom incarnate is Jesus' praise to the Father for hiding "these things from the wise and the intelligent" and revealing them to infants as was his "gracious will" (Matthew 11:25-26). The theme is picked up in the next verse:

> All things have been handed over to me by my Father; and no one knows the Son except the Father, and no one know the Father except the Son and anyone to whom the Son chooses to reveal him. (Matthew 11:27)[64]

Then Wisdom's invitation follows to those disciples who will take up the restful "yoke" of learning the "things" handed over to the Son from the Father (Matthew 11:28-30).[65]

If the synoptics, particularly Matthew, speak of Jesus as the Wisdom of God, the gospel of John is more pervasive in demonstrating a relation

---

and Sophia: Wisdom Tradition and the Gospels" in *Aspects of Wisdom* (see n. 58, above), 1-16.

[62]Matt. 23:34-36; and Luke 11:49-51, where in v. 49 this is attributed to "the Wisdom of God." See Robinson "Jesus as Sophos," 1-4.

[63]Matt. 23:37-39; Luke 13:34-35; Lillie, "Matthew's Wisdom Theology," 135-36; cf. Wilckens, σοφί α κτλ. in *TDNT* 7:515.

[64]See also Luke 10:21-22 with a different setting, just after the reported mission of the seventy. Lillie's "Matthew's Wisdom Theology," 131-33, referring to M. Jack Suggs, *Wisdom, Christology, and Law in Matthew's Gospel* (Cambridge MA: Harvard University Press, 1970) 58, 71-87, 95 [which was unavailable to me]; cf. Robinson, "Jesus as Sophos," 8.

[65]See Lillie, "Matthew's Wisdom Theology," 33-135; and Robinson, "Jesus as Sophos," 11. Both authors refer to Sirach 24:23 and the "yoke" of Torah study, since Wisdom has been identified in Judaism with Torah. See also David E. Orton, "Matthew and Other Creative Jewish Writers," in *Crossing the Boundaries: Essays in Biblical Interpretation* (Leiden: E. J. Brill, 1994) 133-40, who understands Matthew as a scribe who sees himself vested with the authority of Jesus his teacher, claiming the special revelation referred to in this passage.

to the personification of Wisdom in Old Testament and deuterocanonical literature.[66] This personification of Wisdom provides the most convincing background for what is said of the Logos in John 1:1-18.[67]

Paul. The doxological hymn in Romans 11:33-36 at the conclusion of the apostle's apocalyptic argument about God's election of Jews and Gentiles combines Paul the sage and Paul the seer.[68] Paul wants the Colossians (and Laodiceans) to

> have all the riches of assured understanding and have the knowledge of God's mystery, that is, Christ himself, in whom are hidden all the treasures of wisdom and knowledge. (Colossians 2:2-3)

They are facing deceivers who wish to take them "captive through philosophy . . . human tradition, according to the elemental spirits of the universe" (Col. 2:4, 8). Later (2:16-23) Paul mentions ritual observances, worship of angels, dwelling on visions, and ascetic practices which

> are simply human commands and teachings. These have indeed an appearance of wisdom in promoting self-imposed piety, humility, and severe treatments of the body, but are of no value in checking self-indulgence. (2:22-23)[69]

But the *locus classicus* of Paul's wisdom teaching is undoubtedly 1 Corinthians 1:18–2:16. First, it must be said that full-blown gnosticism belongs to the patristic period rather than the New Testament period, so Wilckens is mistaken to discuss it before his treatment of the New Testament, and then assume when reaching the Corinthian passage that Paul's opponents are gnostics.[70] Stuhlmacher traces this history of religious error

---

[66]Raymond E. Brown, *The Gospel according to John (i-xii)*, Anchor Bible 29 (Garden City NY: Doubleday, 1966) cxxii-cxxv.

[67]Brown, *The Gospel according to John (i-xii)*, 519-24.

[68]E. Elizabeth Johnson, "The function of Apocalyptic and Wisdom Traditions in Romans 9-11: Rethinking the Questions," in *Society of Biblical Literature 1995 Seminar Papers*, 352-61; cf. Wilckens, σοφί α, *TDNT* 7:518.

[69]Donald K. Berry believes Paul's wisdom teaching includes Col. 1:15-18 as a Christological reinterpretation of Prov. 8:22-31 (*An Introduction to Wisdom and Poetry of the Old Testament* [Nashville: Broadman and Holman, 1995] 3).

[70]Wilckens, σοφί α *TDNT* 7:519-22. So his hypothetical reconstruction of "A Wisdom Myth in Judaism" is also a mistaken understanding of the personification passages we have been studying, which only become "mythological" with heresies opposed by

back to Bultmann's theology relying on Wilhelm Bousset's detection of the influence of ancient mystery cults.[71] Hans Conzelmann has interpreted Paul as a teacher of wisdom.[72] A problem of interpretation is how Paul's wisdom homily fits in with the problem of church division at Corinth over other human teachers, Apollos and Cephas (1 Cor. 1:10-12). Tuckett rejects the thesis of F. C. Baur, recently revived by Goulder, that the early Christian church was dominated by a great split between the Jewish Christian wing, under the leadership of Peter, and the Pauline wing.[73] Lampe finds the key to the fact that in 1:18–2:16 Paul nowhere refers to the party strife directly in his use of a covert mode of speech called a *schema* by the rhetoricians.[74] Johnson sees the wisdom of God as apocalyptic power in the passage.[75] Paul's heavily ironic arguments are based largely on conceptions and traditions at home in Jewish schools of wisdom, and especially apocalyptic conceptions of various sorts. God alone is wise and the source of all wisdom, so human wisdom stands under the judgment of God.[76] Paul uses a number of scriptures to prove

---

Irenaeus and other church fathers, cf. Bernard Lang, *Wisdom and the book of Proverbs: An Israelite Goddess Defined* (New York: Pilgrim Press, 1986) 142-44. So also mistaken are the interpretations of Elizabeth Schüssler-Fiorenza, "Wisdom Mythology and the Christological Hymns," in *Aspects of Wisdom*, 17-41, in interpretation of passages like John 1:1-18; Col. 1:15-20; and Phil. 2:6-11.

[71]Peter Stuhlmacher, "The Hermeneutical Significance of 1 Cor. 2:6-16," in *Tradition and Interpretation in the New Testament*, ed. Gerald F. Hawthorne with Otto Betz (Grand Rapids MI: Eerdmans, 1987) 330-31. Stuhlmacher thinks this is important enough to give a history of interpretation of the 1 Cor. passage from Luther and the Reformers to the present.

[72]Birger A. Pearson, "Hellenistic-Jewish Wisdom Speculation and Paul," in *Aspects of Wisdom*, 43-45, questions whether the theory about a Pauline wisdom school in Ephesus is true or not.

[73]Christopher Tuckett, "Jewish Christian Wisdom in 1 Corinthians," in *Crossing the Boundaries*, ed. Stanley E. Porter et al. (New York: E. J. Brill, 1994) 201-19.

[74]Peter Lampe, "Theological Wisdom and the 'Word about the Cross': The Rhetorical Scheme in 1 Corinthians 1–4," *Interpretation* 44/2 (April 1990): 117-31. Paul is trying to prove that human speech about God cannot be absolute, party spirit growing out of "wisdom of the world" is theosophy nullifying the power of the cross.

[75]E. Elizabeth Johnson, "The Wisdom of God as Apocalyptic Power," in *Faith and History*, ed. John T. Carrole et al. (Atlanta: Scholars Press, 1990) 134-48. The wisdom and power do not belong to the preachers or the Corinthians but to God, so Paul indicts the whole community for its foolishness.

[76]Pearson, "Hellenistic-Jewish Wisdom Speculation," 50-51.

his point.[77] In the critical passage of 2:6-16 Paul uses key expressions of the terminology of his opponents without capitulating to their position.[78]

Stuhlmacher makes the most of Paul as wisdom teacher in this passage.[79] The crucified Christ whom Paul proclaims is "the power of God and the wisdom of God" (1 Cor. 1:24) in line with the personification in Proverbs 8:22-31. Paul says:

> But we speak God's wisdom, secret and hidden, which God decreed before the ages for our glory. (1 Cor. 2:7)

Then he says one can only understand these mysteries, "even the depths of God," by the Spirit of God given us by God (1 Cor. 2:10-12) and adds "But we have the mind of Christ" (1 Cor. 2:16).

James. Finally in the New Testament, the Book of James is closely related to Jewish Wisdom Literature.[80] Wisdom is not personified, but appears in James 1:5 as a gift of God free for the asking.[81] James, as wisdom teacher, warns against this vocation (James 3:1) because of the dangerous potential of the human tongue, which none can tame (James 3:8). The opposite things that come from the same mouth, blessing and cursing, and so forth, may be compared to the difference between earthly and heavenly wisdom (James 3:10-16):

> But the wisdom from above is first pure, then peaceable, gentle, willing to yield, full of mercy and good fruits, without a trace of partiality or hypocrisy. (James 3:17)[82]

---

[77]For example, 1 Cor. 1:19 (Isa. 29:14); 1:20 (allusion to Isa. 19:11; 44:25); 1:30 (Jer. 9:22); 2:16 (Isa. 40:13); 3:19ff. (Job 5:12-13; Psalm 94:11); see Pearson, "Hellenistic-Jewish Wisdom Speculation," 49.

[78]Pearson, "Hellenistic-Jewish Wisdom Speculation," 50-51. Pearson rather turns their terminology back against them, 52-58.

[79]Stuhlmacher, "The Hermeneutical Significance of 1 Cor. 2:6-16," 332-42.

[80]Donald E. Gowman, "Wisdom and Endurance in James," *Horizons in Biblical Theology* 15 (1993): 145-53.

[81]Gowan "Wisdom," 145, citing a definition by J. A. Kirk as "the divine power which makes possible steadfastness under testing and thus leads to perfection." Gowan finds this definition particularly in the martyr tradition of Judaism in 4 Maccabees.

[82]James 3:17 sums up the *parenesis* on wisdom in the Book of James.

Wisdom in Patristic Literature

One of the clues for my narrowing the focus of this history of interpretation to those passages which personify Lady Wisdom, or in which she speaks, is the selectivity of patristic writers. Wilken says:

> Except for discussions of the personification of wisdom in the development of Christology and the debates over the interpretation of Prov. 8:22, "The Lord created me [Wisdom] in the beginning of his ways," in the trinitarian controversies, the study of wisdom has been but a minor tributary alongside the great river of patristic thought.[83]

Berry prefaces his treatment of Justin Martyr and Irenaeus with some general uses of wisdom in the Odes of Solomon, *Doctrina Apostolorum*, the Didache, Barnabas, and 1 Clement.[84] He rightly focuses on Justin Martyr's use of Proverbs 8 in his Dialog with Trypho. In Dialog 61, he says:

> The Word of Wisdom, who is Himself this God begotten of the Father of all things, and Word, and Wisdom, and Power, and the Glory of the Begetter. . . . He speaks by Solomon. . . . The Lord made me the beginning of His ways for His works. From everlasting He established me in the beginning before He had made the earth. . . . I was along with Him.[85]

Berry points out that Arians later used this passage to foster their Christology that Christ was created rather than coeternal with the Father.[86] Iranaeus identified Wisdom at creation in Proverbs 3:19-20, and Proverbs 8:22ff. with Christ as Word and Wisdom as Spirit:

> I have also largely demonstrated that the Word, namely the Son, was always with the Father, and that Wisdom also, which is the Spirit was present with Him, to all creation.[87]

---

[83]Robert L. Wilken, *Aspects of Wisdom*, 143-44.

[84]Berry, *Introduction to Wisdom*, 65-66.

[85]Justin Martyr, *Dialog with Trypho*, in *The Ante-Nicene Fathers*, ed. Alexander Roberts and James Donaldson (repr.: Grand Rapids MI: Eerdmans, orig. 1905) 227-28.

[86]Berry, *Introduction to Wisdom*, 66.

[87]Irenaeus, *Against Heresies* 4.20, in *The Anti-Nicene Fathers*.

Robinson points out that one of the gnostic groups Irenaeus opposed was the Ophites who believed that Sophia became Christ at his baptism and is seen in the healing miracles, but that Christ/Sophia departs from Jesus before his crucifixion. This gnostic adoptionist Christology saw Christ and Sophia as a divine pair which inhabits Jesus temporarily.[88]

Robert Grant introduces gnosticism in his consideration of "the School of Alexandria," summarizing their thoroughgoing cosmic dualism in separating the Father of Jesus (whose teachings were revealed only to them as "spiritual" beings) from the malevolent creator God of the Old Testament.[89] This leads him into a discussion of Clement of Alexandria who exegetes the scriptures based on Philo's allegorical methodology, and first undertook to justify and explain the meaning of the allegorical method.[90] Clement of Alexandria in *Stromateis* cites Proverbs 3:5, 6:23: "Do not preen yourself on your wisdom." Then he offers his explanation:

> Through these he wants to show that actions must follow the Word. . . .
> The paths of wisdom are diverse, but they lead directly to the path of truth, and that path is faith. . . . He adds, "Do not be intelligent in your own eyes" (Prov. 3:7), following godless reasoning of those who are in revolt against God's governments, "but fear God . . . " teach clearly that the fear of God is a movement away from evil. . . . This is the education offered by Wisdom.[91]

This is followed by his comment on Wisdom of Solomon (7:17-20), particularly to

> an enigmatic allusion to spiritual beings in this addition "I have known all that is hidden, and all that is open to view. I was a pupil of Wisdom who formed them all." There in a nutshell you have the profession of our philosophy. The process of learning about these, if practiced under

---

[88]Robinson, "Jesus as Sophos and Sophia," 7, citing Irenaeus, *Against Heresies* 1.30.

[89]Robert M. Grant with David Tracy, *A Short History of the Interpretation of the Bible*, Second Edition, Revised and Enlarged (Philadelphia: Fortress Press, 1984) 52-54.

[90]Grant, *A Short History*, 55.

[91]Clement of Alexandria, *Stromateis: Books One to Three*, trans. John Ferguson in *The Fathers of the Church, A New Translation*, ed. Thomas P. Halton et al. (Washington DC: Catholic University of America Press, 1991) 159.

good government, leads upward via Wisdom, who formed the whole universe, to the ruler of the universe.[92]

Grant sums up Clement's guiding principle of interpretation:

> Faith in Christ, in his person and in his work, is the key to scripture. The Logos who spoke in the Old Testament finally revealed himself in the New, and the Christian is able to understand all scripture in the light of the knowledge which Christ has given . . . the true gnosis which contains the higher truths of the religion.[93]

This leads to Clement of Alexander's greater pupil in the pursuit of wisdom, Origen, the most distinguished member of the Alexandrian school.[94] In his commentary on John 1:1, Origin says:

> Although so many meanings of "beginning" have occurred to us at the present time, we are investigating how we ought to take the statement "In the beginning was the Word. . . . " But it is as the beginning that Christ is creator, according to which he is wisdom. Therefore as wisdom he called the beginning. For wisdom says in Solomon, "God created me at the beginning of this ways for his work," that "the Word might be in the beginning" in wisdom.[95]

Miyako Demura studies Origen's use of the Sophia tradition of Wisdom of Solomon 7:27b, especially in two passages of *Contra Celsum* (iv.3, iv.7) and concludes:

> Sophia, directly and indirectly, plays an important role behind his Christology and gives a dynamic character to his soteriology. . . . [W]e can therefore say that Origen constructs his mystery of Christology not

---

[92]Clement of Alexander, *Stromateis* 160. William R. Schoedel, "Jewish Wisdom and the Formation of the Christian Ascetic," in *Aspects of Wisdom*, 169-99, compares Clement with *The Teachings of Sylvanus* from Nag Hammadi.

[93]Grant, *A Short History*, 56. Clement in *Stromateis* is always defining a true Gnostic against Valentians and other heretics in this Alexandrian context.

[94]Grant, *A Short History*, 56. There follows a perceptive analysis and critique of Origen's allegorical method of interpreting scripture, 57-62.

[95]Origen, *Commentary on the Gospel according to John Books 1-10*, trans. Ronald E. Heine, in *The Fathers of the Church, A New Translation*, ed. Thomas P. Halton et al. (Washington DC: Catholic University of America Press, 1989) 56.

only as Logos-mystic (Logos-Word), but also as Sophia-mystic (Sophia-God, Sophia-Christ).[96]

Roland Murphy sees Origen as one of the giants among biblical interpreters who wielded enormous influence on later generations. For instance, his acceptance of Solomonic authorship for Proverbs, Ecclesiastes, and the Song of Songs, contents of which he summarized in a quote from the prologue to his commentary on the Song of Songs: Proverbs as moral science, Ecclesiastes as natural science, Song of Songs as introspective science, that is, "love of things divine and heavenly, using for his purpose the figure of the Bride and Bridegroom, and teaches us that communion with God must be attained by the paths of charity and love."[97] Then Jerome passes this view on to the medieval period in his commentary on Ecclesiastes 1:1 where he speaks of a threefold category of "beginners" (who live virtuously—Proverbs), "proficient" (who reject what is vain—Ecclesiastes), and "perfect" (who love God—Song of Songs). "Thus, early on, these wisdom books are evaluated in terms of three stages . . . of the spiritual growth of a Christian."[98]

This assumption of Solomonic authorship is not historically correct according to historical-critical opinion today, because as Murphy says,

> One fails to see the richness of the development of the wisdom movement across Israel's history when Proverbs is fitted into the life span of King Solomon. Similarly Qoheleth's dialogue with his time (the Hellenistic period of the third century) is missed if the book is shifted back to the tenth century.[99]

But then Murphy goes on to say that Origen's hermeneutical thrust to attempt to correlate these books with the life of the believer served the needs of his community in making his immense learning practical and relevant.[100] Berry finds other uses of wisdom in the Apostolic Constitu-

---

[96]Mirak Demura, "Origen on Sophia in Contra Celsus's the Double Understanding of the Wisdom of Solomon 7:27," in *Origeniana Quinta*, Papers of the Fifth International Origen Congress, Boston College 14-18 August 1989 (Leuren's University Press, 1992) 174-78.

[97]Roland Murphy, *Wisdom Literature and Psalms* (Nashville: Abingdon Press, 1983) 52-53.

[98]Murphy, *Wisdom*, 52-53.

[99]Murphy, *Wisdom*, 53.

[100]Murphy, *Wisdom*, 53-54. Murphy goes on to evaluate Origin's philosophy and

tions (Hellenistic Synagogal Prayers), and in Athanasius, Cyprian, Ambrose, Jerome, Cyril of Jerusalem, Theodore of Mopsuestia, Augustine, and Gregory the Great.[101]

Conclusion

Time does not permit speaking of wisdom in Maimonides or Aquinas, Luther or Calvin, Spinoza or Hobbes, Hegel or Wellhauson, Gunkel or Baumgartner. About the passages on the personification of Lady Wisdom, my main conclusion is that *hokmah* was never a goddess or hypostatization for Israel or Judaism, but always a personification. Her importance is certainly emphasized by the connection with creation, and the personification has fed into Christian theology about the person of Christ and the Trinity.

---

theology in his great work *On First Principles* in which he raises questions of the text which are very modern. He evaluates the three meanings Origen found in every scripture and his allegorical methods of interpretation, especially Song of Songs.

[101]Berry, *Introduction to Wisdom*, 67-71, of which Athanasius is most important for his defense of Christ's character as uncreated in *Against the Arians*, using Prov. 8:22-30 and 9:1, 68.

Chapter 10

Literary Forms in the Wisdom Literature

W. Dennis Tucker, Jr.

Introduction

In studying the poetry of the Wisdom Literature there are two questions that should be considered: What is the form of this literature? and What are the possible settings of this literature? Several of the more prominent forms will be discussed below, along with texts that illustrate them. In addition, several possible settings for Wisdom Literature will be explored.

Literary Forms

As is true of other sections in the Old Testament, the Wisdom Literature contains a number of different literary forms. Readers may have a general familiarity with some forms, such as the "saying" as found in the book of Proverbs, but some may struggle with the other forms that appear not only in Proverbs, but especially in Job and Ecclesiastes. Yet rather than attempting to understand the form of the literature, most students of the Bible tend to read over the forms with the hope that the message of the text will eventually emerge. Such an approach fails to appreciate the artistic and aesthetic quality of Scripture and may fail to produce a proper reading of the text.

Saying or Proverb. The most common literary form in the Wisdom Literature is the saying or proverb. A saying/proverb may be broadly defined as a "succinct [expression] that registers a conclusion based on experience and the powers of observation."[1] The Hebrew word most often translated as "saying" or "proverb" is *mašal*. The word itself can have one of two meanings: "rule" or "comparison." In some sense the saying in Wisdom Literature encompasses both meanings. As a rule the sayings

---

[1]Leo Perdue, "Proverb," in *Mercer Dictionary of the Bible*, ed. Watson E. Mills et al. (Macon GA: Mercer University Press, 1990) 718.

provide guidance to individuals, enabling them to master life in all of its complexities. But the saying often serves to note the comparisons or relationships that exist in the world. By simply noting the similarities between objects, the saying points to the connected nature of reality as observed through human experience.[2]

The traditional forms of Hebrew poetry appear in the sayings. The sage used synonymous, antithetical, and synthetic styles of poetry to express his observations.[3] While the sage did make use of the synonymous (19:29) and synthetic (21:16) styles, the antithetical style of poetry proved especially useful. In Proverbs 10–15, the sage recounts the differences between the righteous and the wicked, between the wise and the fool. The antithetical form was well suited to illustrate those differences. For example,

> The righteous hate falsehood,
> but the wicked act shamefully and disgracefully. (Proverbs 13:5)[4]

The sage has presented his observation in this verse and in so doing has left the reader with an implicit choice: to live like the righteous or act like the wicked. In general, the proverbs are intended to inculcate some type of moral behavior. Thus, while the sage was careful to craft a literary work that reflected the rigorous demands of Hebrew poetry, his final goal was moral instruction and guidance.

Additional Saying Forms. There are other styles of the saying, such as the "better than" saying. This form is easily recognizable because, routinely, in English translation, the word "better" appears in the first stich and the word "than" appears in the second stich. The purpose of this comparative saying is to indicate that certain types of conduct or behavior are more acceptable than others. Some of these sayings have overtly religious connotations:

> Better is a little with the fear of the LORD,
> than great treasure and trouble with it. (Proverbs 15:16)

---

[2]Leo Perdue, *Wisdom and Creation: The Theology of the Wisdom Literature* (Nashville: Abingdon Press, 1994) 64.

[3]On these forms of Hebrew Poetry, see "The Poetry and Literature of the Psalms" in this volume.

[4]Unless otherwise noted, biblical quotations are from the NRSV.

At other times the saying seems less religious, but instructive nonetheless:

> Better is a dry morsel with quiet
>> than a house full of feasting with strife. (Proverbs 17:1)

Another form that appears in Wisdom Literature is the numerical saying or numerical proverb. This form most likely aided students in learning, serving as a type of mnemonic device.[5] While it may have been a form of entertainment at times, the numerical saying seems to stress the role of reflection, observation, and education. Von Rad states that "the aim of this form of proverb is always the same, the collection of things which are similar where the assertion of similarity is the real surprise element, for regarded in isolation, the cases listed are quite dissimilar."[6] The usual form is x/x+1, "three things . . . four. . . . " The customary numbers are three and four, but other numbers do appear throughout the wisdom corpus.

> Three things are too wonderful for me;
>> four I do not understand:
> the way of an eagle in the sky,
>> the way of a snake on a rock,
> the way of a ship on the high seas,
>> and the way of a man with a girl. (Proverbs 30:18-19)

The opening line of the saying introduces the theme of the saying, with the emphasis being on the second number. Then the sage lists, without explanation, four seemingly unrelated items. Pedagogically, the sage probably hoped the student would reflect on the four items, consider his own observations, and determine the implied meaning.

The last saying form is the "happy" or "blessed" saying. Normally such sayings begin with, or prominently contain, the word "happy" or "blessed." There is an intrinsic link between the behavior of the individual and the resulting happiness. The sage praises those behaviors that

---

[5]James L. Crenshaw, "Wisdom," 225-64 in *Old Testament Form Criticism*, ed. John Hayes (San Antonio: Trinity University Press, 1974) 236; rev. and repr. as "Wisdom (1974)," 45-77 in Crenshaw, *Urgent Advice and Probing Questions. Collected Writings on Old Testament Wisdom* (Macon GA: Mercer University Press, 1995) 54ff.

[6]Gerhard von Rad, *Wisdom in Israel* (Nashville: Abingdon, 1972) 36.

lead to that state of blessedness. For example, in Proverbs 14:21, the sage writes:

> Those who despise their neighbors are sinners,
>> but happy are those who are kind to the poor.

The emphasis is on the fact that those who help the poor actually discover the meaning of the good life. This saying is not meant to indicate who has the happy life (that is, only those who help the poor), but rather is meant to be instructive as to how one obtains the good life (that is, by helping the poor one finds the blessedness of life).

Riddle. The riddle is one of the more enigmatic forms of Wisdom Literature. The author depends upon the natural ambiguity of language to accomplish his purpose. Words and phrases are selected whose general meaning is common knowledge, but their nuanced meanings may serve to conceal special connotations for the intended audience. The only pure form of the riddle in the Old Testament occurs not in the Wisdom Literature, but in Judges 14:10-18, when Samson offered his riddle to the Philistines. While there are no "pure" riddles in the Wisdom Literature, the form has left its imprint. In Prov. 1:6, there appears to be an equation made between the riddle and the saying. Crenshaw has argued that a number of riddles exist in Proverbs, but only in disintegrated form.[7] For example, in Proverbs 16:15, the author speaks about the king, but in ambiguous language:

> In the light of a king's face there is life,
>> and his favor is like the clouds that bring the spring rain.

The reader is left to ponder what the author meant by the king's face bringing life and how his favor resembles the clouds.[8] While the meaning may seem obvious upon first reading, a second reading is necessary to glean the meaning. Thus, the reader is challenged to examine each riddle and to move beyond the surface meaning to the deeper, intended meaning.

Allegory. Two allegories appear in the wisdom corpus, Proverbs 5:15-23 and Ecclesiastes 12:1-7. Each of the allegories, while resembling a

---

[7]Crenshaw, "Wisdom," 242 (rev. repr. 58ff.).
[8]Other examples include Prov. 5:1-6; 5:15-23; 6:23-24; 20:27; 23:27; 23:29-35; 25:2-3; 27:20.

riddle, actually provides an admonition. In Proverbs 5:15-23, the author stresses the wisdom in marital fidelity. The allegory centers around the image of a cistern. By the end of the pericope, this image has been clearly defined for the reader and, as a result, the allegory is explained.

> Drink water from your own cistern,
> > flowing water from your own well. . . .
> Let your fountain be blessed,
> > and rejoice in the wife of your youth. . . . (Proverbs 5:15, 18)

The second allegory, Ecclesiastes 12:1-7, is a description of approaching death.

Hymns. Even though this literary form is typically associated with the book of Psalms, it does appear in Wisdom Literature, primarily in the book of Job.[9] In form, these hymns are quite similar to the hymns found in the Psalter and in other poetic texts in the Old Testament.[10] In many of the wisdom hymns, the primary theme is the relationship between God and creation. The poet affirms throughout that it is wisdom that serves as the primary contact between the two parties, yet this wisdom is not always so easily accessible. In perhaps the most famous wisdom hymn, Job 28, the reader is told:

> [Wisdom] is hidden from the eyes of all living,
> > and concealed from the birds of the air. . . .
> God understands the way to it,
> > and he knows its place. (Job 28:21, 23)

In a similar vein, Proverbs 8 recounts how Lady Wisdom stands on the street corner, singing her hymn to those in the marketplace. And like the writer of Job, she explains that wisdom, though difficult to find, is worth the search.

> For whoever finds me, finds life

---

[9]See Job 5:9-16; 9:5-12; 12:13-25; 26:5-14; 28; Proverbs 8. In later wisdom literature, particularly in the Wisdom of ben Sirach, this form is used regularly. For example, see 1:1-10; 10:14-18; 24:1-22; 39:12-35. Three lament songs have been identified in this work as well, 33:1-13a; 36:16b-22; 51:10-11.

[10]For a helpful survey of the forms of biblical prayer and hymns, see Patrick D. Miller, *They Cried to the Lord: The Form and Theology of Biblical Prayer* (Minneapolis: Fortress, 1994).

and obtains favor from the LORD;
   but those who miss me injure themselves. . . . (Proverbs 8:35-36a)

While these two hymns address the qualities of wisdom, other hymns found in Job praise God for his qualities both as redeemer and creator.

Disputation. This form of Wisdom Literature is found primarily in the book of Job. The alternating speeches that take place between Job and his consoling friends illustrate this particular form. In the form of a powerful lament, Job questions why tragedy has visited him (chapter 3). The three friends, Eliphaz, Bildad, and Zophar, each appear prepared to defend the ways of God through traditional wisdom theology. Then at the end of each speech, Job offers a rebuttal of sorts. For example, in chapters 4–5 Eliphaz answers Job's lament. In turn, in chapters 6–7, Job responds to Eliphaz. The function of these extended speeches is to allow for adequate presentation of the arguments from traditional wisdom theology. In addition, these speeches allow Job the opportunity to build a serious and damaging critique of that worldview. As the book concludes, even God enters the disputation, in Job 38–41.

Rhetorical questions also play a critical role in the disputation speeches of Job.[11] Each of Job's friends skillfully uses rhetorical strategy in the construction of his argument: Elipaz, 4:7; 15:2, 7-9, 11-14; Bildad, 8:3, 11; 18:4; Zophar, 11:2, 7, 10; and Elihu, 34:13, 17-19, 31-33; 36:19, 22. Even Job employs this technique in his own defense (6:5, 11, 22; 7:12; 9:12; 12:9; 13:7-9). The nature of the questions usually demands a response in the negative: "No" or "Of course not." In 11:2-3, Zophar asks two rhetorical questions:

Should a multitude of words go unanswered,
   and should one full of talk be vindicated?
Should your babble put others to silence,
   and when you mock, shall no one shame you? (Job 11:2-3)

The expected response from Job (and the reader) would be "of course not," thus justifying the need for Zophar to respond to the claims of Job in chapters 9–10.[12]

---

[11]Rhetorical questions appear in other wisdom texts as well. The author of Ecclesiastes makes extensive use of rhetorical questions. For example, see Ecc. 2:2; 3:9; 4:11; 5:5; 6:8; 7:13; 10:14.

[12]On the use of rhetorical strategies in Wisdom Literature, see James L. Crenshaw,

Rhetorical questions even appear in the speeches by God, but they demand a slightly different response. Whereas the questions in the speeches of Job and his friends elicit a negative response, some of the questions in the speeches of God tend to elicit a response such as "I do not know" or "I was not there." In 38:4a, 5, God questions Job:

Where were you when I laid the foundation of the earth? . . .
Who determined its measurements—surely you know!
　　Or who stretched the line upon it? (Job 38:4a, 5)

A proper response would be something like "I was not there." Even more demanding of Job are the questions in 38:24:

What is the way to the place where the light is distributed,
　　or where the east wind is scattered upon the earth? (Job 38:24)

There can only be one response for Job—"I do not know"—which is expressed in Job's silence. The questions by the Creator force Job to recognize his own creatureliness. Throughout the book, Job has demanded to speak to God on equal footing, yet through this series of powerful rhetorical questions, Job realizes the impossibility of such a request, and he is finally forced to admit in 40:4: "See I am of small account; what shall I answer you?" The rhetoric of God has accomplished its intended goal.

Autobiographical Narrative. This form of Wisdom Literature is sometimes referred to as "confession" or "reflection."[13] Central to the work of the sage is observation and experience. These two avenues enable the sage to consider the world around him and to glean its wisdom. These insights then become the subject matter of the autobiographical narrative. Although autobiographical narrative does appear in Proverbs (4:3-9;

Education in Ancient Israel, ABRL (New York: Doubleday, 1998) 133-37; also see Crenshaw's "Wisdom and Authority: Sapiential Rhetoric and Its Warrants (1982)," 326-43 in *Urgent Advice and Probing Questions,* esp. 332-37. Crenshaw explains the strategies in terms of three categories: *ethos, pathos,* and *logos. Ethos* is the appeal to the character of the speaker (cf. Job 8:8-10). The rhetoric of *pathos* appeals to the emotion of the hearer (cf. Job 33:14-18). And the rhetoric of *logos* appeals to the coherence of the argument—its logical consistency. These strategies can be found throughout the speeches of Job and his friends.

[13]See Roland Murphy, *Wisdom Literature: Job, Proverbs, Ruth, Canticles, Ecclesiastes and Esther,* FOTL (Grand Rapids MI: Eerdmans, 1981) 130; and Crenshaw, "Wisdom," 256-58 (rev. repr. 70-71).

24:30-34) and in the Psalms (37), it dominates the book of Ecclesiastes.[14] Most scholars consider Ecclesiastes 1:12–2:26 as representative of the autobiographical narrative. In this text, the writer begins by relating his desire to obtain wisdom:

> I, the Teacher, when king over Israel in Jerusalem, applied my mind to seek and to search out by wisdom all that is done under heaven. . . . And I applied my mind to know wisdom and to know madness and folly. (Ecclesiastes 1:12-13a, 17a)

The remainder of the book recounts his findings based on experience. The use of anecdotes, personal stories, and examples throughout the book contribute to the autobiographical feel of the entire book.There are also words and phrases that enhance the autobiographical nature of Ecclesiastes. Many of these appear in the opening narrative (1:12–2:26), and continue to appear throughout the book. For example, the author employs the first person pronoun (*'ánî*) frequently (twenty-nine times). In addition to the appearance of the first person pronoun, a number of verbs relating to observation and experience appear in the first person. The primary formula used in the autobiographical narrative is "I saw . . . and I have seen." This appears in close proximity with the verb "to pass by."[15] For example, in Psalm 37:35-36a, the psalmist has employed two of the three verb forms:

> I have seen the wicked oppressing,
>   and towering like a cedar of Lebanon.
> Again I passed by, and there were no more. (Psalm 37:35-36a)

The writer of Ecclesiastes has opted for a slight variation in the autobiographical narrative formula. The verb "to pass by" does not appear in Ecclesiastes. Instead, while the author still makes extensive use of the verb "I saw" (1:14; 2:24; 3:10, 16; 4:1, 4, 15; 5:17; 6:1; 7:15; 8:9, 10; 9:11, 13; 10:5, 7), the author opts for other verbs that connote observation: "I said in my heart" (1:16; 2:1, 15; 3:17); "I gave my heart" (1:13, 17: 8:9, 16); "I know" (1:17; 2:14; 3:12, 14; 8:12). Together, these verbs

---

[14]Tremper Longman contends that the entire central portion of the book (1:12–12:7) is an extended autobiographical narrative. See *The Book of Ecclesiastes*, NICOT (Grand Rapids MI: Eerdmans, 1998) 15-24.

[15]Crenshaw, "Wisdom," 256 (rev. repr. 70).

not only emphasize the personal nature of the search, they demonstrate the method of acquisition of knowledge: observation and experience.[16]

The Setting in Life

The forms of Wisdom Literature mentioned above emerged from various settings in the life of Ancient Israel. While the literature is not explicit in all cases, it does hint at several possible settings where the forms and ideas of Wisdom Literature may have been developed and taught.

Family. The patriarchal nature of the Israelite family demanded that the father assume the primary responsibility for instruction. Within the family, the father acted as the resident sage, instructing the sons in the traditions of the family and of local wisdom. Many of the proverbs that seem to come from this setting focus on agricultural imagery, self-control, and proper relationships: misbehavior in any of these areas could have dramatic consequences on the family, in particular, and the local tribe in general. The phrase "my son"[17] appears throughout the Book of Proverbs (1:8, 10, 15; 2:1; 3:1, 11, 21; 4:10, 20; 5:1, 20; 6:13, 20; 7:1; 19:27; 23:19, 26; 24:13, 21; 27:11), reflecting the familial context of ancient Israelite education. [18]Although the father acted as the primary sage in matters of education, the mother did teach, and her teachings were considered authoritative (6:20; 10:1; 15:20; 20:20; 23:22, 25; 28:24; 31:1, 10-31). In the opening chapter of Proverbs, the sage mentions the instruction of both father and mother.

> Hear, [my son], your father's instruction,
>   and do not reject your mother's teaching. (Proverbs 1:8)

That the "mother's teaching" appear in parallel construction to the "father's instruction" suggests that while the father may have acted as the

---

[16]In addition to the use of these verbs, the autobiographical narrative actually employs a number of different genres. Throughout the opening chapters of Ecclesiastes, there are proverbs, sayings, rhetorical questions, and even woe oracles. These other genres, used in the service of the autobiographical narrative, assist the author in presenting his "finds."

[17]The "son" of the text routinely has been changed to "child" in certain modern, politically correct versions, including TEV and CEV, NJB, and NRSV. (Some recent versions have retained the original, notably the REB, NAB, and of course the NJV.)

[18]Sages sometimes referred to their students as "my son." The metaphorical use of this phrase seems to have been lifted from the familial context, where it represented the intimate relationship between the father and son.

primary teacher in the family, the mother also played an important role in the education of the children.

Royal Advisor. The organization of Israel into a monarchy prompted the emergence of a number of different occupations. Certain advisors or sages, for example, served the monarchy primarily as counselors. While it is questionable whether there was a formal organization known as "the royal court," there were individuals who did provide wise advice to the monarch. The narratives concerning the reigns of David, Solomon, and the other monarchs mention such advisors.

One of the more famous examples of a royal court advisor is in 2 Samuel 16:20-23. In this text, Absalom seeks the wisdom of Ahithophel, a court advisor. Ahithophel speaks his words of advice to Absalom, which Absalom follows. Then the narrator explains:

> Now in those days the counsel that Ahithophel gave was as if one consulted the oracle of God; so all the counsel of Ahithophel was esteemed, both by David and by Absalom. (2 Samuel 16:23)

The members of the royal court occupied more than just an ancillary role in the functioning of the empire. They often represented the wisdom of God to those in power. First Kings 3–11 recounts the story of the reign of Solomon. Throughout the narrative, there are reminders that Solomon was the wise king *par excellence* and that, as a result, the royal court under Solomon epitomized the role of wise counsel. From the beginning of his reign when he prays for and receives a "wise mind," until the end when the Queen of Sheba "could not believe her own eyes" due to the wisdom and rule of Solomon, the reign of Solomon is characterized by the various facets of wisdom. In 1 Kings 3, he decides between two women which one is the actual mother of a child. Because of his judicious and wise decision, all Israel "perceived the wisdom of God was in him." A chapter later, Solomon is called "wiser than anyone else" (1 Kings 4:31). His abilities included composing proverbs and songs (1 Kings 4:32). The wisdom of Solomon appeared encyclopedic, with his wide-ranging knowledge of the various forms of flora and fauna in the region (1 Kings 4:33). Together these stories indicate that the nature of the court under Solomon exemplified the pursuit of wisdom.

Portions of the Book of Proverbs may best represent the form of wisdom developed and passed on in the royal court. The clearest example appears in Proverbs 25–29, a section entitled "Other proverbs of Solomon that the officials of King Hezekiah of Judah copied" (25:1). The first eight verses make explicit reference to the king and his court. The remainder of the proverbs appear more general in nature, but still reflect the work of the "officials of King Hezekiah" in the preservation of wisdom. This would suggest that while members of the royal court served as advisors, as was the case with Ahithophel, they also served as preservers and recorders of tradition.[19]

School. The third possible setting for the transmission of wisdom is the school. In the Old Testament, there is little explicit reference to a school. The text most often cited to support the notion of a school appears in the Wisdom of Ben Sirach:

> Come to me, all you that need instruction,
>   and learn in my school. (Sirach 51:23 TEV)

"My school" in the original Hebrew and Greek is literally "house of study," "house of learning" (KJV), or "house of instruction" (NAB, NRSV). Thus, by the second century BCE, there probably were small residential academies in Jerusalem with an emphasis on teaching and instruction. The larger question of whether schools existed in Israel prior the second century BCE is vigorously debated, with no clear answer available.[20]

Although no official school building has been recovered, there are possible hints of a school in the biblical literature. Some texts suggest that some type of training existed during the period of the monarchy (1 Kings 12:8, 10; 2 Kings 10:1, 5-6), and other texts suggest the presence of temple school (Isaiah 28:9-13).[21] In addition, there are inscriptions that suggest the presence of some type of educational institution in Palestine, perhaps as early as the eighth century, if not earlier.[22] These types of institutions may be more aptly understood as guilds that

---

[19]Joseph Blenkinsopp suggests that under Hezekiah, Jerusalem reached its social and economic zenith, thus paving the way for "a social and economic infrastructure capable of generating, or at any rate, of supporting, a genuine literary tradition": *Sage, Prophet, and Priest* (Louisville: Westminster/John Knox, 1995) 32-33. Despite this claim, Blenkinsopp is careful to avoid separating these individuals into an official class.

[20]For a thorough treatment on the issue of schools in Ancient Israel, see Crenshaw, *Education in Ancient Israel*, 85-113; see also Crenshaw, "The Sage in Proverbs (1990)," 406-16 in *Urgent Advice and Probing Questions*, esp. 409-11.

[21]Perdue, *Wisdom and Creation*, 72-73.

[22]Crenshaw, *Education in Ancient Israel*, 100-108.

trained young men in the scribal tradition. If such guilds did exist, the collection and preservation of written materials such as annals, records, and even wisdom material such as proverbs may have been taken place in those groups.

Summary. While it may be impossible to determine the exact setting in life of all of the wisdom corpus, some general observations can be made. The family unit was probably the primary setting for the distribution of wisdom and the education of the young. But the importance of the family unit for education did not cease with the organization of Israel into a nation. The family played a critical role in education throughout the history of the nation.

As noted above, with the rise of the nation, certain institutions developed, namely, the royal court and the "school." These institutions did not replace the family, but served to enhance the educational opportunities of young people in the community. These schools probably not only reaffirmed the moral education received at home, but also sought to train students in other matters including legal matters and political affairs, as well as literary activity such as writing and copying.

Conclusion

The authors of the Wisdom Literature used various forms to express their message. Quite often they would intermix and combine different forms in an effort to increase the poetic quality of their writings. Students who wish to read competently the Wisdom Literature cannot do so without an adequate understanding of those forms. These forms aid in conveying meaning.

Students who read Wisdom Literature must also keep in mind that these texts emerge from real life. Students typically mistake Wisdom Literature as material that is only academic or theoretical in nature. But as Roland Murphy has said, these materials "are not the creation of a study desk; they grew out of human situation and needs."[23] By searching for the setting in life for these literary forms, not only does one engage in good form criticism, one discovers the connection that these books had and continue to have with the world around us.

---

[23]Roland Murphy, *The Tree of Life*, ABRL (New York: Doubleday, 1990) 4.

Chapter 11

Biblical Wisdom
in Its Ancient Middle Eastern Context ·

Thomas Smothers

The Hebrew Bible provides abundant witness to Israel's contacts with the surrounding nations. War, trade and commerce, the inclusion of peoples from other nations with different religions and cultures, insured that Israel could not pursue its life in isolation. The struggle by some to maintain Israel's identity and distinctiveness was unceasing and often bitter. Israel was always conscious of itself as one among many.

It is impossible to study ancient Israel's literature in isolation. The study of the covenant tradition is enhanced by the knowledge of the form and content of international treaties. Israelite law must be compared and contrasted with ancient Middle Eastern law codes and legal practices. The study of the prophetic movement in Israel received new impetus with the recovery of texts describing prophetic activiy in Mesopotamia and in the northwest Semitic area, particularly the texts from Mari mentioning prophetic activity and the reports of their statements. The study of Israelite religion and the classical Hebrew language has been put on a new level with the discovery of the texts from Ugarit. Comparative study has long since become *de rigeur* for responsible exegetes, for only by comparative study can the areas held in common with other nations, as well as the unique features of Israel's thought and the thought of each of the other nations, be fully appreciated.

Several references in the Hebrew Bible indicate that Israel knew about, and in some instances, was acquainted with the wisdom traditions

---

ˑThis essay is offered in grateful appreciation to Professor Marvin Tate, colleague and friend, who, in his long and distinguished career, has introduced many generations of students to the joys of the study of the wisdom literature, and has helped them gain an understanding of the crucial and essential place of the wisdom literature in the life of faith.

of its neighbors (see below on Proverbs 22:17–24:22). Genesis 41:8, Exodus 7:11, and Isaiah 19:11-15 refer to the wise men of Egypt and their activities relating to dream interpretation and providing wise counsel. First Kings 4:30 (MT 5:10) states that "Solomon's wisdom surpassed the wisdom of all the people of the east, and all the wisdom of Egypt." The wisdom of the Edomites is referred to in Jeremiah 49:7 and in Obadiah 8. First Kings 10:1-5 relates that the queen of Sheba visited Jerusalem to test Solomon's wisdom with riddles and that Solomon answered all questions.

The recovery in the last century and a half of a significant portion of the wisdom literature from Israel's neighbors allowed these biblical references to take on new life and depth, and has made it possible to read the Bible in as broad a context as possible. Wisdom traditions dealt with common human concerns, concerns that know no national, religious, cultural, or ethnic boundaries: how to succeed in life and, when success was not gained, how to deal with the problems of life and the disappointed expectations that forced one to question the correctness of religious and societal norms. The commonality of human experience does not, of course, blur the unique contributions each culture made in wisdom teaching and speculation.

A basic problem in the comparative study of Israelite wisdom literature and other Middle Eastern literature is that of the definition of wisdom. Biblical scholars, who have traditionally used the term "wisdom" to refer both to the prudential, instructional literature of Proverbs and Sirach and to the philosophical books of Job and Qoheleth, have also been in the habit of labeling "Wisdom Literature" those non-Israelite documents that parallel in content and somewhat in form the biblical books. Specialists in Egyptian Literature, while noting that the term wisdom used in this way was not native to Egypt, have tended to follow this practice.[1] But scholars of Mesopotamian literature have been less receptive to the idea of "Wisdom Literature" as a rubric. Lambert has argued that although this term is used for convenience for some Mesopotamian texts, it is foreign to ancient Mesopotamia, and "since Wisdom as a category in Babylonian literature is nothing more than a group of texts which happen to cover roughly the same area, there is no precise canon by

---

[1]R. J. Williams, "The Sage of Ancient Egypt in the Light of Recent Scholarship," *Journal of the American Oriental Society* 101/1 (1981): 1.

which to recognize them."[2] In a similar vein, Buccellati, after identifying "wisdom" themes in several kinds of Mesopotamian literature reflecting both folk tradition and the sophisticated scholarly output of the schools, concludes that he cannot identify wisdom with a literary genre because wisdom themes are scattered throughout a variety of literary forms which, in turn, reflect a wide range of environments. Thus he cannot identify a coherent textual canon which might be called "Wisdom Literature." He prefers to view wisdom as an intellectual phenomenon in itself, and to keep wisdom separate from literature.[3]

All of this is, of course, more than just quibbling over terms. These are attempts to be reflective, exegetical, and descriptive. In any case, if one is going to advocate comparative study of ancient Middle Eastern "wisdom" literature, the parameters of the study have to be set. Without trying to define wisdom or to identify its social settings or all of its literary genres, this brief essay will take as its point of departure the books of Proverbs, Qoheleth, and Job and the issues raised in them, and will identify and briefly discuss texts from other parts of the ancient Middle East that parallel them in content, concerns, and, where possible, in literary genre. Readers who consider the biblical wisdom books alongside similar treatments from the Middle East will be able to judge for themselves the values of comparative analysis.

Prudential Wisdom

Prudential wisdom literature consists of proverbs, aphorisms, admonitions, and riddles designed to show the way to success and to life. This kind of literature is pragmatic, confident of its goals and methods, concerned to preserve and treat as normative the traditions and teachings of respected sages, and often assumes a well-known divinely ordained order of reality for the human world to which persons may conform themselves by appropriating wisdom teaching.

From ancient Egypt have come several texts which may be compared with the book of Proverbs. These texts are labeled *sboyet*, "instruction." Although *sboyet* may not be called a wisdom genre since it includes

---

[2]W. G. Lambert, *Babylonian Wisdom Literature* (Winona Lake IN: Eisenbrauns, 1996) 1-2.

[3]Giorgio Buccellati, "Wisdom and Not: The Case of Mesopotamia," *Journal of the American Oriental Society* 101/1 (1981): 44.

several kinds of texts which are not collections or proverbial sayings, all texts so labeled have the goal of imparting instruction.[4] Of particular importance here are those instructions which take the form of gnomic sayings, at least in part.

The *Instruction of the Vizier Ptah-hotep*[5] comes from some time in the Old Kingdom. The instruction was for Ptah-hotep's son whom he prepared to succeed him in office. The chief emphasis is on the ability to speak, that is, the ability to give sound counsel to the king in a wisdom way and at the proper time. The ability to speak effectively comes from the careful appropriation of the tested ideas of the ancestors. The wise man is the one who listens and obeys. "When hearing is good, speaking is good."[6] Practical advice appropriate for successful life at court includes renunciation of arrogance, support of justice, being wary of the strange woman, generosity in sharing wealth, and aloofness from an emotional opponent. The work concludes with a contrast between the wise man and the hot-tempered or hotheaded man, a major theme in the Book of Proverbs (15:18; 22:24; 29:22).

The *Instruction for King Meri-ka-re*[7] reflects the confused conditions between the Old and Middle Kingdoms. The king instructs his son not to depend too much on royal prerogatives, but rather to adopt a pragmatic approach: promote the good of society because it will be to your personal advantage. Again, the ability to speak is central: "be a craftsman in speech." Truth comes already "fully brewed." Wisdom is to conform to the traditions of the ancestors. The young king is counseled to practice patience, respect people and their property boundaries, protect the helpless, reject covetousness and the showing of partiality, and, finally, revere the god and be punctilious in religious observance. The pragmatic motivation for all this instruction is clear: do these things because they work and are to your advantage.

---

[4]Williams, "The Sages of Ancient Egypt," 7.

[5]"The Instruction of the Vizier Ptah-hotep," trans. John A. Wilson, in *Ancient Near Eastern Texts*, ed. James B. Pritchard (Princeton NJ: Princeton University Press, 1955) 412-14.

[6]Ibid., 414.

[7]"The Instruction for King Meri-ka-re," in *ANET*, 414-18. For a more recent translation, see Mirian Lichtheim, "Merikare," in *The Context of Scripture*, vol. 1, *Canonical Compositions from the Biblical World*, ed. W. W. Hallo (Leiden: Brill, 1997) 61-66.

The *Instruction of King Amen-em-het*[8] from the time of the Twelfth Dynasty, reflects unsettled conditions and is pessimistic in tone. The work consists mainly of a description of troubles during the king's reign despite his exemplary life. He counsels his son to beware of making intimate friends because they often lead a rebellion. What is significant about this brief work is its realistic assessment of the "ideal" life: it implies that traditional wisdom teaching about the way to gain success had failed in the case of this king.

Whereas the previous instructions were for courtiers and kings, the *Instruction of Ani*,[9] also a Twelfth Dynasty work, offers instructions for the common people aimed at success in everyday life, reflecting the increasing importance of the growth of middle-class life.[10] Thus, Ani instructs his son to establish a stable home while he is still young, to beware of the strange woman, to practice guarding his tongue (the "truly silent" motif), to refrain from getting drunk, to prepare for his death, to eschew fraud, to be frugal, to show respect for elders, and to be generous to the needy. The epilogue features perhaps a growing resistance to unreflective dependence on traditional instruction, for the son objects that he is incapable of such high standards, and that he does not like to be forced to follow a life which requires virtues he does not have. Ani answers that even animals learn from experience and thus defends traditional instruction.

The *Instruction of Amenemope*,[11] dating from the Ramesside period, is elegant and comprehensive. Lichtheim suggests that "With this long work, the Instruction genre reaches its culmination."[12] The work consists of thirty chapters of prudential wisdom, focusing not so much on success or on getting ahead in life, as on a life of moderation and balance. Chapter 30 begins with these words:

Look to these thirty chapters,

---

[8]"The Instruction of King Amen-em-het," in *ANET*, 418-19; Lichtheim, "Amenem-het," in *The Context of Scripture*, 66-68.

[9]"The Instruction of Ani," in *ANET*, 420-21; Lichtheim, "Instruction of Ani," in *The Context of Scripture* 110-15.

[10]Lichtheim, "Instruction of Ani," 110.

[11]"The Instruction of Amen-em-opet," trans. Wilson, in *ANET*, 421-25; Lichtheim, "Instruction of Amenemope," in *The Context of Scripture*, 115-22.

[12]Lichtheim, "Instruction of Amenemope," 115.

They inform, they educate;
They are the foremost of all books,
They make the ignorant wise,
If they are read to the ignorant
He is cleansed through them.[13]

In the introduction to a central section of Proverbs, 22:17–24:22, there are included these words:

Have I not written for you thirty sayings
    of admonitions and knowledge,
to show you what is right and true,
    so that you may give a true answer
        to those who sent you? (Proverbs 22:20-21)

This mention of the thirty sayings as well as the many similarities and parallels in content strongly suggest that the author of this unit in Proverbs was acquainted with the Instruction of Amenemope.[14]

The *Instructions of Onchsheshonqy*,[15] dating perhaps to the last part of the fifth century BCE, consists of some 550 or more sayings, proverbs, aphorisms, and admonitions. The narrative frame relates that Onchsheshonqy had been accused of involvement in a plot agaist the throne, and, although innocent, he was imprisoned. He spent the years recording his sayings on potsherds for the instruction of his son. The instructions themselves are of much the same type and content as the other works just surveyed.

Finally, I should mention the *Satire on the Trades*,[16] a work known from texts from the Eighteenth and Nineteenth Dynasties. On the journey to enroll his son Pepi in the school for scribes, Dua-Khety extolled the advantages of the scribal profession by satirizing no fewer than eighteen

---

[13]Ibid., 121-22.

[14]For a comparative treatment, see Glendon Bryce, *A Legacy of Wisdom: The Egyptian Contribution to the Wisdom of Israel* (Lewisburg and London: Bucknell University and Associated University Presses, 1979).

[15]Berend Gemser, "The Instructions of Onchsheshonqy and Biblical Wisdom Literature," *Supplements to Vetus Testamentum*, Congress Volume 7 (Leiden: E. J. Brill, 1960) 102-28.

[16]"The Satire on the Trades," trans. Wilson, in *ANET*, 432-34; Lichtheim, "Dua-Khety or The Satire on the Trades," in *The Context of Scripture*, 122-25.

other professions. The work ends with a small collection of practical advice, typical of the other instruction literature, intended to help the young scribe maintain his status and dignity in the profession and in society.

The amount of prudential wisdom recovered from the Mesopotamian areas is not nearly so extensive, but is of equal importance for the comparative study of biblical wisdom. Collections of Sumerian wise sayings[17] put together from a large number of tablets, give a good impression of Sumerian observations on secular life, on how to achieve success and avoid failure. These sayings consist of proverbs, observations on the natural order from which wisdom for living may be abstracted, observations on the consequences of unwise and immoral behavior, and admonitions in imperative form. Many of these observations are relevant for any time and any culture. They formed a basic part of the student curriculum because sometimes the teacher's exemplar is followed by the student's copy on the same tablet.

The *Instruction of Shuruppak*[18] from the early second millenium, known also from Akkadian fragments, purports to be addressed by Shuruppak to his son, Ziusudra, the hero of the flood story (Ut-napishtim in the Akkadian version). These instructions, often in the form of admonitions (note the repetitive beginning, "do not"), deal with the problems and temptations of normal life and how to deal effectively with them. Typical of wisdom teaching in general, the instructions are pragmatic, counseling right behavior out of self-interest.

The *Counsels of Wisdom*[19] comes from perhaps the Cassite period. Although the beginning is lost, the reference to "my son" and the entire contents confirm that the document takes the standard form of instruction of father to son. The areas of concern are those characteristic of wisdom instruction all over the ancient Middle East: guard your speech, avoid disputes, do not retaliate, treat the poor with consideration, stay away

---

[17]Bendt Alster, "Sumerian Proverb Collection 3," in *The Context of Scripture*, 563-67. For a complete and up-to-date edition of the Sumerian proverbs, see Alster, *Proverbs of Ancient Sumer: The World's Earliest Proverb Collections* (Bethesda MD: CDL Press, 1997).

[18]Alster, "Shuruppak," in *The Context of Scripture*, 569-70.

[19]W. G. Lambert, *Babylonian Wisdom*, 96-107; "Counsels of Wisdom," trans. R. H. Pfeiffer, in *ANET*, 426-27.

from one who is not your wife, guard the possessions of your master, be religious because it is proper and it pays.

The *Advice to a Prince*[20] dates from the late Assyrian period and counsels any prospective ruler to avoid policies that would cause his downfall. The document employs the literary style of omens: "If . . . then . . . ," in which the apodosis spells out the threatened consequences. The emphasis is on social justice and seems to have been inspired to protect the special interests of Sippar, Nippur, and Babylon.

It is surprising and disappointing that the excavations at Ugarit have not yet brought to light collections, or even examples, of wisdom instruction written in Ugarit. Found at the site, however, were fragments of a document written in Akkadian which is of the genre of instruction. RS 22.439[21] contains the instruction of a man to his son about how to travel safely and how to behave properly so as to achieve success. He was to guard his tongue, leave the property of others alone, avoid the strange woman, avoid strife, and other issues similar to the *Counsels of Wisdom*. The instruction claims to be in accord with the learning of the ancestors and therefore authoritative. This document is not an example of Canaanite wisdom, but it shows that the scribal school stood in the tradition of the *Instruction of Shuruppak* and the *Counsels of Wisdom*.

Reading the Book of Proverbs alongside these examples of instructional literature reveals the common ground shared by international wisdom. Many a proverb and instruction may be exchanged without loss or harm to any other tradition. And of course, the common structure and commonality of content of Proverbs 22:17–24:22 and the *Instruction of Amenemope* is obvious. But comparative analysis can take us farther. Instructional or didactic literature was based on the appeal to authority. The father passed on the traditional learning of the ancestors, and it was the task of the would-be wise man to appropriate what was tried and true, hallowed by antiquity, and to invent nothing. The didactic method employed in Proverbs is similar, as witnessed in the constant appeal to audition (Proverbs 1:8; 2:1; 3:1; 4:1; passim). The way to life is given by

---

[20]Lambert, *Babylonian Wisdom*, 110-15.

[21]J. Nougayrol, "Sagesses (R.S.22.439)," in *Ugaritica V, Mission de Ras Shamra XVI*, ed. J. Nougayrol, Ch. Virolleaud, C. F. A. Schaeffer (Paris: Imprimere National, 1968) 273-90; Duane E. Smith, "Wisdom Genres in R.S. 22.439," in *Ras Shamra Parallels 2*, ed. Loren R. Fisher (Roma: Pontificium Institutum Biblicum, 1975) 215-47.

the father and the mother, not discovered by the son. Also it is clear that in the wisdom traditions the emphasis was on the individual and his welfare, not on the nation as such, and on the corollary of individual retribution. It can no longer be argued that the concept of individual retribution made its appearance in Israel only in the time of Jeremiah and Ezekiel. And many of the ethical concerns in Proverbs, such as just weights and measures, the evils of bribery, caring for and being generous toward the poor, are paralleled in the Egyptian and Mesopotamian instructions. These were common concerns of the wise in all cultures, so that it can no longer be argued that Israelite wise men derived all of their ethical teachings from the prophets.

Finally, the relative reserve toward the cult in Proverbs is an orientation characteristic of international wisdom. References to cult or religion are those which tend to enjoin religious participation as part of the life of any person, usually in order to gain success.

Speculative Wisdom

It was inevitable that the generally positive and hopeful view of human life promised by the wise teachers—if only people would follow the normative practices and teachings passed down from the ancestors—would be brought into question by the facts of human experience. The wise men themselves, along with others who dealt with the vagaries of an inconsistent and often incomprehensible world, faced forthrightly the mystery of why the righteous and innocent were rewarded with suffering and injustice, while the wicked were recompensed with prosperity. The documents from Egypt and Mesopotamia which gave voice to a more speculative, or even more pessimistic, view of life took the forms of social criticism, protest literature, or dialogue about the possibility of finding meaning in life.

The *Admonitions of Ipuwer*[22] from ca. 2000 BCE is a work of social criticism which describes the chaos and the reversal of social norms in Egypt. An unnamed king is accused of being responsible, and even the sun god Re, is criticized for failing to perceive the evil in human nature. The hot-tempered man says, "If I knew where god is, I would serve him."

---

[22]Nili Shupak, "The Admonitions of an Egyptian Sage: The Admonitions of Ipuwer," in *The Context of Scripture*, 93-98; "The Admonitions of Ipuwer," trans. Wilson, in *ANET*, 441-44.

The *Complaints of Khakheperre-sonbe*[23] composed during the Middle Kingdom also describe the chaotic state of Egyptian society. The author wished he had new words "void of repetitions; not maxims of past speech, spoken by the ancestors." But his complaints take the usual form and use the standard modes of expression. The work may suggest that both standard language and traditional wisdom instruction were not fully capable of dealing competently with the realities of life.

The *Tale of the Eloquent Peasant*,[24] coming from the time of the Middle Kingdom (Twelfth or Thirteenth Dynasty), tells the story of a man who, having been unjustly divested of his property, carried his complaint to the high steward. The peasant was so eloquent of speech that the high steward reported the case to the king. The king directed the steward to be silent, to let the peasant talk, and to put in writing all his speeches. The needs of the peasant and his family were to be provided without his knowing their source. One is reminded of the prologue to the Book of Job where the sufferings of Job are put in a context about which he never knew. Nine times the peasant appeared before the high steward to protest, and finally he was vindicated. Although injustice is the theme, it seems that ultimately the work is a justification of the art of eloquent and effective speech, a central concern of the teachers of traditional wisdom.

The *Dispute over Suicide*,[25] or the *Dispute of a Man with his Ba*, probably reflects unsettled conditions just prior to the Middle Kingdom. A man, distressed over the apparent supremacy of injustice and disorder, sees no solution but to commit suicide, and he tries to get his *ba* (soul, or other self) to agree to share his fate. The *ba* resists at first, but finally agrees to honor the man's decision.

From Mesopotamia, the *Dialogue between a Man and His God*,[26] known only from an Old Babylonian document, appears to focus on the problem of theodicy. A man's burdens (probably illness) became too heavy, and he cried out to his god for relief. Following the standard the-

---

[23]Shupak, "The Complaints of Khakheperre-sonb," in *The Context of Scripture*, 104-106.

[24]Shupak, "The Eloquent Peasant," in *The Context of Scripture*, 98-104; "The Protests of the Eloquent Peasant," trans. Wilson, in *ANET*, 407-10.

[25]"A Dispute over Suicide," trans. Wilson, in *ANET*, 405-407.

[26]Benjamin R. Foster, "Dialogue between a Man and his God," in *The Context of Scripture*, 485.

ology, he assumed that he suffered because of some wrong he had committed, but he protested: "the wrong I did, I did not know." And although the text becomes fragmentary at this point, he seems to have blamed his god for much of his trouble. But the god responds with healing and with assurance of divine favor, and counsels the man to care for the needy.

I Will Praise the Lord of Wisdom (*Ludlul bêl nêmeqi*),[27] coming from the Cassite period in Babylonia, follows the same pattern as the preceding *Dialogue*. An official found himself in dire straits, forsaken by the gods, by the court, and by family and friends. The clergy with all their esoteric arts were unable to discover the reason for his misfortune. Prayers were unavailing. He suffered as one who had committed impiety, although he protested his innocence. In his bewilderment he asked:

> Who knows the will of the gods in heaven?
> Who understands the plans of the underworld gods?
> Where have mortals learnt the way of a god?[28]

Various diseases and physical disabilities assaulted him, but still the diviners and exorcists could neither determine the cause of his troubles, nor predict how long the sufferer would have to remain in distress. In his fitful sleep, he had three dreams in which three figures presage his deliverance, and upon awakening, he discovered his illness was over. There follows a lengthy and detailed reversal of each of his maladies along with his declaration that Marduk, who is the lord of wisdom, had heard his prayers finally and had restored him.

The purpose of this poem was obviously to praise Marduk for his power to deliver the sufferer and to affirm that cultic faithfulness eventually did pay off. But this orthodox resolution does not really solve the problem of theodicy. The sufferer did not know what sin he had committed, although it was obvious to him that he had failed in some way. The sticking point is that the ways of the god are unfathomable. The ideas of the "hiddenness" of the god and the inscrutability of divine ways place in jeopardy the possibility of finding meaning in life.

---

[27]Foster, "The Poem of the Righteous Sufferer," in *The Context of Scripture*, 486-92; Lambert, *Babylonian Wisdom*, 21-62; Pfeiffer, "I Will Praise the Lord of Wisdom," trans. Pfeiffer, in *ANET*, 434-37.

[28]Lambert, *Babylonian Wisdom*, 41.

The *Babylonian Theodicy*[29] is in the form of a dialogue between a sufferer and a friend who offers orthodox responses. The sufferer complains that his parents had died while he was still a child, and consequently he had been placed in a disadvantageous position in life. His friend responded that all have to die and that experience shows that the pious get wealthy anyway. The sufferer asked, "Can a happy life be a certainty?" The friend answers that a life that seeks justice will experience the kindness of the gods. And so the dialogue continues. If the gods are kind and just and if people receive the just rewards of their deeds, then why does human experience indicate the opposite? In the *Theodicy*, the orthodox friend resorts to the same argument that the sufferer in *Ludlul* raised in a question: "The purpose of the gods is as remote as the netherworld . . . divine purpose is as remote as innermost heaven." And the friend defended the gods with the observation that they endowed people from birth with lies and falsehood, so what can a person expect? The theodicy problem remains unsolved, with the poem ending with the sufferer's petitions to the gods for help.

The *Dialogue of Pessimism*[30] reports a conversation between a man and his slave. Every kind of activity proposed enthusiastically by the master is praised by the slave who emphasizes its positive features. When the master despondently reverses each of his intentions, the slave follows suit by pointing out the negative or dangerous features of each activity. Finally, the master asks, "What then is good?" To which the slave replies, "To have my neck and your neck broken and to be thrown into the river of good." When the master threatened to kill the slave and to send him ahead to the underworld, the slave replied that his master would not outlive him three days, by which he meant either the master could not survive without the services of his slave, or that the master would see immediately that death solves all problems and promptly follow the slave there. Whether this dialogue is viewed as a serious philosophical work or as

---

[29]Foster, "The Babylonian Theodicy," in *The Context of Scripture*, 492-495; Lambert, *Babylonian Wisdom*, 63-89; "A Dialogue about Human Misery," trans. Pfeiffer, in *ANET*, 438-40.

[30]Lambert, *Babylonian Wisdom*, 139-49; Alasdair Livingstone, "Dialogue of Pessimism or the Obliging Slave," in *The Context of Scripture*, 495-96; "A Pessimistic Dialogue between Master and Servant," trans. Pfeiffer, in *ANET*, 437-38.

satire, or perhaps as a combination,[31] the problem of finding meaning in life is highlighted, and the proposed solution—suicide—is taken seriously.

From Ugarit has come a tablet written in Babylonian which reads like a miniature of *I Will Praise the Lord of Wisdom*. R.S. 25.460[32] is a single tablet with about forty-five lines that are legible. The sufferer complains that his oracles are obscured ("muddy"). The diviners and exorcists could not explain his illness, nor could they predict a time limit for it. But in this account, he was not abandoned by his family. He could not sleep; he ate his tears as his food. But then Marduk came to his rescue, although there is full acknowledgement that Marduk was the one who had smitten him.

> He confined and bound me,
> He broke me to pieces and broke me off.
> He scattered me and poured me out.
> He who poured me has gathered me.
> He who threw me down has exalted me.[33]

Like *I Will Praise the Lord of Wisdom*, this poem is a hymn of praise for Marduk, but unlike the longer poem, it lacks—at least in it present fragmentary condition—philosophical pondering over the ways of the god.

Also from Ugarit have come three fragmentary bilingual tablets (Sumerian and Akkadian) whose contents, consisting of sayings or maxims, are closely related and partly overlapping. R.S. 25.130,[34] the longest fragment, is in dialogue form. One voice laments the human condition, the other offers traditional answers representative, no doubt, of orthodox theological thought. The following is a tentative translation arranged to indicate a possible identification of the alternating lament and answer sections:

> Where are those great kings [of old]?
> Women do not conceive, do not give birth anymore?
>
> Like the heaven is remote, the hand [. . .]
> Like the underworld is deep, no one knows it.

---

[31]Lambert, *Babylonian Wisdom*, 139-41.
[32]Foster, "A Sufferer's Salvation," in *The Context of Scripture*, 486; J. Nougayrol, "(Juste) Souffrant (R.S. 25.460)," in *Ugaritica V*, 265-73.
[33]My translation of lines 35-39.
[34]Nougayrol, "R.S. 25.130," in *Ugaritica V*, 293-97.

The life of all [the earth?] is blinded.
A life without light, does it not return to death?
In exchange for the happiness of a day, there is a day of stupor;
The year passes with 30,000 [disasters?].

With Ea, the primordial plans are traced,
According to the divine pleasure the lots are cast.
Men do not themselves know what they have done.
The meaning of their days and nights is found with the gods

Has no one assigned forced labor for mankind?
Has no one spoken evil about mankind?
Has no one held the weak in contempt?

The crippled man will pass the swift man,
The rich man will beg from the hand of the poor.
This is the lot of the faithful.

Works such as these from the nations surrounding Israel—with which the books of Qoheleth and Job resonate in so many ways—place the limits of human understanding at the center of the human dilemma. Humans complained that they did not always know what they had done to cause the wrath of heaven to fall on them; neither did they understand the ways of the deity. They recognized that the one who caused the suffering was the only one could restore, but who knew whether or on what basis the deity would deliver them? That such speculative, often heterodox and pessimistic, literature survived and sometimes attained a sort of "canonical" status, confirms that doubt and honest questioning in the face of an opaque world had a legitimate place in the life of the person who struggled for faith.

Conclusion

The issues raised in these nonbiblical sources are quite similar to the issues raised in the Wisdom Literature of the Hebrew Bible. While there are obvious points of departure between the works, they retain the same goal: to understand and master life in all of its complexities.

Chapter 12

The Canonical Shape
of the Wisdom Literature

Gerald Keown

> The heart of the canonical process lay in transmitting and ordering the
> authoritative tradition in a form which was compatible to function as
> scripture for a generation which had not participated in the original
> events of revelation. The ordering of the tradition for this new function
> involved a profoundly hermeneutical activity, the efforts of which are
> now built into the structure of the canonical text.[1]

While no attempt will be made in the following pages to defend or
challenge the specific methodological approach proposed by Brevard
Childs, the preceding quotation offers an appropriate starting point for a
discussion of the "canonical shape" of the wisdom literature. The following pages represent an attempt to identify ways in which hermeneutical
goals were achieved through the canonical shape given to the wisdom
books that function within the canon of scripture.

For the purposes of this essay, canonical shape is treated in two
different ways. Initial discussion focuses on the shape that was given to
the wisdom tradition as a whole and the impact "wisdom" has as a result.
In addition, each corpus has its own "shape" that requires attention.

There are differing ways biblical scholars respond to the hermeneutical patterns of the canonical text, but there is a clear consensus among
current Old Testament scholars that attention to the hermeneutical activity
of the biblical tradition offers much more fruitful returns than the
obsession earlier scholars had with historical concerns.

This essay focuses specifically on the hermeneutical impact of one
part of the larger canon, the wisdom literature. Childs includes only

---

[1]Brevard S. Childs, *Introduction to the Old Testament as Scripture* (Philadelphia:
Fortress Press, 1979) 60.

Proverbs, Job, and Ecclesiastes in his discussion of wisdom and the canon, choosing to work with the Hebrew canon. He bases that decision on the process of selection which, he argues, Pharisaic Judaism used to distinguish those books that were consciously included in the canon from a much wider collection of noncanonical books used with varying degrees of authority in the larger community.[2]

It is possible to defend limiting one's attention to the Hebrew canon for the same reasons Christians have chosen to use the smaller canon across the generations. At the same time, some recognition of the role the larger canon has played across those same generations seems necessary. At least for Catholic Christians, the so-called Apocrypha is also a part of the canon, and the apocryphal wisdom books are worthy of attention. While the majority of the discussion below relates to Proverbs, Job, and Ecclesiastes, brief attention is also given to Sirach and Wisdom.

At the outset, it is worthwhile to explore some of the possible ways the wisdom literature as a whole participates in the larger confessional role of the canon. Just what role does wisdom play, and is that role unique?

There seems to be a human tendency, especially evident in the arena of religion, to harmonize the disharmonious. When one turns to sacred writings, the tendency is ever present. If one approaches the literature of the Old Testament with some degree of objectivity, the amazing variety of its contents is undeniable. Everything from fable to saga to soap opera to court history can be readily discerned. Such variety of form and content can prove theologically troubling. One response is to minimize the differences and attempt to identify the theological commonality that binds all of the "different" parts into a purposeful whole. To some degree, that response can be defended, and many interpreters operating from a faith perspective employ it. The danger comes when common purpose is identified in ways that ignore the intrinsic variety and plurality of the text. Is it possible to continue to affirm the authority claims of scripture, yet also recognize and affirm the great diversity of thought within the various texts? Can authoritative scripture challenge, even contradict, itself?

The two preceding questions may partly explain why such elaborate attempts have traditionally been made to "interpret" textual inconsistencies and tensions so as to eliminate them. The common assumption seems

---

[2]Childs, *Introduction*, 67.

to be that any tensions, much less ideas which are inconsistent with one another, must be eliminated or explained lest they blemish the "holy" book. Such an assumption overlooks the possibility that the power of the message may be due in part to its reality and honesty. Life itself is filled with contradictions and tensions. Why should the book of faith not mirror life in that regard?

The wisdom literature offers a microcosm of all of scripture in addressing the dilemma noted above. Proverbs offers, for the most part, a simplistic view of life with few gray areas. Life lived according to the "rules" brings reward. Life which violates the "rules" is certain to bring disaster. In Proverbs, wisdom is pragmatic and minimally related, at least in explicit ways, to the spiritual sphere. The key focus is upon how to live.

If the Book of Proverbs were the sole representative of Israel's wisdom literature, there would be little tension, no contradiction. The two major wisdom books that accompany Proverbs in the Hebrew canon do not follow the pattern of Proverbs. On the contrary, at many points Ecclesiastes and Job appear to be direct challenges offered to the simplistic system of Proverbs. The assumptions of the "wise" in Proverbs are mentioned only to be challenged and all but dismissed as clearly false. What is perhaps most interesting is that Job and Ecclesiastes take dramatically different approaches, but both alike seem to reject the straightforward philosophy of Proverbs.[3]

The dramatic contrast between the themes of Proverbs and those of the other two wisdom books provides canonical shape to the wisdom literature. How does one account for the dramatic tensions that exist between the wisdom books? Do Job and Ecclesiastes represent rejections of the philosophy of Proverbs? Is there a middle ground? Is it possible that the questions raised by the dramatic differences mirror what real life presents to ordinary mortals?

It is worth noting that the tensions in Israel's wisdom tradition are also present in the wisdom literatures of Egypt and Mesopotamia. The tensions may represent less a contradiction than a different wisdom expression. The proverb, or maxim, is found universally, and with much the same impact. The concern is usually pragmatic, the observation simplistic and to the point. In larger philosophical essays, very different

---

[3]See James L. Crenshaw, *Ecclesiastes* OTL (Philadelphia: Westminster, 1987) 23.

approaches are apparent. Just as Job and Ecclesiastes raise disturbing questions about life and its events, similar questions appear in the *Babylonian Theodicy*. Newsom, in her commentary on Job, has documented well the striking similarities between these two works.[4] R. B. Y. Scott has also called attention to similar themes found in the Egyptian work, *A Dispute over Suicide*.[5] The tendency to question traditionally held assumptions is not unique to Israel.

Walter Brueggemann has provided a persuasive description of the way such diverse expressions functioned in Israel's life of faith, specifically within the book of faith. In his *Theology of the Old Testament*, Brueggemann proposes the paradigm of testimony such as is common to the courtroom.[6] By its nature, testimony is never of one fabric only. Testimony is often at odds with countertestimony. It is this dichotomy that Brueggemann identifies as essential to understanding the diversity and variety of the Old Testament message. Like a courtroom witness, Israel offered testimony about God and the world. At its core, the testimony affirmed the principles that made life possible and God trustworthy. Nevertheless, the "core" testimony was not the only testimony. Life confronted Israel with numerous events, especially tragedies and injustices, which directly challenged the core testimony. This countertestimony was not ignored, but was embraced as central to Israel's understanding of faith.

Yahweh was trustworthy. Yet, that affirmation did not overlook those troubling times and events when Yahweh's presence was either not discernible, or worse, when Yahweh seemed enemy to Israel.

The shape of Israel's wisdom literature should not be reduced to the simplest common denominator, but accepted with all of the tensions, even contradictions, inherent in it. Such an approach does not weaken or dilute the message of the wisdom literature. On the contrary, it makes it possible to acknowledge the raw honesty of the biblical message that, rightly understood, gives it even greater force. It resonates with life as it has

---

[4]Carol A. Newsom, "The Book of Job," *The New Interpreter's Bible*, vol. 4 (Nashville: Abingdon, 1996) 329-33.

[5]R. B. Y. Scott, *The Way of Wisdom in the Old Testament* (New York: MacMillan, 1971) 32 (see *ANET*, 405-407).

[6]Walter Brueggemann, *Theology of the Old Testament* (Minneapolis MN: Fortress, 1997) 119-22.

been, is, and will be experienced across human history. Furthermore, it is not a unique quality limited to wisdom literature. As Brueggemann illustrates in his *Theology*, the interplay between testimony and counter-testimony is found throughout the Old Testament.

What may be said about the individual wisdom books? Is there a canonical shape/hermeneutical function to be discerned in the books individually?

Proverbs

Biblical scholars have tended to disagree about the "shaping" of Proverbs. McKane, for example, insists that the content of Proverbs originally consisted of pragmatic secular wisdom which was later molded to address theological concerns.[7] Von Rad, on the other hand, stresses the absence of artificial division between sacred and secular in Israel's wisdom tradition. According to von Rad, the foundation of wisdom in the "fear of Yahweh" should not be seen as a later interpolation.[8] He would insist that the apparent secular nature of Proverbs is built upon theological assumptions held in common with Torah and Prophets. Theological presuppositions provide a foundation which may appear hidden to the reader. Crenshaw observes that "religious sentiments were consciously allowed to interpret older texts" in Proverbs, so that to separate the secular from the sacred is "sheer conjecture."[9] Whether von Rad is correct or not, Crenshaw's observation is a valid one. If there is a purely secular strain in Proverbs, it is impossible to isolate it.

The structure of Proverbs is perhaps the best clue to its "shape." There is consensus among scholars that Proverbs 1–9 provides a crucial introduction to the more diverse texts that follow, and which are judged by most to be the older material of Proverbs. Childs calls the first nine chapters the "framework" of Proverbs, "establishing a religious perspective from which he (the biblical writer) intended the rest of the book to be understood."[10]

---

[7]William McKane, *Proverbs*, OTL (Philadelphia: Westminster, 1977) 8-10.

[8]Gerhard von Rad, *Wisdom In Israel* (Nashville: Abingdon, 1972) 61-62.

[9]James L. Crenshaw, *Old Testament Wisdom: An Introduction* (Atlanta: John Knox, 1981) 92.

[10]Childs, *Introduction*, 552-53.

Proverbs 10–29 evidences common patterns with other literary traditions of the ancient world. The relationship between similar sayings in Israel and those from other cultures has been widely discussed. The distinctiveness of Israel's use of common traditions is somewhat difficult to establish. The "fear of Yahweh" is sometimes identified as the means whereby the typical is given unique standing, though it could perhaps be argued that wisdom sayings in other literary contexts have at least as much connection to appropriate "gods."

The key themes of Proverbs may be heard with theological underpinning, but that is not the only way to hear them. For example, the classic duality of Dame Wisdom and Dame Folly may be connected to theological understandings, but may as easily be heard as a contrast between the choices a person faces which may have no religious connection. The "right" choice may involve obeying the teacher's instruction, avoiding overindulgence, industry rather than laziness. The right choice is paying suit to Lady Wisdom. The one who makes the wrong choice falls prey to the seduction of Dame Folly. The numerous uses of the seductress in Proverbs may not be as much a disturbing negative portrayal of women as it is an extension of the contrast between wisdom and folly personified.[11] The contrast may be given theological weight, but may also be purely pragmatic.

Whether the images of Proverbs are given significant theological impact or not, they represent the straightforward assumptions about life that characterized what is usually called normative wisdom in Israel. The themes encountered fit well within Brueggemann's "core testimony." To live a certain way leads one to success. There is reward to the one who is "wise." This normative way of thinking is reinforced and stated even more forcefully in the works that are the latest in the wisdom corpus, Sirach and the Book of Wisdom. They will be discussed at greater length below. In between the normative thought of Proverbs and the reaffirmations of it which emerge as the latest contributions to the wisdom corpus in Sirach and the Book of Wisdom, one finds another point of view. Job and Ecclesiastes offer very different perspectives on life, and perhaps on God.

---

[11]Roland E. Murphy, *The Tree of Life: An Exploration of Biblical Wisdom Literature* (Grand Rapids MI: Eerdmans, 1990) 17.

Job   → righteous suffering

For the first time in all of wisdom literature, the Book of Job introduces the idea of righteous suffering. There is no such concept in Mesopotamian wisdom. Obviously, this idea presents a radical challenge to normative understandings regarding good and evil. The consistent assumption in proverbial wisdom is that those who are righteous experience the reward commensurate to their deeds. Likewise, the evil person can expect appropriate consequences. Job challenges the norm.

The shape of Job dramatically affects the impact of its message. Apart from the narrative introduction, the issue of theodicy is much less troubling. One could assume that Job's protests of innocence are not well founded. His peevish response to friends and to God would make that deduction seem correct. The narrative, however, establishes Job's righteousness through the unchallengeable testimony of Yahweh. One must then come to terms with the unthinkable, a righteous person who suffers. The dialogues of Job are transformed by the narrative. Job's protests are validated. His complaints cannot be cavalierly dismissed. When the friends respond in that fashion, they are the ones indicted by the reader because of the privileged information the reader possesses.

The repetitive nature of the dialogues, and the apparent breakdown of the established pattern in the third speech cycle, also help establish the "shape" of Job. The intensity of discussion is heightened by repetition. The disturbance of structure is more than a disturbance of form; it parallels the disturbance of theological worldview created by Job's suffering and his resultant protest.

Elihu voices standard commitments regarding God and the world, but, because of what has preceded his speech, he is heard as little more than a buffoon. The Elihu speech is often interpreted as a desperate attempt to rescue normative theology from the attack present earlier in Job. That may be an accurate explanation of its origin. If so, it is not successful.

The climactic exchange between Job and Yahweh moves the focus nearer to normative views. Job's radical complaints are challenged, not because Job has no reason to complain, but on the basis of the character of God which dwarfs any sense of injustice Job has experienced. Coupled with the narrative conclusion, the effect is unsettling to the reader.

The narrative ending of Job jars the reader as much as anything encountered previously in the book. It is a common reaction to perceive the ending of Job as inappropriate, given what has preceded it. How can a disturbing sequence of dialogue, which has been affirmed as legitimate by Yahweh, be undercut by a seeming return to "normative" understandings about life? Job's restoration seems more affirming of the friends' position than to the legitimacy of his own protest. It is as if the overturning of orthodoxy which Job's dialogues accomplish is itself overturned.

As Newsom has observed, the tensions created by the book's ending may well be deliberate.[12] Normative wisdom is not set aside nor invalidated. Neither is Job's righteous suffering ignored or explained away. The dilemma presented is just that, a dilemma, one which arises not just in literary spheres, but in life as it is experienced.

Does God reward the righteous? Is God always just? Does God always come to the rescue of the righteous? Can God be experienced as hostile by the righteous? As disturbing as such an outcome is, all of the preceding questions can be answered in the affirmative. The message of Job creates tension, not just because of its challenge to normative theological presuppositions, but also because of its retention of so much that is normative when Job's saga is concluded.

Without question, the message of Job introduces radical questions into the arena of faith. Job is required to take the chaotic into account, not as consequence of evil, but as part of creation itself. The impact is disquieting not just to Job. It is the rare modern reader who does not find such an idea disturbing. Nevertheless, the directness of the challenge is not that unusual within the broader biblical message. The challenge of faith is not to identify the unquestioned resolution of life's dilemma, but, as in Job's case, to accept the trustworthiness of God in the face of chaos.[13]

Ecclesiastes

The book of Ecclesiastes presents many readers of the Bible with serious problems. What one encounters in the words of Qoheleth seems very different from what has always been assumed to be biblical truth. The conventional piety which is common in the book of Proverbs is not the norm. The conclusion of Qoheleth that "all was vanity and a chasing after

---

[12]Newsom, 634-37.
[13]See Newsom, 628-29.

wind" (2:11) is somewhat removed from standard confessions of faith or appeals to faith. Whereas Job at least links deed and consequence, "Qoheleth discerns no moral order at all."[14]

Towner describes Qoheleth as "the most real of the realists of the sacred writers."[15] The distinctive features of Ecclesiastes which are filled with skepticism have been explained in a variety of ways. The explanations tend to address the "distinctive" nature of Ecclesiastes in a manner that Childs argues fails "to deal seriously with the canonical role of the book as sacred scripture of a continuing community of faith."[16] Childs explains tensions, even contradictions, which occur in Ecclesiastes as the result of "shifting contexts" common to the book as the writer at times accepts, at other times refuses to accept, the rationale of traditional wisdom.[17]

How does one comprehend the "canonical shape" of such a writing? More important, how does one understand its connection to the other wisdom writings that are part of the canon of scripture?

The text of Ecclesiastes illustrates dramatically the attention to raw reality alluded to earlier in this essay. While there is no question that Qoheleth challenges too-easily held assumptions about piety and its rewards, there is likewise no ignoring the truth of Qoheleth's words. As Towner points out, one may not wish to hear what Qoheleth has to say, but one is hard pressed to challenge its validity.[18]

The key question may be whether or not one should identify Qoheleth as a thoroughgoing cynic. Has Qoheleth rejected completely the assumptions of the more normative sages? According to Crenshaw, Qoheleth lost trust in the goodness of God and the central tenets of earlier wisdom.[19] Crenshaw nevertheless refers to the clear acknowledgment by Qoheleth of God's generosity, though it is generosity which is experienced arbitrarily. There is never any possibility that Qoheleth would choose not to believe in God. Qoheleth may have been a skeptic, but there was never

---

[14]Crenshaw, *Ecclesiastes*, 23.

[15]W. Sibley Towner, "The Book of Ecclesiastes," *The New Interpreter's Bible*, vol. 5 (Nashville: Abingdon, 1997) 267.

[16]Childs, *Introduction*, 583.

[17]Childs, *Introduction*, 587.

[18]Towner, "The Book of Ecclesiastes," 267.

[19]Crenshaw, *Old Testament Wisdom*, 128.

any doubt regarding God's existence or power.[20] Furthermore, as Murphy observes, even when he was in conflict with wisdom teaching, he employed the methodology of wisdom and had an ambivalent attitude toward wisdom.[21]

It may be more appropriate to speak of Qoheleth's "wisdom" as a reframing of wisdom's boundaries rather than as a rejection of wisdom altogether. To return to Brueggemann's model, Qoheleth offers an excellent example of countertestimony. It is not, however, a rejection of faith's central tenets. It simply brings a reality check into the equation. Qoheleth offers "a valuable witness in the Bible to the mystery of God."[22] Crenshaw urges the same tolerance on the part of modern readers for Ecclesiastes "that his original audience extended to one whose radical ideas challenged virtually everything they cherished."[23]

The Old Testament does not offer a portrait of unexamined faith, but by means of tension-producing texts like Qoheleth it probes the difficult issues which every human being must at some point contemplate. Faith is not thereby set aside, but is held with more humility. It might be possible to view the world from an arrogant theological perspective if only Proverbs presented wisdom's case, but Ecclesiastes eliminates the possibility of arrogance.

Sirach and the Book of Wisdom

The two wisdom books from the larger canon, Sirach and the Book of Wisdom, should no doubt be treated somewhat differently than Proverbs, Job, or Ecclesiastes. There is no question but that both are influenced by Hellenistic ideas.[24] Both also support an orthodoxy more consistent with Proverbs than anything related to the difficult struggles of Job and Ecclesiastes. Nevertheless, these (clearly later) books in the wisdom corpus have contributions to make that should not be overlooked.

Sirach is almost certainly the older of the two. The reference in Sirach 50 to the priest Simon offers the best evidence for dating.

---

[20]Crenshaw, *Old Testament Wisdom*, 136-37.

[21]Roland E. Murphy, *Ecclesiastes*, WBC (Dallas: Word, 1992) lxiii.

[22]Murphy, *The Tree of Life*, 58.

[23]Crenshaw, *Ecclesiastes*, 53.

[24]It should be noted that Hellenistic influence is widely argued for Ecclesiastes as well. See Murphy, *Ecclesiastes*, xliii-xlv.

Crenshaw's discussion convincingly supports a date between 200 and 180 BCE.[25] The similarity in the use of wisdom forms between Sirach and Proverbs is immediately obvious to any reader. The similarity extends to content. Whether it is deliberately modeled on Proverbs 1:7 or not, Sirach 1:11-20 offers an expanded discussion on the "fear of the Lord." There is also the same emphasis on the desirability of gaining wisdom, though Sirach identifies wisdom much more closely with the "commandments of the Lord" than does Proverbs.

As Crenshaw notes, the Hellenistic influences in Sirach, though present, are not nearly as important as the biblical influences which are found throughout the book.[26] Sirach departs from the patterns of earlier wisdom in the way explicit use is made of Torah and Prophets. Historical events in Israel's salvation history are alluded to or implied often, with obvious focus in Sirach 44–50, where Sirach extols the deeds of the ancestral heroes from Noah to Simon the priest. There is no direct repudiation of the emphases of Job or Ecclesiastes, but one looks in vain to discover any of the tensions of those works in Sirach. The assurance of Sirach is focused on the reliability of God to provide for those who seek and find wisdom.

One interesting contrast between Sirach and the Book of Wisdom involves their respective assumptions regarding death. Sirach considers death to be final and looks for no reward beyond it. The Book of Wisdom, on the other hand, finds many of the troubling questions of Job and Ecclesiastes answered by a belief in life after death. For the Book of Wisdom, it becomes a means whereby God balances the inequities of life.

Both Sirach and the Book of Wisdom include an emphasis on care for the poor and oppressed. This is a theme found in all of the wisdom books. The Book of Wisdom gives sufficient attention to justice that the tone sounds remarkably like that found in the Book of Amos. The "wisdom" connection is the identification of justice with wisdom. It is wisdom that sustains and upholds justice.

Sirach and the Book of Wisdom also share an understanding of testing as purification.[27] Both also move beyond the earlier wisdom works

---

[25]James L.Crenshaw, "The Book of Sirach," *The New Interpreter's Bible*, vol. 5 (Nashville: Abingdon, 1997) 610-13.

[26]Crenshaw, "Sirach," 625.

[27]Sirach 2:5; Wisdom 3:4-6.

to include specific references to individuals and events from the larger biblical tradition.

To ignore the contributions made by these two later wisdom books would be a serious error. One may not be fond of Sirach's attitude toward women, and there are doubtless reasons to maintain a distinction between either of these two works and the more accepted canon, but there is also much which rings familiar and true to any reader of the Bible. A brief sketch of a few examples illustrates this.

Sirach 11:18-19 sounds remarkably like the setting for Luke's Parable of the Rich Fool, and the Book of Wisdom's emphasis on immortality is little removed from ways in which the New Testament employs this same theme.[28] Hebrews 11 personifies "faith" in presenting a hall of fame of faith's heroes. With a simple shift from "faith" to "wisdom," the Book of Wisdom 10:1-21 presents a similar catalog of heroes who achieved through wisdom's gift what the heroes of Hebrews achieved through faith.

The Book of Wisdom directly challenges the conclusions of Ecclesiastes, and presents a very different approach than Job, but does not dismiss cavalierly the issues which are so tension-producing in either book. There is a fundamental difference in outlook that governs the Book of Wisdom's response to pain and suffering, and to those dilemmas confronted in life which may seem to affirm the victory of evil. The difference in approach between the Book of Wisdom and Job or Ecclesiastes is certainly no greater than that found in the New Testament.

Conclusions

Canonical shape is treated in this essay as more related to hermeneutical function than literary structure. The concern is the way in which the wisdom literature operates as a part of the canon of scripture.

Proverbs, Job, and Ecclesiastes are to be heard as part of the same message which is communicated by Torah and Prophets. While von Rad's conclusions may not be beyond question, there is good reason to affirm the importance of wisdom's contribution to the larger biblical message. Even though the theological emphasis is from a different perspective, it

---

[28]See also Michael Kolarcik, "The Book of Wisdom," *The New Interpreter's Bible*, vol. 5 (Nashville: Abingdon, 1997) 507. Kolarcik calls attention to the similarity between Wisdom 7:25-26 and 2 Corinthians 3:18.

is difficult to ignore the way the wisdom literature invites serious theological reflection. The very different approaches to understanding life and God found in Proverbs on the one hand, and in Job and Ecclesiastes on the other, are often perceived as intractable difficulties. Brueggemann's suggestion in his recent *Theology* offers a very different way of assessing those differences. It is important that one be willing to hear the varied voices of wisdom, or, for that matter, the varied voices which are present throughout the canon. If the tensions, even apparent contradictions, are heard as indispensable to the full witness of faith, perhaps the reader of today will have more in common with an ancient Israelite than might be imagined.

Murphy offers needed counsel with regard to scholarly assessments of the wisdom tradition that applies well here. He speaks of the "crisis" of wisdom which is often presumed to exist within the wisdom tradition, yet points out the absence of any sense of crisis in the Bible itself. "There is no record that the book of Ecclesiastes was received with consternation."[29] In other words, the greatest dilemmas confronted by interpreters of the varied voices of wisdom may be of their own making.

The "shape" of wisdom is incomplete without at least some awareness of the contributions of Sirach and the Book of Wisdom. These two later works may have more to offer to the contemporary student of wisdom than is often assumed.

There is no simple summary statement which can possibly encompass the dilemmas facing the interpreter of the wisdom literature. Nor can one provide analysis to address adequately Child's description of canonical shape. The works themselves offer convincing enough evidence of the value in the attempt. Finally, the words of Sirach perhaps apply to this essay and its intended focus, if not necessarily in the manner Sirach intended. Understanding that which challenges all of our faculties is a worthwhile goal, but one to be approached with humility.

All wisdom is from the Lord,
    and with him it remains forever. (Sirach 1:1 NRSV)

---

[29]Murphy, *Ecclesiastes*, lxi.

Chapter 13

The Scope of Theology
in Wisdom Literature

Carol S. Grizzard

Introduction

The scope of theology in Wisdom Literature is the same as it is throughout the canon. These books deal with the broad questions raised by the
rest of the Bible: Who is God? Who are people? and What is and what
should be the relationships among them? The concern with divine/human
and human/human relationships runs through all parts of the Hebrew
Scriptures. Proverbs, Ecclesiastes, and Job nonetheless do constitute a unit
within the canon in two ways. In the first place, these books tend to focus
more on the individual than on the clan, tribe, or nation. The Torah deals
with specific characters—Abraham, Joseph, Moses—but their stories are
told largely in order to explain the origins of Israel in God's purpose. The
material devoted to the words and actions of the kings and prophets in
the Nebi'im provides a theological interpretation of the development of
the nation, the attempts made to bring it back into line when it departed
from its mission, and its eventual fall. While Wisdom Literature does
make general statements about the human condition and how people
should and should not live, it focuses on concerns raised by living in
society rather than on how to form, lead, or change society.

In the second place, Wisdom Literature is cross-cultural. Characteristics such as a practical, human-centered approach and the search for order
appear in both Israel's Wisdom Literature and that found in Egypt and
Mesopotamia. Proverbs quotes at least one non-Israelite with the same degree of authority as Israelites (31:1 and probably 30:1), and none of the
characters in Job appear to be Hebrew. At the same time, events and
ideas that have permeated earlier biblical literature are not found here.
There are no references to matriarchs and patriarchs, Exodus, conquest,
covenants, or other elements of Israel's understood history, and no dis-

tinctly Israelite rituals or locales of worship are discussed (although worship and sacrifices in general are mentioned).

This practical, individualized nature of Wisdom coupled with its cross-culturalism has sometimes led scholars to consider these books to be less authentically Israelite and less religious than the rest of the canon, particularly when salvation-history studies were dominant in the field.[1] This cannot be justified. Certainly other sections of the Hebrew Scriptures show common forms and ideas with other cultures: the similarity of the Mosaic covenant in the Torah to older ancient Near Eastern (ANE) treaty forms is well attested, and there were kings who were believed to rule by the divine will in cultures other than Israel's.[2] Prophecy was not unique to that society either. If evidence of participation in the wider ANE culture makes biblical literature impure, Proverbs, Ecclesiastes, and Job are not alone in being affected.

While some elements of Israel's Wisdom do draw on material found outside the nation, other elements come from firmly within Israel herself. Biblical Wisdom is obviously monotheistic, unlike the Wisdom traditions of other societies. The personal Hebrew name *Yahweh* along with the more generic *Elohim* is used here as elsewhere in the Hebrew Scriptures. The importance of ethical behavior is stressed in all parts of the Hebrew canon even though (or perhaps because) it does not come naturally to imperfect human beings. Wise men and women figure in stories in the Deuteronomistic History (2 Samuel 13:3; 14:1-24; 20:14-22), as does interest in God's gift of a wise mind (1 Kings 3:5-14, especially v. 12). Finally, while the Creator aspect of God is emphasized more often in Wisdom than in Torah or Nebi'im, it is certainly found in those traditions as well. Biblical Wisdom Literature has its own distinctive approach to these elements that are important in Israel's other writings, but that does not make it an intrusion into the Bible any more than the prophetic cynicism where the cult is concerned is out of place in a canon that includes Leviticus.

---

[1]Walther Eichrodt, *Theology of the Old Testament*, vol. 2, trans. J. A. Baker (Philadelphia: Westminster, 1967) 81-83. For further discussion, see James L. Crenshaw, "Prolegomenon," *Studies in Ancient Israelite Wisdom*, ed. James L. Crenshaw (New York: KTAV, 1970) 1-60; repr.: "Studies in Ancient Israelite Wisdom: Prolegomenon," in *Urgent Advice and Probing Questions. Collected Writings on Old Testament Wisdom* (Macon GA: Mercer University Press, 1995) 90-140.

[2]John Bright, *A History of Israel*, 2nd ed. (Philadelphia: Westminster, 1972) 34-41, 146-47.

Basic Issues in Wisdom Literature

Most of the Hebrew Scriptures deal with the question "What does it mean to be the people of God?" This question is answered in various ways as the nation of Israel is traced from its ancestors through slavery, liberation, victory, civil war, defeat, exile, and return to a homeland that has become part of a huge empire. The Wisdom teachers or sages are not concerned with this particularly Israelite question but with a more generally human one: "How can we live life to its fullest and best?"[3] This is a question that engages all people regardless of time, place, or philosophy. In answering it, Wisdom Literature deals with four basic issues: (1) How do we learn? (2) How can we be satisfied in life? (3) What connection is there between our actions and the circumstances of our lives? and (4) What can we expect from God? These are all theological issues, going to the heart of God, humanity, and the divine/human and human/human relationships.[4] Proverbs, Ecclesiastes, and Job do not offer identical approaches or answers to these questions. Some of the theological generalizations of Proverbs are challenged and rethought in the other two more reflective Wisdom books. We will look at each of these issues individually and trace them through the three canonical Wisdom books.

How do we learn? This is the most basic question. Until we know how to acquire knowledge—what sources we can trust—we can answer no other questions. Gerhard von Rad says that "experience presupposes a prior knowledge of myself; indeed it can become experience only if I can fit it into the existing context of my understanding of myself and the world."[5] Establishing that context is the goal of the Wisdom tradition. Consequently, one of its most basic issues concerns how we can develop the framework that enables us to interpret our lives. From what sources can this knowledge be drawn? Wisdom Literature is rationally rather than supernaturally oriented and therefore teaches that we learn from reflection

---

[3]Donn F. Morgan, *Between Text and Community: The Writings in Canonical Interpretation* (Minneapolis: Fortress Press, 1990) 41.

[4]These questions are put in the plural in spite of the literature's orientation towards the individual because the basic setting of all three canonical books is Wisdom devotees generalizing about the human situation from what they have discovered or been taught.

[5]Gerhard von Rad, *Wisdom in Israel*, trans. James D. Martin (Nashville: Abingdon Press, 1972) 3.

on observation and experience, both our own and others'. "Rationally oriented" in no sense means "atheistic"; rather, it means that the Wisdom teachers believe that God created the human mind with the ability to notice and interpret and that these gifts enable us to understand. The Wisdom books generally focus on the human perspective rather than on describing God's purposes or state of mind as do the Torah (cf. Gen. 1:26; 3:22-24; 6:5-8; 12:1-3; Exodus 3:1–4:23; 32:1-35) and Nebi'im (cf. Joshua 1:2-9; 1 Samuel 8:1–9:17; 2 Samuel 7:5-16; 11:27; Isaiah 1:1-31). Job 38-42, which is an exception to this, will be discussed later. While the sages say that God created Wisdom and wants people to find it, nonetheless our individual searches for Wisdom are humanly initiated. Unlike Abraham, Moses, and the prophets, sages are not "called." When asked how to find the answer to a perplexing philosophical problem, a teacher of Torah, a prophet, and a sage would agree that the questioner should study what others have learned about God and humanity. But the first two might well also suggest praying for God to resolve the dilemma by sending a vision or revelation—something no person could make happen. The sage would be more likely to tell the petitioner, "God gave you a mind; you figure it out."

It comes therefore as no surprise that all three canonical Wisdom books take the form of one or more sages presenting what they have learned. In Proverbs this is explicitly designated as a parent-child or teacher-student relationship (cf. 1:8; 2:1; 4:10; 5:1, etc.). Ecclesiastes does not name an audience in this sense, but Qoheleth (Hebrew for "the Teacher") is clearly instructing others in what he has learned and what he has found impossible to learn.[6] In Job, the title character, his friends, and Elihu all come from the Wisdom tradition and debate their now-differing reactions to it. From the friends' perspective, the argument boils down to Eliphaz's contention that Job is abandoning the fear of the Lord, which means he is no longer speaking like a wise man (15:1-6; cf. Proverbs 1:7). In each of these books, observation is the most frequently cited source of knowledge:

A glad heart makes a cheerful countenance,
　　but by sorrow of heart the spirit is broken.

---

[6]In this essay, "Ecclesiastes" refers to the book and "Qoheleth" to the sage whose teaching makes up its bulk.

The mind of one who has understanding seeks knowledge,
    but the mouths of fools feed on folly.
All the days of the poor are hard,
    but a cheerful heart has a continual feast. (Proverbs 15:13-15)[7]

The sun rises and the sun goes down,
    and hurries to the place where it rises.
The wind blows to the south,
    and goes around to the north;
round and round goes the wind,
    and on its circuits the wind returns.
All streams run to the sea,
    but the sea is not full;
to the place where the streams flow,
    there they continue to flow.
All things are wearisome;
    more than one can express;
the eye is not satisfied with seeing,
    or the ear filled with hearing. (Ecclesiastes 1:5-8)

"Think now, who that was innocent ever perished?
    Or where were the upright cut off?
As I have seen, those who plow iniquity
    and sow trouble reap the same." (Job 4:7-8)

Aside from the personification of Wisdom herself (to be discussed later),
divine inspiration is seldom credited; the visions cited in Job 4:12-21 and
33:15-18 are rare exceptions to this. Indeed, these books make it clear
that such a source of knowledge is not to be expected (Ecclesiastes 5:2;
Job 11:7-12).

    This human-centered, observation-based characteristic is used in
different ways in the three canonical books. Proverbs takes a practical
approach to reward and punishment, stating that those who follow
Wisdom will prosper and those who do not will face disaster (1:32-33).
This book's methodology is perhaps best shown in the discussion of
adultery begun in 6:20. There is never any doubt that adultery must be
avoided; this attitude is, of course, completely compatible with the Torah
and the Nebi'im. But the *reason* for avoiding adultery is illuminating. At
no point in this discussion does the sage say that *God* will punish

---

[7]All biblical quotations are from the New Revised Standard Version.

adulterers; it is rather the wronged husband who will refuse to give up his revenge (6:32-35). This behavior has been observed frequently enough to become a proverb. Notice verse 32: "he who commits adultery has no sense"—one of the most stinging condemnations in Wisdom Literature. It is surely possible to argue whether or not God is behind the husband's vengeance, but the fact that the husband is taking vengeance is inarguable. Since the sages say that God established Wisdom before the world (8:22-31), they would argue that God created the moral order that leads to the husband's revenge. Nonetheless, human beings and not God are used as threats in this situation. Claus Westermann notes that the proverbs, while presenting the hearer with choices, stack the deck by pointing out that to choose for Wisdom is in "your own best interest."[8] Such an argument might well convince people of the value of the moral life when the more overtly religious approach of Torah and Nebi'im failed to impress them.

Reflection on observation does not make Qoheleth as optimistic as the sages quoted in Proverbs. No matter what kind of person you are, he says, you will die: "How can the wise die just like fools? So I hated life, because what is done under the sun was grievous to me; for all is vanity and a chasing after wind" (2:16-17). In 3:18-21 his observation takes him farther:

> I said in my heart with regard to human beings that God is testing them to show that they are but animals. For the fate of humans and the fate of animals is the same; as one dies, so dies the other. They all have the same breath, and humans have no advantage over the animals; for all is vanity. All go to one place; all are from the dust, and all turn to dust again. Who knows whether the human spirit goes upward and the spirit of animals goes downward to the earth?

The sage's observation of death leads him to conclude that not only does the wise one ultimately end up like the fool, but that there is no reason to think that human beings have any advantage over animals in the end. Here Qoheleth shows the limits of the traditional Wisdom teaching: it cannot go beyond what people can observe. This means he does not look for justice after death. This does not lead him, however, to believe that

---

[8]Claus Westermann, *Roots of Wisdom: The Oldest Proverbs of Israel and Other Peoples*, trans. J. Daryl Charles (Louisville: Westminster/John Knox Press, 1995) 133.

there is no point in being wise (or human), because his observations have also taught him that living in accordance with Wisdom leads to a better life even if it does not affect that life's end:

> There is nothing better for mortals than to eat and drink, and find enjoyment in their toil. This also, I saw, is from the hand of God; for apart from him who can eat or who can have enjoyment? For to the one who pleases him God gives wisdom and knowledge and joy; but to the sinner he gives the work of gathering and heaping, only to give to one who pleases God. (Ecclesiastes 2:24-26)

While Qoheleth is not as cheerful as the sages in Proverbs, he is not a purveyor of gloom. He is frustrated by the fact that the meaning of life is hidden (1:12-14; 3:11; 7:14; 11:5), but he has nonetheless observed many joys in life. He states in 5:18-19:

> This is what I have seen to be good: it is fitting to eat and drink and find enjoyment in all the toil with which one toils under the sun the few days of the life God gives us; for this is our lot. Likewise, all to whom God gives wealth and possessions and whom he enables to enjoy them, and to accept their lot and find enjoyment in their toil—this is the gift of God. (Cf. also 2:24-25; 9:7-10; 11:8)

The Book of Job shows its participation in the Wisdom tradition by also coming from a human-centered, rational perspective. This is seen in two ways. In the first place, although God is actually a character in the book, the humans do most of the talking, thus stressing the role of the human perspective throughout the book. The fact that the Satan is permitted to destroy Job's riches, family, and health leaves open the possibility that even God does not know whether the accusations about Job are true[9]; nevertheless, in the bulk of the book (chapters 3-37) God does not appear and we have no indication of how God is reacting to the speeches of the human characters. This is noteworthy for being the longest section in the Hebrew Scriptures without God's speech or action (while the Psalms seldom quote God directly, they do frequently speak of divine intervention in Israel's or the psalmists' past). The dialogue or debate[10]

---

[9]David Noel Freedman, "Is It Possible to Understand the Book of Job?" *Bible Review* 4 (April 1988): 31-33.

[10]Both terms are often used to refer to the poem cycle in 3:1–42:6, although it quickly becomes a series of monologues with little interaction.

among the five characters shows their attempts to deal with Job's life, but God is conspicuously absent.

In the second place, reflection on observation is again the accepted and expected way to learn. All the human characters use observation to back up the points they make (cf. Job 4:7-11; 12:7–13:1; 18:5-21; 20:4-29; 36:24-33). The *interpretations* given to what they observe, however, differ greatly. Everyone in the book agrees on Job's current situation. Their disagreement is over how to understand it: do Job's calamities mean that his previously accepted reputation as a wise and righteous man was undeserved or that the belief that the wise and righteous do not suffer is wrong? The friends and Elihu take the first position (4:7-8; 8:4-7; 11:1-6; 20:1-29; 34:11), but the book as a whole ultimately comes down on the side of the second (1:1, 8; 2:3; 42:7). This difference in interpretation is based on how the characters understand the relationship between human beings and God, which is the fourth basic issue in Wisdom Literature.

How can we be satisfied in life? The second issue in Wisdom Literature builds upon the first. All people in all times and places want their basic needs filled and some degree of happiness besides. Now that human observation and reflection have been established as the method for learning, what does that method teach about satisfaction and how to achieve it?

Wisdom Literature suggests many things that can lead to happiness: Wisdom itself (Proverbs 4:5-9), a good marriage (Ecclesiastes 9:9), many descendants in whom to take pride (Job 1:2; Proverbs 17:6), loyal friends (Ecclesiastes 4:9-12), righteousness (Proverbs 16:8), having a relationship with God (Job 29:1-4), a good reputation (Proverbs 22:1), taking joy in work (Ecclesiastes 5:18), and correct priorities (Proverbs 15:16), among others. But there is something even more basic than any of these things, something without which they cannot exist. It is *order*. Wisdom Literature advocates order in relationships, in work, in habits, and in outlook. Those who live according to order will be satisfied. Proverbs 1:33 is one of the best expressions of what constitutes "the good life": Wisdom says,

> but those who listen to me will be secure
> and will live at ease, without dread of disaster.

Other ways of thinking might talk about finding joy in taking risks, changing society, and doing things that have never been done before.

Wisdom Literature does not value these things. (In fact, Ecclesiastes 1:9 eliminates the possibility of the last by saying there is nothing new under the sun.) To the sages, security is necessary for a good, complete, satisfactory life, and nature teaches that that is available through order.

Wisdom Literature refers frequently to nature to support the value of order (cf. Job 8:11-15; Proverbs 6:6-11; Ecclesiastes 1:5-9). This is done for at least four reasons. First, it is easy to observe nature, and all the cultures that participated in the Wisdom movement had the natural world (but not their individual histories and traditions) in common. Second, nature itself is basically orderly: there is a rainy season and a dry, harvest comes at the end of summer and not winter, and darkness does not come in the middle of the day. This enables us to plant and to plan. Third, when this natural order is broken—when the expected weather patterns shift, a harvest does not occur, or an eclipse leads to a noon that looks like night—terror results, and frequently drought, famine, and death. Fourth, the sages teach that this order in nature is no accident but is part of God's intentional act of creation.

Each of the canonical Wisdom books sees order as integral to life, but each has a different perception of that order. In Proverbs, living according to Wisdom means living prudent, orderly lives (cf. 3:19-21; 6:6-11, 20-35; 10:4-5; 11:15; 12:8; 13:15; 19:11; 21:23; 25:28). The description of drunkenness in 23:29-35 makes the point clear: you do not want to be drunk and disorderly. The reason for this is found in 8:22-36. Note the verbs used to describe the divine act of creation in verses 27-29:

> When he *established* the heavens . . .
> . . . *made firm* the skies above,
>   when he *established* the fountains of the deep,
> when he *assigned to the sea its limit,*
>   so that the waters might not transgress his command,
> when he *marked out* the foundations of the earth. . . .

This is the language of making secure, of setting boundaries, of creating order (cf. also Job 38:4ff.). This section says that Wisdom is the first of God's creations, prior to the earth itself. Wisdom helped create the world.[11] This means that Wisdom is not something that was added later,

---

[11]"Master worker" in 8:30 can also be translated as "little child," but the former reading is preferable. Not only does it make the position of Wisdom stronger, but the idea of

a valuable luxury if we can find it. Wisdom and the order it represents are part of the fabric of the world, and therefore they are vital for any success in the world. No wonder the sages say,

> The beginning of wisdom is this: Get wisdom,
> and whatever else you get, get insight. (Proverbs 4:7)

Living in such an orderly world makes for a secure life.

Qoheleth agrees that order is a fundamental part of the world, but the order praised in Proverbs is boring and frustrating to him. In Ecclesiastes 1 the sage recites the predictability of nature—the rising of the sun, the blowing of the wind, the flowing of the streams—and ends with

> All things are wearisome;
> more than one can express;
> the eye is not satisfied with seeing,
> or the ear filled with hearing.
> What has been is what will be,
> and what has been done is what will be done;
> there is nothing new under the sun. (vv. 8-9)

This sense of ennui leads Qoheleth to conclude that no one is remembered by later generations: only "the earth remains forever" (verse 4). The book's most famous passage is 3:1-8:

> For everything there is a season,
> and a time for every matter under heaven:
> a time to be born, and a time to die; . . .

and on through thirteen other pairs of opposites. This image of order holding killing and healing, tearing and sewing, loving and hating in dynamic tension is complex and all-inclusive, but it gives Qoheleth no satisfaction. The next verse reads, "What gain have the workers from their toil?" (3:9). Why work for peace or healing or love when order may necessitate war or killing, or hate? Why *should* people be remembered when the world proceeds despite their efforts and desires? Order is seen here as stifling all possibility of human accomplishment. There seems to be no room in such a world for freedom or spontaneity.

Wisdom as a participant in the creation of the earth is also found in the noncanonical Israelite Wisdom tradition (Wisdom 7:22) and in the New Testament (John 1:1).

The characters in Job all originally assume that order is a basic fact of life. Part of Job's frustration and anger is that he believes that what has happened to him shows that order has broken down and he wants it back (9:13-24; 13:13-28; 29:1–31:40). If order was functioning as he once understood it, he would again be the wealthy patriarch of the book's first five verses. This perceived break in the way things should be leads him to say (in language reminiscent of the laments in Psalms) that God is tormenting him:

> When I say, "My bed will comfort me,
>   my couch will ease my complaint,"
> then you scare me with dreams
>   and terrify me with visions,
> so that I would choose strangling
>   and death rather than this body. (7:13-15)

and

> know then that God has put me in the wrong,
>   and closed his net around me.
> Even when I cry out, "Violence!" I am not answered;
>   I call aloud, but there is no justice.
> He has walled up my way so that I cannot pass,
>   and he has set darkness upon my paths. . . .
> He breaks me down on every side, and I am gone,
>   he has uprooted my hope like a tree.
> He has kindled his wrath against me,
>   and counts me as his adversary. (19:6-8, 10-11; cf. also 10:10-22)

It is not until the divine speeches of chapters 38–41 that we come to see that order is not the dependable cycle celebrated in Proverbs and debated here, nor is it the repetitive regime found in Ecclesiastes. God describes a Creation of power and wonder, filled with constellations and singing stars (38:7, 31-33), barely controllable seas (38:8), strong oxen, fierce horses, and far-seeing birds (39:1-30), and creatures yet more powerful and harder to control (40:15-18; 41:1-34). Here we find a wild world of terrible beauty where anything can happen and a God who, far from supervising a predictably running machine, is constantly balancing the violent forces and creatures that populate it. It is a world where chaos is controlled and limited, not destroyed . . . exactly as we see God handling the never-again-mentioned Satan of chapters 1 and 2. The fact that Job's corner of the world is troubled does not mean that the cosmos is out of balance; he has spoken of things he does not understand (38:2; 42:3). This is a vision that incorporates both order and vitality, one that leaves God and people with something to accomplish.

How, if at all, do our actions affect the circumstances of our lives? This third basic issue in Wisdom thought builds on the second. Is there any way we can guarantee the receiving and keeping of that which satisfies us? How pervasive is the basic order? Does it guarantee that I get what I deserve?

According to the book of Proverbs, there is a moral order in life. An inevitable relationship exists between the kinds of lives people lead and the things that happen to them. Those who regulate their lives with the same order that is readily apparent in the natural world have the security of knowing that their lives will not be overturned by catastrophe; those who refuse to listen to Wisdom find calamity and chaos:

> No harm happens to the righteous,
> > but the wicked are filled with trouble. (12:21)

and

> Misfortune pursues sinners,
> > but prosperity rewards the righteous.
> > > (13:21; cf. also 1:32-33; 3:13-35; 10:9; 11:21; 12:7; 21:7)

This leads to two kinds of people: the wise and the foolish. Many of the proverbs in this book compare these positive and negative models, making clear which one is to be followed:

> Those who trouble their households will inherit wind,
> > and the fool will be servant to the wise. (11:29)

(Some other examples are in 10:1, 14; 12:15-16; 13:1, 16; 15:14; and 17:24.)

The book of Ecclesiastes also presents this doctrine of just desserts. Qoheleth begins his discussion of the moral order in 3:16-17. As he observes wickedness flourishing even in "the place of righteousness," he says, "God will judge the righteous and the wicked, for he has appointed a time for every matter, and for every work"—an outcome he cannot observe. The book ends by urging the hearers to keep God's commandments: "For God will bring every deed into judgment, including every secret thing, whether good or evil" (12:14). But in between Qoheleth notices that the doctrine he believes in does not always work in life, and as noted above he cannot see resolution in an afterlife. In 4:1-3 he returns to the issue of undeserved suffering, noting what he *can* see:

> the tears of the oppressed—with no one to comfort them! On the side of their oppressors there was power—with no one to comfort them. And I thought the dead, who have already died, more fortunate than the living, who are still alive; but better than both is the one who has not yet been, and has not seen the evil deeds that are done under the sun.

By 7:15 he has moved to, "In my vain life I have seen everything; there are righteous people who perish in their righteousness, and there are wicked people who prolong their life in their evildoing"—a denial of a moral order in this world. This grieves him, but he cannot deny that there are people, both good and evil, whose circumstances in life are not what their lives should have earned. Even so, his realization that there is not perfect justice in the world does not keep him from valuing life: "Even those who live many years should rejoice in them all" (11:8).

Ecclesiastes 2 presents the sage as a man of wealth, power, and many pleasures. When he speaks of injustice under the sun, he refers to general situations he has observed and not experienced. The Book of Job, however, presents us with a test case. Job is the best possible person (in the first verse he is called "blameless"; God also refers to him so in 1:8 and 2:3) who undergoes horrendous losses and suffering (1:13–2:10). The book of Ecclesiastes questioned the connection between human action and later circumstances. The book of Job ultimately says that there is no connection. The issue is first raised by the Satan in chapters 1 and 2. He suggests that Job's piety is intended to buy him wealth and, after the first round of disasters, life. And perhaps it is. While Job genuinely regrets the loss of his former close relationship with God (10:11-12; 29:1-25), he is driven even more by his burning sense that justice has not been done him. He is innocent of wrongdoing and therefore should not have to endure the tragedies that have overtaken him. He believes that his blameless life should have guaranteed him security and happiness. On this ground he challenges God to meet him in court (9:3-24) and is confident that he will win the case (13:13-18; 23:1-7). He never challenges either God or his friends on the grounds that he (or anyone else) has always known that undeserved suffering is a reality. His challenge is based on his personal experience of that suffering and his knowledge that he has done nothing wrong (31:1-40).

Here we see the wisdom method of learning through reflection on observation and experience at work again. Job and his friends have all observed Job's previously well-respected life (4:2-6; 29:1-25) and his current misery (2:11-13). This gives each of them a choice: how will they interpret these observations? It is impossible to believe both in Job's goodness and in the doctrine of moral order. If people get what they deserve, then devastated Job cannot be good. If devastated Job is good, then there is no connection between actions and later circumstances. Eliphaz, Bildad, Zophar, and Elihu, forced to choose between Job and their doctrine of moral order, choose their doctrine and trash their friend (4:7-8; 8:4-7; 11:1-6; 20:1-29; 34:11). They are so determined to uphold this doctrine that they offer a low view of human beings in general: Bildad says people are maggots and worms (25:5-6). They are insistent on his admitting guilt because if Job suffers undeservedly, then so could they, and they cannot face the possibility that they cannot control their lives with their own actions. Job therefore experiences not only the pain of his disasters and the shock of discovering that the world does not work the way he thought it did but also the further agony of being blamed for his loss of wealth, children, and health. It seems to be this, rather than the disasters themselves, that drives him to the edge of blasphemy. Until the friends appeared, he was *speaking* piously even if he was thinking otherwise (1:21; 2:10; note "with his lips" in the latter verse). He could ease his situation if he confessed his own guilt, even if he said only that he must have sinned but did not know how. But Job is a man of integrity. He will not admit guilt that he knows is not his, although to do so would change his companions from shrieking theologues into the compassionate friends they originally intended to be.

What can we expect from God? The fourth and final basic issue in Wisdom Literature asks what our reflections on our observations and on the events of our lives tell us about God. Proverbs speaks frequently of the "fear of Yahweh," a phrase familiar in both Torah and Nebi'im. The first occurrence of this phrase in Proverbs is in 1:7:

> The fear of the Lord is the beginning of knowledge;
>   fools despise wisdom and instruction.

Proverbs 14:26-27 refers to the fear of Yahweh as life and refuge; similar statements are found in 16:6; 19:23; and 22:4. Qoheleth sees the fear of God as vital (5:7; 7:18); Ecclesiastes 8:12b-13a says, "I know that it will be well with those who fear God, because they stand in fear before him, but it will not be well with the wicked." Job's blamelessness is illustrated by his fear of Yahweh (1:1, 8; 2:3), and Eliphaz fears that Job's rebelliousness is "doing away with the fear of God" (15:4). The repeated use of this phrase in biblical Wisdom shows how important it is to take God seriously. But what exactly does that mean? How does God function in our lives?

In general, the Wisdom Literature sees God as the Creator of all that is and as the distant and mysterious judge of human behavior. Job 12:7-10 illustrates God's creative function:

> But ask the animals, and they will teach you;
>   the birds of the air, and they will tell you;
> ask the plants of the earth, and they will teach you;
>   and the fish of the sea will declare to you.
> Who among all these does not know
>   that the hand of the Lord has done this?
> In his hand is the life of every living thing
>   and the breath of every human being.

A few of the many other passages depicting God as the Creator and sustainer of the natural world are Proverbs 8:22-36, Ecclesiastes 11:5, and Job 38:1–41:34.

God's rewarding the righteous and punishing the wicked is connected to the idea of the created moral order, already discussed. All three Wisdom books accept this to some degree, although Ecclesiastes and Job both observe against Proverbs that this judgment does not always affect life on earth. The Wisdom books, like most of the Hebrew Scriptures, are reluctant to make statements about a life after death that cannot now be observed.[12] For Qoheleth and Job, therefore, the apparent injustice

---

[12]There is no mention of life after death in any of the covenants. It is seldom mentioned in the Hebrew Scriptures. To many of the biblical writers, human life is brief and upon death a person's shade invariably exists in Sheol separated from all that made life good, including God (cf. 1 Samuel 28:3-19; Psalms 6:5; 30:8-9; 88:4-12; 103:15-18; 115:17). A more positive view is also found in Psalms (49:5, 13-15; 73:24-26) and in the

occurring in life is a serious problem where the doctrine of the moral order is concerned (Ecclesiastes 3:18-21; 5:13-16; 6:3-6; Job 9:25-35; 14:1-22). This is not an issue in Proverbs since no exceptions to the doctrine are mentioned.

All three books see God as distant and mysterious. Proverbs affirms God's watchful judgment (15:3) but adds that God's knowledge is hidden from humans (25:2) and never mentions any possibility of a close divine-human relationship or direct revelation. This distance is lessened, however, because of the presentation of God's Wisdom as highly accessible. Wisdom frequently speaks in the person of a woman searching for men on the street (1:20-33; 8:1-21) and preparing a feast in her home for those who need her (9:1-16).[13] At times this character has been called a "hypostasis," meaning that she is not a literary device but is being presented as an actual divine entity separate from God. Wisdom Literature in the Apocrypha moves towards treating Wisdom as a separate figure (Ecclesiasticus 14:20–15:8; 24:19-22; Wisdom of Solomon 8:2-4), but this move is not completed in the canonical material. Here she is clearly *not* divine but is given priority as God's first creation, the "master workman" helping to create all that came later (8:22-36). This character is a personification of one of God's attributes in much the same way that

---

Nebi'im (Isaiah 26:19; Daniel 12:2-3), based largely on the ideas that (1) a relationship with an eternal God must also be eternal and (2) the apparent lack of justice in this life requires an afterlife in which there is appropriate reward and punishment—the issue at stake in this discussion.

[13]It is noteworthy that the cultures that developed Wisdom Literature consistently personified Wisdom as female. They did the same with her opposite, the adulteress (6:20–7:27). The characterizations are amazingly similar: neither stays at home but is out in the street (1:20; 7:11-12; 8:1-3) seeking men (1:21; 7:13-15; 8:4) to come to her well-prepared house (7:16-17; 9:1-6), although the results of their encounters differ greatly (1:33; 6:31-35; 7:21-23). These eternal opposites are represented as women because these images developed in a patriarchal culture: "For a patriarchal discourse in which the self is defined as male, woman qua woman is the quintessential other" (Carol A. Newsom, "Woman and the Discourse of Patriarchal Wisdom: A Study of Proverbs 1–9," *Women in the Hebrew Bible: A Reader*, ed. Alice Bach [New York: Routledge, 1999] 89). These characters are both attractive and dangerously powerful; thus they are personified as "the opposite sex." Notice that Proverbs sees finding a good wife as a gift of God (18:22; 19:14), as is finding Wisdom herself, and that the description of "the good wife" that makes up the book's last chapter shows a woman who, like Wisdom, is not limited to her home but goes out in public, seeking out the needy and doing business with men (31:14, 16, 18, 20, 24).

poets may address Love or Justice without assuming that such conscious entities actually exist. "Lady Wisdom" is not being presented as a divine being in her own right.[14] Nonetheless, this personification does show an aspect of God reaching out to people. Wisdom is eager to be helpful, which in Proberbs keeps God from seeming to be wholly inaccessible.

As in Proverbs, in Ecclesiastes and Job God is distant; unlike Proverbs, these books do not use the personified Wisdom reaching out as a helpful liaison between divine and human.[15] Therefore these books are more explicit about God's distance. Qoheleth says:

> Never be rash with your mouth, nor let your heart be quick to utter a word before God, for God is in heaven, and you upon earth; therefore let your words be few. (Ecclesiastes 5:2)

We cannot understand God's purposes or ways (1:12-14; 3:11; 7:14; 11:5). In Job, while the friends and Elihu tell Job to repent before God (5:8, 17; 8:5-7; 11:13-14; 33:12-28), they hold out no hope that God might respond to his complaint in any way.[16] No one can find out "the deep things of God" (11:7-12); the deity is far away in heaven (22:12). Job himself understands this. In speaking of God, he says:

> If I go forward, he is not there;
> or backward, I cannot perceive him;
> on the left he hides, and I cannot behold him;
> I turn to the right, but I cannot see him. (23:8-9)

God is so removed that human righteousness does not affect him:

> "Can a mortal be of use to God?
> Can even the wisest be of service to him?
> Is it any pleasure to the Almighty if you are righteous,
> or is it gain to him if you make your ways blameless?"

---

[14]For a further discussion of the nature of Wisdom's personification or hypostasis in the canon and apocrypha, see James Wood, *Wisdom Literature: An Introduction*, Studies in Theology 64 (London: Duckworth, 1967) 94-109.

[15]Job 28 says God values and understands the way to Wisdom (23–28), but here there is no personification and Wisdom does not speak.

[16]In 11:5-6 Zophar wishes that God would speak to Job and instruct him in "the secrets of wisdom," but he clearly does not expect this to happen since he then proceeds to instruct Job himself—and his topic is the impossibility of knowing God's ways.

asks Eliphaz (22:2-3; cf. 35:6-8). Elihu has the last human speech in the book before God's:

> "Out of the north comes golden splendor;
>   around God is awesome majesty.
> The Almighty—we cannot find him;
>   he is great in power and justice,
>   and abundant righteousness he will not violate.
> Therefore mortals fear him;
>   he does not regard any who are wise in their own conceit."
>
> (37:22-24)

It is in this context that we must view the divine speeches that immediately follow in chapters 38–41. In other parts of the Hebrew canon God frequently speaks and intervenes, but not here. After the constant assertions that God is distant and will not respond to Job, these speeches come as a surprise to the reader as well as to the characters. No one expects this to happen. None of the human characters except Job speak again; the simple fact of God's speech to Job silences them. But these speeches may surprise the readers, at least, in two other ways. For thirty-seven chapters we have been focusing on the terrible things that have happened to a righteous person, eavesdropping on Job's protestations of his innocence and the injustice of God in the face of the others' refusal to accept anything he says. When God answers Job from the whirlwind, we might expect to hear compassion and perhaps apology for Job's specific losses or response to the points of his complaint. We might even expect to hear God say, "Well, Job, one day the heavenly beings came to present themselves before me, and the Satan also came among them. . . . " But the first surprise is that we do not. As we have already seen, God speaks only of the complicated and vital cosmos Job does not understand, one in which it is necessary to keep the forces of chaos in line.

The second surprise is that this satisfies Job. All of his points are left unanswered, but Job rests his case. Why? It is because God answered him. Against all odds, God answered him. That is more important than anything God could have said. Job was not forsaken in his pain even though he thought he was. He thought that he had lost God on top of everything else, and now he knows that was not true. God's presence gives Job the perspective with which to deal with his pain. So Job says:

> "I had heard of you by the hearing of the ear,
>   but now my eye sees you;
> therefore I despise myself,
>   and repent in dust and ashes." (42:5-6)

The fact that Job's agonized charges have obviously been heard lets him move past the tragedies and clears the way for God and Job to renew their relationship. It is in the light of this renewed relationship that the restoration of Job's fortunes must be regarded. This is not the doctrine of moral order kicking back in; by now, that doctrine has been reduced to quivering bloody shreds. But God is still free to bless and blame, just as Job and the others were free to make their choices. At the book's end God affirms that Job and not his pious friends spoke the truth (42:7) and Job acts as he did at the beginning, interceding in prayer for others (1:5; 42:8). But neither we nor the characters are as we were at the story's beginning. We now know that good and bad fortune are not earned. Job's experience has changed everything for him. Neither its personal nor theological effects are negated by Job's new children and wealth; anyone who has lost a child knows that later and much-loved children do not end the grief. His perception of himself, the world, the nature of order, and God have all been affected as well. Now Job knows that God is a real being, not a philosophical construct, and God knows that Job will refuse to give up on God even in great suffering.

This personal interaction between God and Job is unprecedented in Wisdom Literature. All of Job's knowledge of Wisdom did not prepare him for what he had to face. That is why he demands a divine encounter. His friends do not feel the need for such an encounter; neither did Job, apparently, before he was confronted with the unexpected capriciousness of life. This is therefore a book for those who find that the conventional religious responses, whether Wisdom or not, are no longer sufficient. It does not answer the question of why bad things happen to good people, nor does it intend to. Rather, it models the honest anger, loyalty strong enough to question, and desperate searching hope needed to hang onto God with integrity when God has not fulfilled what we thought of as the divine job description. The Book of Job says that in such cases it is the human perception of that job description that needs to change. The stories of Israel's ancestors, rulers, and prophets as well as of Jesus and those who followed him make clear that keeping people safe and happy is not

God's task, no matter how much Job and others might want it to be. When tradition fails, something more is needed. Norman C. Habel says, "[Job] did not find wisdom but he found God. That experience makes all other claims to knowledge relative."[17] That experience gave him what he needed to continue in the fear of the Lord. Notice, however, that the Book of Job does not abandon Wisdom. What Job finds is still a Wisdom God speaking of Creation and order. In Qoheleth's grappling with the issue of death we saw the limits of the traditional Wisdom approach. In Job we find an expanded Wisdom tradition that is flexible enough to adapt to situations that the traditional teaching could not handle.

Conclusion

Biblical Wisdom Literature contains the teaching of the sages, just as the Torah gives the perspective of priests and other legal minds, the Nebi'im provides the prophetic approach, and Psalms shows the work of poets. They are all part of Israel's religious tradition. They all affirm and praise the One God, Creator of heaven and earth, who provides humanity with standards of behavior and with the means to live up to them. The priests constantly offered sacrifices that they said were ordained by God to mark seasons and holidays as well as events in the lives of the nation and of individuals. The prophets, too, claimed a revelation from God. In their case, the divine word dealt with issues and concerns in the political present. The Wisdom sages did not generally claim divine authority for their teaching. They spoke to and for the vast majority of Israel, the people who received no personal word from God. They learned about God by studying God's Creation, including humanity. They found evidence of God's power and purposes in the rhythms of nature and urged their followers to incorporate that order into their own lives even as they also acknowledged that there would always be matters they could not understand. From what they learned by their own and others' observation they decided that it is important to live in an orderly manner, that a righteous life is still better than an evil one even when it involves undeserved suffering, and that the divine/human bond is incredibly strong.

---

[17]Norman C. Habel, "Of Things beyond Me: Wisdom in the Book of Job," *Currents in Theology and Mission* 10 (1983): 154.

Chapter 14

Unresolved Issues in Wisdom Literature

James L. Crenshaw

Eurocentric male dominance in the interpretation of Wisdom Literature during the first three-quarters of the twentieth century has eased in the last twenty-five years. The rich variety of voices has introduced new questions and applied different presuppositions to the ancient corpus. By highlighting the male perspective of the texts and by searching for the significance of depicting wisdom as female, feminist readings[1] have been particularly suggestive, but Asian and liberationist interpretations have also widened the parameters of investigation and forced interpreters to question their own assumptions about the worldview hidden within the literature.[2]

The sharpest challenges to the reigning hypotheses fashioned by white males have, nevertheless, arisen largely in their own circle, harsh rhetoric from other interest groups notwithstanding. The most extreme view dismisses the entire literary corpus and professional sages as a figment of the imagination.[3] More moderate revisionists raise the issue of correctly

---

[1]Among contributions by feminist scholars, certain works stand out, notably, Claudia V. Camp, *Wisdom and the Feminine in the Book of Proverbs*, BLS 11 (Sheffield: Almond Press, 1985); Carole R. Fontaine, *Traditional Sayings in the Old Testament*, BLS 5 (Sheffield: Almond Press, 1982); and Carol A. Newsom, "Woman and the Discourse of Patriarchal Wisdom: A Study of Proverbs 1-9," 142-60 in *Gender and Difference in Ancient Israel*, ed. Peggy L. Day (Minneapolis: Fortress Press, 1989). Athalya Brenner, ed. *A Feminist Companion to Wisdom Literature* (Sheffield: Sheffield Academic Press, 1995) also includes some important essays on various topics. Women interpreters at the front ranks of sapiential scholarship include Miriam Lichtheim and Nili Shupak in Egyptian studies, Helga Stadelmann and Ada Wischmeyer on Sirach, Dorothea Sitzler and Katherine J. Dell on the Book of Job, and Jutta Hausmann and Gerlinde Baumann on Proverbs.

[2]The minimal interest shown by liberation scholars (Gustavo Gutierrez being the exception) is puzzling, although the themes from Exodus and the prophetic conscience naturally offer much more easily recognizable points of contact.

[3]R. N. Whybray, *The Intellectual Tradition in the Old Testament*, BZAW 135 (Berlin

identifying the extent of Wisdom Literature,[4] its unity,[5] and its consistency over time.[6]

Fact or Fiction

The designation "Wisdom Literature" has no Hebrew or Aramaic equivalent in the Old Testament. The modern construct derives from the prominence of the word *hokmah* and various synonyms in the books of Proverbs, Job, Ecclesiastes, Sirach, and Wisdom of Solomon. The authors of these books clearly considered wisdom a worthy acquisition, the bestower of long life and its desirable assets, or they reflected on its hiddenness and special relationship with the deity. Such unbridled speculation came very close to philosophy, for its mythic ruminations eventually equated wisdom with the divine thought process.[7]

By analogy, interpreters of Egyptian and Mesopotamian literature dubbed certain texts "wisdom" because of their similarity with the above-mentioned biblical books.[8] The occasional caveat indicates early acknowledgment that nonbiblical sources contained omen texts presuppos-

---

and New York: Walter de Gruyter Verlag, 1974) and Stuart Weeks, *Early Israelite Wisdom*, OThM (Oxford: Clarendon Press, 1994). Whybray later revised his views, largely because an intellectual tradition needs trained guardians other than people who have large estates.

[4]Claus Westermann, *Der Aufbau des Buches Hiob* (Stuttgart: Calwer Verlag, 1977) and *Roots of Wisdom* (Louisville: Westminster/John Knox, 1995). On formal grounds, Westermann excludes the Book of Job from wisdom literature.

[5]The impact of critical theory has been felt acutely where interpreters using tools of literary analysis have sought to demonstrate the integrity of texts that on other presuppositions have seemed totally disjointed. Irony·has come to the forefront in analyses of the Book of Job, especially by Carol A. Newsom, "The Book of Job," *The New Interpreter's Bible*, vol. 4, ed. Leander E. Keck et al. (Nashville: Abingdon Press, 1996) and Yair Hoffman, *A Blemished Perfection: The Book of Job in Context*, JSOTSup 213 (Sheffield: Academic Press, 1996).

[6]Katharine J. Dell, "On the Development of Wisdom in Israel," *VTS* 66, Congress Volume Cambridge 1995 (Leiden: E. J. Brill, 1997): 135-51.

[7]Michael V. Fox, "Ideas of Wisdom in Proverbs 1-9," *JBL* 116 (1997): 613-33.

[8]A growing restlessness over this practice is detectable, particularly in Miriam Lichtheim, *Moral Values in Ancient Egypt*, OBO 155 (Göttingen: Vandenhoeck & Ruprecht, 1997).

ing a magical base, as well as noun lists compiled for scribal instruction, and laments.[9]

Once the analogy was made, the move also occurred in the other direction. Biblical interpreters began to use ancient Near Eastern texts to fill in gaps of knowledge about the composition and function of Proverbs, Job, and Ecclesiastes. This move led to the supposition that Israelite sages served royal administrators, composing educational texts to instruct fellow courtiers.[10] The cultural gap between the courts of Egypt and Mesopotamia on the one hand, and Israel, on the other hand, was largely ignored.[11] Perhaps the decisive reason for overlooking Israel's differences in administrative development was this: linking them provided an explanation for the presence of foreign material in the Book of Proverbs. If courtiers graced the courts of Solomon or even Hezekiah, the incorporation of portions of the *Instruction of Amenemope* in the Book of Proverbs makes sense, as do the "sayings" of Agur and Lemuel's mother.[12]

A major difficulty remained, however, for the overwhelming impression given by the Book of Proverbs is that of instruction within the family in small villages,[13] whereas few indications of courtly interests have survived. Parents convey vital information to their children, preparing them to cope with whatever circumstances they encounter. Clues derived from Sumerian Wisdom Literature, where the references to fathers and sons function metaphorically for teachers and students,[14]

---

[9]Onomastica, once thought to signify sapiential activity, have been shown to belong to the wider community of intellectual productivity. See Michael V. Fox, "Egyptian Onomastica and Biblical Wisdom," *VT* 36 (1986): 302-10.

[10]W. Lee Humphreys, "The Motif of the Wise Courtier in the Book of Proverbs," in *Israelite Wisdom: Theological and Literary Essays in Honor of Samuel Terrien*, ed. John G. Gammie et al., 177-90 (Missoula MT: Scholars Press, 1978) could find very little evidence of court wisdom in the Bible.

[11]Friedemann Golka, *The Leopard's Spots* (Edinburgh: T. & T. Clark, 1992) makes this point with telling effect.

[12]A suitable explanation for the overlap of texts from the Bible with other literature from the ancient Near East has yet to appear. Can one really imagine this phenomenon apart from trained sages utilizing similar literature from neighboring cultures?

[13]Westermann, *Roots of Wisdom*, argues that the Book of Proverbs originated in tiny villages and reflects the intimacy of family life.

[14]The problem is twofold: at what point, if ever, did the Hebrew words for *father* and *son* assume a metaphorical sense, and how can one detect the moment when such metaphors lost vitality?

suggested that the same may occur in Israel. Although the allusion to maternal instruction lacks a parallel outside the Bible, it has not been considered sufficiently weighty to nullify the evidence of metaphorical language.

When the mode of composition entered the picture, matters were further complicated. The primacy of oral instruction within the family and the unsettled question of the extent of literacy in Israel left many unre-solved issues.[15] The frequent appeal within Proverbs for a hearing, together with the total absence of any reference to reading a text and copying it so that teachers could make corrections, gave a different im-pression from that generated by similar texts in Egypt and Mesopotamia.[16] The resulting uneasiness was only minimally assuaged by the knowledge that literate people in the ancient world, few in number, read aloud.

The books of Job and Ecclesiastes, moreover, seemed ill-suited as parental instruction for young boys; like Sirach and Wisdom of Solomon, they raised theoretical questions more appropriate for a learned audience. Did such texts offer guidance to advanced students, or did they represent serious intellectual activity of ordinary adults who sought answers to existential questions?[17] The striking use of *hakamim* in Ecclesiastes as a technical term and ben Sira's high regard for sages when compared with other professions imply that something more than parental advice has found expression.[18]

Whatever its origin and locus, this literature assisted in the formation of character and the socialization process.[19] It went a long way toward

---

[15]Susan Niditch, *Oral World and Written Word: Ancient Israelite Literature*, LAI (Louisville: Westminster John Knox, 1996) and James L. Crenshaw, "The Primacy of Listening in Ben Sira's Pedagogy," in *Wisdom, You are My Sister*, ed. Michael L. Barré, 172-87, CBQMS 29 (Washington: Catholic Biblical Association of America, 1997).

[16]Why have no scribal texts with teacher's corrections survived in ancient Israel? Why do books such as Proverbs and Sirach lack specific features of didactic technique?

[17]An advanced level of cognition is presupposed by the books of Job and Ecclesiastes. It is remotely possible that the gnomic expressions in the Book of Proverbs belong to a similar setting, for serious philosophical thinking can take the form of epigrams (Pascal, Wittgenstein).

[18]The technical use of *hakamim* cannot be proven beyond doubt, but the evidence seems to favor such use in the epilogue to Ecclesiastes, and Ben Sira seems to presuppose it (James L. Crenshaw, "Sirach," *NIB* 4).

[19]William P. Brown, *Character in Crisis: A Fresh Approach to the Wisdom Literature of the Old Testament* (Grand Rapids MI: Eerdmans, 1996).

shaping a worldview, making explicit the things to cultivate and those to avoid. In this precarious environment, a certain kind of woman seems to have posed the gravest danger to young men.[20] Alongside this peril from seductive words and limbs, other dangers lurked, especially drunkenness, lack of control of one's temper, and malicious talk. Very little in this socialization applies solely to prospective courtiers; the vast majority of the instructions and warnings were intended for society at large.

Identifying a Specific Type

The force of the argument against professional sages comes from things other than the absence of this class among the lists of officials in Solomon's bureaucracy.[21] If sages existed in Israel, why did they not compose unique literature? Their failure to do so has raised the issue of correctly identifying a type.[22] The argument, necessarily circular, goes like this. Certain books within the Bible share various features: nonrevelatory address, concentration on humankind, emphasis on what promotes positive results in society, concern for unraveling life's mysteries, an absence of sacred traditions relating to Moses, David, or the patriarchs. One naturally assumes that these features indicate the presence of Wisdom Literature, and when they are absent, the texts belong to another category.

A degree of slippage can be detected even within the three classic texts, especially the Book of Job. Both divine revelation through theophany and a profusion of laments suggest either that the type has been too rigidly defined or that other texts have a claim to inclusion in Wisdom Literature.[23] The widespread incorporation of Yahwistic tradition in Sirach and Wisdom of Solomon, together with the inclusion of sentence-like literature in texts such as Tobit, imply that the interests commonly

---

[20]Christa Maier, *Die "fremde Frau" in Proverbien 1-9*, OBO 144 (Fribourg: Universitätsverlag, 1995) and Bernard Lang, *Wisdom and the Book of Proverbs: An Israelite Goddess Redefined* (New York: Pilgrim Press, 1986).

[21]Weeks, *Early Israelite Wisdom.*

[22]James L. Crenshaw, "Method in Determining Wisdom Influence upon 'Historical' Literature," *JBL* 88 (1969): 129-42; repr.: 312-25 in *Urgent Advice and Probing Questions. Collected Writings on Old Testament Wisdom* (Macon GA: Mercer University Press, 1995).

[23]The necessity for a more sophisticated approach to classification has claimed the attention of Giorgio Buccellati, "Wisdom and Not: The Case of Mesopotamia," *JAOS* 101 (1981): 35-47.

-the meaning of life

wisdom and the psalms

attributed to the sages may have been broader than usually thought. Similarly, the posing of intellectual queries about life's meaning in the face of injustice and physical suffering is not limited to the books of Job and Ecclesiastes, but comes to expression in several psalms, notably 37, 49, and 73.[24] Should these psalms be included in Wisdom Literature? Most specialists have thought so, but what about other texts in the Psalter? Should learned psalmography be attributed to sages, and does the same judgment apply to so-called torah psalms like 119? Do indications of educational intent signify sapiential composition, particularly those psalms based on a reading of sacred history—the exodus and wanderings in the wilderness, for example? Are such "midrashic" readings a precursor to Sirach 44-50? Do meditative and self-reflective psalms such as 139 derive from groups who place a premium on cognitive achievements?

The sages did not hold a monopoly on intellectual queries demanding a high degree of sophisticated thinking. The wrestling with the issue of theodicy by the prophetic books of Habakkuk and Jonah[25] suggests that certain problems were universal. Similarly, some rhetorical features seem to have found utility in various settings, which explains their presence in wisdom and prophetic books. The sages were not the only ones interested in controlling their destiny or in the written word.[26]

The resulting dilemma has hampered the study of Israelite wisdom, for interpreters have not been able to agree on what constitutes the phenomenon. Some of them collapse the literature into a single corpus; when the wisdom texts themselves remain silent about traditional Yahwism, they simply take it for granted.[27] Others view the lack of national particu-

---

[24]On Psalm 73, see James L. Crenshaw, *A Whirlpool of Torment*, OBTh (Philadelphia: Fortress Press, 1982) 93-109.

[25]The problem also surfaces in the Book of Genesis, on which see James L. Crenshaw, "The Sojourner Has Come to Play the Judge: Theodicy on Trial," in *God in the Fray: Essays in Honor of Walter Brueggemann*, ed. Tod Linafelt et al., 83-92 (Minneapolis: Augsburg Fortress Press, 1998).

[26]Gerhard von Rad's attempt to explain the Joseph narrative as a type of wisdom literature has increasingly come under attack ("The Joseph Narrative and Ancient Wisdom," 292-300 in *The Problem of the Hexateuch and Other Essays* [Oxford: Blackwells, 1966]). Moshe Weinfeld, *Deuteronomy and the Deuteronomic School* (Oxford: Clarendon Press, 1972) has failed to convince many readers.

[27]Roland E. Murphy, *The Tree of Life: An Exploration of Biblical Wisdom Literature*, 2nd ed. (Grand Rapids MI: Eerdmans, 1996) has made this point repeatedly.

larities and "special" revelation as proof that wisdom constitutes an alien body devoid of salvific content.[28]

These issues have thus far resisted resolution. A recent wrinkle concerns the affinities between wisdom and apocalyptic, especially in light of developments at Qumran and the postbiblical traditions associated with Enoch, a notable figure in both wisdom and apocalyptic.[29] Does the extraordinary character of God in the Book of Job pave the way for introducing additional apocalyptic concepts into the wisdom tradition?[30]

The affinities between Wisdom and Torah seem distant because the texts do not confirm a postulated common origin in the clan, about which very little can be known.[31] Why do sages remain quiet about the law until the second-century Ben Sira, who takes the unexpected step of equating the Mosaic legislation with a highly developed concept of personified Wisdom. Despite this extraordinary move, a minimum of legal data occurs in Sirach. Either Ben Sira did not take the identification seriously, or he used the broadest possible language when referring to the law.

The meager evidence in Proverbs and Ecclesiastes does not lend support to the view that a group of scribal traditionists was responsible for composing Deuteronomy. The superficial similarities between this book and Wisdom Literature and the substantial differences suggest that the two derive from different circles. A test based on vocabulary hardly carries conviction, for any number of factors easily skew such compilations.[32]

Perhaps the search for a particular type should be guided by the knowledge that categories in biblical literature have considerable flexibil-

---

[28]Horst-Dietrich Preuss, *Einführung in die alttestamentliche Weisheitsliteratur*, UT 383 (Stuttgart: Kohlhammer Verlag, 1987); his view was vigorously opposed by Franz-Josef Steiert, *Die Weisheit Israels—ein Fremdkörfer im Alten Testament?* FThSt (Freiburg: Herder Verlag, 1990).

[29]John J. Collins, *Jewish Wisdom in the Hellenistic Age*, OTL (Louisville: Westminster/John Knox, 1997).

[30]The character of God in this book comes closer to the classic *Urgott*, a distant creator deity, than to the biblical Yahweh.

[31]An intrinsic connection between law and wisdom has been associated with the period of the clan (Erhard Gerstenberger, *Wesen und Herkunft des "apodiktischen Rechts,"* WMANT 20 [Neukirchen: Neukirchener Verlag, 1965]).

[32]Only when a given word has a unique sense in wisdom literature can one reasonably assume exclusive use, but even this instance may be purely accidental.

ity.[33] Prophecy, for instance, includes both narrative and oracle. The former prophets consist largely of a view of history in which prophetic proclamation exercises controlling power, and the latter prophets comprise oracles and visions, with occasional biographical narrative and meditation. This broad characterization of the prophetic literature still leaves out the Book of Jonah, a story about a prophet, and Malachi, a series of discussions with an audience largely about matters of purity. If one takes into consideration prophecy at Mari and neo-Assyrian texts, even more latitude is necessary, given the prominent place of divination here as opposed to its role in ancient Israel.[34] A similar situation exists in Torah, which includes far more than legislation, whether casuistic or apodictic. A story of the beginnings of the cosmos and peoples of the earth, replete with genealogies, and an account of family conflict introduce the corpus in which legal matters later find expression.

Unity

In one sense the individual books in the wisdom corpus lack unity; so does the collection as a whole. This statement applies most directly to the Book of Proverbs, which has at least eleven separate collections,[35] but also to the other books. Although modern interpreters have made valiant efforts at understanding the Book of Job as a work of literary integrity,[36] it nevertheless has strong indications of developmental stages. Similarly, Ecclesiastes shows signs of later adjustments to soften its pessimism.[37] As a product of a different culture from that reflected in the books of Job and Ecclesiastes, one that prizes authorship, Sirach seems to derive from a single mind, except for the translator's prologue. Wisdom of Solomon,

---

[33]David L. Petersen, "Rethinking the Nature of Prophetic Literature," in *Prophecy and Prophets*, ed. Yehoshua Gitay, 23-40, SBLSS (Atlanta: Scholars Press, 1997).

[34]Simo Parpola, *Assyrian Prophecies*, and Marti Nissinen, *References to Prophecy in Neo-Assyrian Sources*, vols. 9 and 7 respectively in State Archives of Assyria (Helsinki: Helsinki University Press, 1997 and 1998).

[35]Anthologizing is not unique to Israelite wisdom, for it also plays a significant role in prophetic books, particularly Isaiah.

[36]Hoffman, *A Blemished Perfection*.

[37]Michael V. Fox, *Qohelet and His Contradictions*, JSOTSup 71 (Sheffield: Almond Press, 1989); a major revision will appear shortly under the auspices of Eerdmans Publishing Company.

too, was crafted by a highly educated person, one steeped in Greek thought and fully at home in the niceties of the Greek language.[38]

The book of Ecclesiastes comes close to philosophical speculation in the Greek sense. Despite its sustained argument that everything is futile or absurd, the book still has occasional collections of unrelated sayings. The modern reader gets the impression that the author incorporated earlier material into the work, sometimes without comment and occasionally with corrections to bring it into line with the rest of the book.[39] The most glaring indications of editorial intention occur here, however, for the book concludes with two epilogues that most likely derive from a later hand than that of the author of what precedes. This judgment rests on style, tone, and content. The first epilogue, which refers to the author in the third person and makes an assessment of his role among the wise, reads almost like an epitaph. The second epilogue, more distant and cooler in tone, introduces entirely different views from those championed by Qoheleth. Torah piety, fearing God, and keeping the commandments now sums up the human requirement, and the prospect of divine judgment awaits everyone.

The affinities between the final epilogue in Ecclesiastes and torah piety as reflected in Sirach have been pointed out.[40] Has an editor attempted to align the two books theologically? It has even been conjectured that an editor has brought the Book of Proverbs into the same theological ambiance by the addition of the prologue in the initial collection (Prov 1:2-7). The centrality of the fear of Yahweh as the avenue to acquiring wisdom, in other words the importance of religion for becoming wise, seems to function almost as a buzz word here. A similar theme finds expression in the poem (chap. 28) that comes after Job's dialogue with his three friends and before his great oath of innocence.[41]

---

[38]Armin Schmitt, *Weisheit* (Würzburg: Echter, 1989) and David Winston, *The Wisdom of Solomon*, AB 43 (Garden City NY: Doubleday, 1979).

[39]R. N. Whybray, "The Identification and Use of Quotations in Qoheleth," *VTS 32. Congress Volume Vienna 1980* (Leiden: E. J. Brill, 1981) 435-51.

[40]Gerald F. Sheppard, "The Epilogue to Qoheleth as Theological Commentary, *CBQ* 39 (1977): 183-89, and idem, *Wisdom as a Hermeneutical Construct*, BZAW 151 (Berlin and New York: Walter de Gruyter Verlag, 1980).

[41]On this poem, see above all Stephen A. Geller, "Where Is Wisdom? A Literary Study of Job 28 in Its Setting," in *Judaic Perspectives on Ancient Israel*, ed. Jacob Neusner, Baruch Levine, and E. S. Frerichs, 169-75 (Philadelphia: Fortress Press, 1987).

Consistency over Time

If one assumes that wise men existed in ancient Israel as a professional class, it follows that the literature they produced ought to have a high degree of consistency. Certain themes should come to prominence, together with stylistic features and vocabulary. The search for characteristically wisdom themes has been only moderately productive. In the Book of Proverbs, one can identify certain central features such as pithy sayings about human nature and animals, along with intentionally didactic instructions conveying strong moral suasion, but this type of teaching recedes to the background in the very different Book of Job. Here the dialogical literary form, first with human partners in dispute and subsequently with the dominant voice being identified as the deity, give an entirely different impression. Moreover, the narrative that frames the dialogue links this text with a significant body of literature from elsewhere in the ancient Near East.[42]

With Ecclesiastes another literary form emerges, this time a quasi-philosophical exploration of the nature of reality. Moreover, the author formulates a thesis and endeavors to demonstrate its validity. Only here and there do moral maxims occur, and in some instances they are poorly integrated into the argument.[43] Sirach reverts to sayings and instructions, but these are joined in such a way as to create sustained treatments of various topics, a rare occurrence in the latest section of the Book of Proverbs and entirely missing in earlier collections. Sirach goes beyond its predecessors in introducing hymnic texts. Like Proverbs, Ben Sira includes hymns about personified wisdom, and like the Book of Job he praises the creator for the majesty of the universe. The unprecedented paean of famous men in the Bible has been seen as an attempt to create a national myth,[44] and its Hellenistic characteristics have caught inter-

---

[42]Besides the Joban parallels, one thinks of the *Aramaic Sayings of Ahikar* and the *Instruction of Onkhsheshonqy.*

[43]James L. Crenshaw, *Ecclesiastes*, OTL (Philadelphia: Westminster Press, 1987); Fox, *Qohelet and His Contradictions*; Roland E. Murphy, *Ecclesiastes*, WBC 19a (Dallas: Word, 1988), and Choon-Leong Seow, *Ecclesiastes*, AB 18c (New York: Doubleday, 1997).

[44]Burton O. Mack, *Wisdom and the Hebrew Epic: Ben Sira's Hymn in Praise of the Fathers* (Chicago and London: University of Chicago Press, 1985).

preters' eyes. Although Wisdom of Solomon continues some of the earlier emphases such as celebrating wisdom's virtues, it does so in an entirely new manner. The linguistic difference alone cannot explain this shift, even if the author has become thoroughly Hellenized. The ambiguity of death issues in a sustained argument in which an immortal soul complicates matters, at least for anyone trained in traditional Jewish thought.[45] The author uses Greek categories and rhetoric with telling effect, both in praising wisdom and in midrash-like interpretation of the Exodus.

How can this development from moral maxims, often lacking religious significations, to fervent religious passion with apocalyptic inclinations be explained? All efforts to trace the various stages of Wisdom Literature have suffered from an absence of reliable historical data. The few attempts to specify a linear development have been criticized on several counts, largely because of the failure to recognize an oral stage alongside a literary one and the assumption that a secular tradition preceded a religious one.[46] The claim that wisdom moves resolutely within creation[47] runs the risk of trivializing the kind of thought underlying the majority of collections in the Book of Proverbs. Perhaps one should qualify this dictum, thus leaving room for everyday maxims with specific moral functions, rather than submitting these to the cosmic ramifications of another kind of wisdom altogether. Both anthropocentric and cosmocentric wisdom probably existed from the beginning.[48] The former may actually have consisted of two very different types of sayings, those with no religious intentions and others with theological purposes. Even

---

[45]Michael Kolarcik, *The Ambiguity of Death in the Book of Wisdom 1-6: A Study of Literary Structure and Interpretation*, AnBib 127 (Rome: Editrice Pontificio Instituto Biblico, 1991).

[46]Dell, "On the Development of Wisdom in Israel." Curiously, she uses my introductory study of wisdom to describe views that she considers in need of revising, but in several important instances she acknowledges that I do not share the view she rejects. Her interpretation needs considerable nuancing to show how I have consistently challenged operative assumptions in the discipline. See the revision of the above work (*Old Testament Wisdom: An Introduction*, rev. and enl. [Louisville: Westminster John Knox, 1998]).

[47]The reader will recognize Walther Zimmerli's well-known dictum from 1964: "Wisdom thinks resolutely within the framework of a theology of creation," in "The Place and Limit of Wisdom in the Framework of Old Testament Theology," *SJTh* 17 (1964): 147.

[48]Leo G. Perdue, *Wisdom in Revolt*, JSOTSup 112 (Sheffield: Almond Press, 1991).

the ones that appear secular from the modern standpoint must be understood against the background of a thoroughly religious society. This acknowledgment does not settle the debate over the extent to which modern interpreters may assume that Yahwistic monism has infused the sayings in Proverbs. On that issue, a minimalist position seems more appropriate than a maximalist one.

The long-held assumption that Wisdom Literature is ahistorical has been effectively challenged,[49] but how far can one go in the other direction? With Sirach and Wisdom of Solomon, the effects of adverse historical developments can certainly be detected, giving rise to fervent prayer and apocalyptic expectations of relief from persecution. A similar conclusion may apply to the Book of Job but, like Proverbs, it conceals the social circumstances of its origins. The exilic and postexilic environment provided the matrix within which much of the Wisdom Literature took shape, but almost nothing of this social context has found expression. Even Ecclesiastes has left few clues about its actual date of composition; the author's concerns transcend historical circumstances.[50]

Conclusion

The current controversy over the existence of professional sages in ancient Israel, and consequently a specific corpus of Wisdom Literature distinct from the rest of the Old Testament has arisen within the ranks of biblical criticism. Modern interpreters have resisted the tendency to view their conclusions as final, for they have understood their work as a process in need of constant refinement. The evidence has always been subject to multiple readings.

On the issue of a professional class of sages, the scant evidence seems to point to gifted intellectuals who combined the earlier product of instruction in the family with intellectual pursuits of a quite different

---

[49]Hans-Heinrich Schmid, *Wesen und Geschichte der Weisheit*, BZAW 101 (Berlin and New York: Walter de Gruyter, 1966).

[50]Hence the sharp differences among interpreters regarding the date of the book (mid-third century according to most critics); much earlier in the views of Seow and Daniel C. Fredericks, *Qoheleth's Language: Re-evaluating Its Nature and Date*, ANETS 3 (Lewistown NY: Mellen Publishers, 1988); but see Antoon Schoors, *The Preacher Sought to Find Pleasing Words: A Study of the Language of Qoheleth* (Leuwen: University Press, 1995).

kind. Eventually such individuals may have functioned as teachers in schools,[51] but this remains uncertain until Ben Sira.[52] Can one really imagine the first stages of philosophy that occur in Ecclesiastes, or even the intellectual dispute in the Book of Job, apart from a circle of advanced thinkers?[53]

The peculiarities of language and style that characterize Wisdom Literature seem to confirm the existence of actual professional sages in Israel. Nevertheless, major problems remain, for the Book of Job employs stylistic features more at home elsewhere than in sapiential enclaves that produced the Book of Proverbs—or even Sirach and Wisdom of Solomon.

A professional group of sages may have had diverse interests. That would explain the lack of unity within the several bodies of literature attributed to them. If a few sages sought to shape the different books in a way that would suggest some grand scheme, one should not be surprised. A theological agenda need not alter the entire document, when introductory and concluding coda could orient the material in a given direction.

Still, the wisdom corpus was consistent only to a certain point. Orientation toward human beings existed in tension with cosmic focussing. Perhaps the same people held both views, but that seems less likely than positing separate circles for the two perspectives. In any event, describing a linear development of wisdom tradition, except in broad strokes, has proved enormously difficult. More progress has occurred in the literary realm than in the historical or social domain. The greatest challenge facing scholars at the beginning of the twenty-first century is to describe the social setting of wisdom over the years.

---

[51]James L. Crenshaw, *Education in Ancient Israel: Across the Deadening Silence*, ABRL (New York: Doubleday, 1998).

[52]Even Ben Sira's reference to a house of study has been read as a metaphor referring to the book itself: Oda Wischmeyer, *Die Kultur des Buches Jesus Sirach*, BZNW 77 (Berlin and New York: Walter de Gruyter Verlag, 1994) 175-76.

[53]See James L. Crenshaw, "Qoheleth's Understanding of Intellectual Inquiry," in *Qohelet in the Context of Wisdom*, 205-24, BETL 136 (Leuwen: University Press, 1998); Oswald Loretz, "Anfänge jüdischer Philosophie nach Qohelet 1, 1-11 und 3, 1-15," *UF* 23 (1991): 223-44; and idem, " 'Frau' und griechisch-jüdische Philosophie im Buch Qohelet (Qoh 7, 23-8, 1 und 5, 6-10)," *UF* 23 (1991): 245-64.

Contributors

H. Wayne Ballard, Jr. . . . . Campbell University

William H. Bellinger, Jr. . . . . Baylor University

James L. Crenshaw . . . . Duke University Divinity School

Nancy L. deClaissé-Walford . . . . McAfee School of Theology

Joel F. Drinkard . . . . . The Southern Baptist Theological Seminary

Robert C. Dunston . . . . Cumberland College

Carol Stuart Grizzard . . . . Pikeville College

Gerald Keown . . . . M. Christopher White School of Divinity

M. Pierce Matheney, Jr. . Midwestern Baptist Theological Seminary

Daniel S. Mynatt . . . . Anderson College

James D. Nogalski . . . . Lombard, Illinois

Thomas Smothers . . . . . The Southern Baptist Theological Seminary

W. Dennis Tucker, Jr. . . . . Ouachita Baptist University

John D. W. Watts . . . . . The Southern Baptist Theological Seminary

Indexes

Scripture References

Old Testament

Name and Subject Index